THE CONSTITUTION OF THE EUROPEAN UNION

This book provides a contextual analysis of the constitution of the European Union, which, unlike most constitutions, does not belong to a state. Rather, the EU is an international organisation that has moved beyond the features of international law into a terrain very close to the municipal law of federal states. Many features we take for granted in nation-states are non-existent, or contested, in the Union. There is no European Union constitutional text in the proper sense; the 'Constitutional Treaty' signed by the Member States in 2004 failed spectacularly in the process of popular ratification. The Union's founding texts were international treaties – international law, not constitutional law. And yet, over time, legal doctrine put into place by the European Court of Justice in Luxembourg has led to constitutional attributes of Union law, and political practice, led by the Commission, has mirrored these attributes, complementing a de facto constitutionalist environment. As a consequence, we have seen a steady re-ordering of the functional boundaries of the Member States, followed by a nascent re-ordering of the imagined boundaries of political community and self. All of this is constitutionalism writ large: legal doctrines, institutional arrangements, political practices, and their implications for legitimacy, democracy, and political self-imagination, and together they form the subject of this fascinating book.

EU Constitutionalism in Context
Pictorial Narrative

This image is formed from a series of iconic references to elements associated with the European Union. At its summit are a series of hands and wrists, clad in formal suits. The third hand is using a compass to sketch out the institution's original form. Immediately below are the yellow stars on blue referring to the familiar European Union flag. In addition, a solitary egg is depicted at the point of the compass to recognise the fundamental importance of the Single Market.

In the middle ground, on the left hand side, continuity and tradition stretching back to ancient Greece assumes the mythological form of Europa and the Bull. By way of contrast, at the central core of the composition, conjuring the spirit of twentieth century modernist architecture stands the geometrically rectangular symmetrical shape of the European Court of Justice in Luxembourg, also symbolically representing the rationality of European Union law. The colours and rhythms within the right hand rectangle also reflect those in the flags of the EU nation states.

On the right hand side, a trilogy of eminent contributors to the European project watch over the scene as it unfolds: Konrad Adenauer (German Chancellor 1949–63), Jean Monnet (architect of European integration), Jacques Delors (President of the Commission in the 1980s). Beneath them, a cascading scroll represents the original Treaty of Rome of 1957, accompanied by Beethoven's 'Ode To Joy', selected as the anthem for the European Union.

Putachad
Artist

Constitutional Systems of the World
General Editors: Peter Leyland, Andrew Harding, Benjamin L Berger, Rosalind Dixon and Heinz Klug

In the era of globalisation issues of constitutional law and good governance are being seen increasingly as vital issues in all types of society. Since the end of the cold war there have been dramatic developments in democratic and legal reform, and post-conflict societies are also in the throes of reconstructing their governance systems. Even societies already firmly based on constitutional governance and the rule of law have undergone constitutional change and experimentation with new forms of governance and their constitutional systems are increasingly subjected to comparative analysis and transplantation. Constitutional texts for practically every country in the world are now easily available on the internet. However, texts which enable one to understand the true context, purposes, interpretation, and incidents of a constitutional system are much harder to locate, and are often extremely detailed and descriptive. This series seeks to provide scholars and students with accessible introductions to the constitutional systems of the world, supplying both a road map for the novice and, at the same time, a deeper understanding of the key historical, political, and legal events which have shaped the constitutional landscape of each country. Each book in the series deals with a single country or a group of countries with a common constitutional history, and each author is an expert in their field.

The Constitutional Systems of the following nations have so far been covered by the series:

Australia
Republic of Austria
Belgium
Brazil
Canada
China
Commonwealth Caribbean
Czechia
European Union
Finland
France
Germany
Hong Kong SAR
Independent Central Asian States
India
Indonesia
Ireland
Israel
Italy
Japan
Malaysia
Mexico
Myanmar
New Zealand
Pakistan
Romania
Russian Federation
Singapore
South Africa
Spain
Taiwan
Thailand
United Kingdom
United States
Vietnam

Link to series website
www.bloomsbury.com/uk/series/constitutional-systems-of-the-world/

The Constitution of the European Union

A Contextual Analysis

Ulrich Haltern

•HART•
OXFORD • LONDON • NEW YORK • NEW DELHI • SYDNEY

HART PUBLISHING

Bloomsbury Publishing Plc

Kemp House, Chawley Park, Cumnor Hill, Oxford, OX2 9PH, UK

1385 Broadway, New York, NY 10018, USA

Bloomsbury Publishing Ireland Limited, 29 Earlsfort Terrace, Dublin 2, D02 AY28, Ireland

First published in Great Britain 2025

First published in hardback, 2025

Paperback edition, 2025

A catalogue record for this book is available from the British Library.

A catalogue record for this book is available from the Library of Congress.

Library of Congress Control Number: 2024949787

ISBN: HB: 978-1-50998-510-4
ePDF: 978-1-78225-751-6
ePub: 978-1-78225-749-3

Typeset by Compuscript Ltd, Shannon

For product safety related questions contact productsafety@bloomsbury.com

To find out more about our authors and books visit www.hartpublishing.co.uk. Here you will find extracts, author information, details of forthcoming events and the option to sign up for our newsletters.

Acknowledgements

USUALLY, THERE ARE too many people to thank. Not this time. The one person to thank, first and foremost, is Ben Berger, whose wisdom, thoughtfulness, encouragement, patience, and enduring friendship are the only reason this book exists.

I am also grateful to Rosalind Dixon for her insights, to Will Siegmund and Joanne Choulerton for their terrific copy edit, to Putachad Leyland for her cover design, to Tom Adams and everyone at Hart, and to my wonderful Munich team.

Contents

Table of Cases

Table of Legislation and International Materials

Table of National Materials

Introduction

This is a brief book about the European Union's constitutional system of governance. As such, it is inherently different from other books in this series on 'Constitutional Systems of the World', which overwhelmingly cover the constitutions of individual nation-states. The European Union (EU, or Union) is an international organisation, not a state. Its founding text is an international law treaty, not a constitution in the proper sense. The template of 'constitutionalism' may therefore not intuitively suggest itself. However, the Union has moved far beyond the features of international law into a terrain that is very close to the municipal law of federal states. The Union's institutional set-up has insulated many EU decisions from the direct influence of individual Member States (a term of art which, in 'Union speak', is always written with capital letters). Over time, the Union's court, the Court of Justice of the European Union, has put legal doctrine with constitutional attributes into place. The Union's political practices have complemented its institutions, acting more akin to a constitutional system than an international treaty organisation. All these features of the Union complement one another to create a de facto constitutionalism, even in the absence of a proper constitutional document. This de facto constitutionalism has implications for how both the Union and its Member States work and understand themselves, and where European citizens locate Union governance, state governance (which is thoroughly entangled with Union governance), and their own involvement on a scale of legitimacy, democracy, and political self-imagination. Constitutionalism resides not just within the law proper, but also within its context. It is a lived experience[1] – a curious blend of law, history, economics, culture, and institutional arrangements. This understanding of constitutionalism lies at the heart of both this volume and of the 'Constitutional Systems of the World' series.

While the constitutionalist template is, therefore, a good fit for the European Union, its precise format is decidedly different from that of

[1] As Justice Oliver Wendell Holmes famously wrote, 'The life of the law has not been logic; it has been experience' (*The Common Law*, Boston MA, Little, Brown & Company 1881, 1).

states. Many features we take for granted in nation-states are either non-existent in the Union (for instance, political identity) or contested (for instance, what is the Union good for, and who should or should not be a member?). As a consequence of these contested features, much of what the Union is today reflects developments that could have transpired in crucially different ways. The excitement one feels when studying EU constitutionalism arises from this historical contingency: there was no grand plan at the outset, and what unfolded was the product of a unique European variant of constitutionalism. It is my aim in this book to lead the reader through the maze of institutional, political, and legal developments that have produced, and shaped, the constitutional settlement between, and beyond, European state borders. This introduction lays out the major contours of the themes and points of legal and political contestation that are part and parcel of that settlement.

I. THE UNIQUE FORMAT OF EU CONSTITUTIONALISM

The European Union is a union of 27 nation-states in Europe. It is a legal construct, born out of international treaties between European states, and its development has been marked by successive amendments of those treaties. It is the result of a peace process among six Member States that started shortly after World War II. Over time, that number rose to 28 before recently falling to 27 when the United Kingdom left. Approximately 450 million people live in the countries that belong to the European Union. Those countries have equipped the Union with the capacity to pass laws that are legally binding upon the Member States, which is unique among international organisations. The Union has, over the decades, passed innumerable laws. Their legal effect is, depending on the legislative instrument, more than that of a national law: Union law enjoys direct effect within its Member States, and it can override Member State law. What the Union does, therefore, has immediate effects in the countries that have joined it. It is governed by a host of institutions seated mostly in Brussels, with names such as 'the Council', 'the European Council', 'the Committee of Permanent Representatives', 'the European Commission', 'the European Parliament', 'the European Central Bank', and 'the Eurogroup'.

And therein lies a problem. When the President of the European Council visits the head of state of a country, people who hear the news tend to be slightly confused: Who is that, what is the European Council, and whom or what does he represent? When the President of the European Commission visits a week later, people tend to be even more confused: Now who is she, what is the European Commission as opposed to the European Council, and whom or what does she represent? Matters get worse when the High Representative of the European Union for Foreign Affairs and Security Policy comes to visit. The EU puts out a 'Five Presidents' Report,' and none of the Presidents are a Member State President; they are each President of an EU body (in this case, the Commission, the European Council, the European Parliament, the European Central Bank, and the Euro Area). Much of the confusion people feel about who these representatives are and whom they represent comes from a more general fuzziness as to what the Union is as such.

This fuzziness is no surprise. We tend to understand politics in terms of state institutions, and associate state institutions with specific functions and representational claims. The President of the United States, for instance, is the head of state and leader of the US government, is elected by the American people (via the Electoral College), and interacts with the US legislator, Congress. We have a general idea, at least, what he does, and for whom he speaks.

The same goes for international organisations. When the Secretary-General of the United Nations speaks, we have at least a rough idea what he does, and, perhaps most of all, whom he does *not* represent. The reason is that we have a general idea that international organisations are not states, and that states use international organisations as forums, as regulatory agencies, or as a means to further their agendas. We also know that states cannot be pushed around by international organisations, and that in a breakfast meeting of the UN Secretary-General and the US President, power is unevenly distributed in favour of the US President.

The European Union runs against such understandings. It is no mere international organisation. Even rich and powerful states like France and Germany cannot simply 'use' the Union to further their agendas. Rather, the Union has, in many respects, the power to compel its Member States to behave in a certain way. The Union has its own legislature (Council and Parliament), an executive body that in many respects looks like a government and is completely independent from Member States (the Commission), a Court with real teeth (the Court of Justice of the European Union), and laws that are immediately effective in the Member States and constitute a real European rule of law.

At the same time, the European Union is emphatically not a state. It does not have a mythical 'We the People', it does not have sovereignty, and its citizens do not have a European political identity in any meaningful sense of the word. Unlike states, the Union does not have the authority to 'act' when it deems it appropriate to act. It can only act when its Member States have authorised it to act through the founding Treaties.

Its position between international organisation and state makes the EU a unique, and strange, animal. Traditional conceptions and understandings of representation, division of powers, and institutional power break down and leave onlookers confused. Non-Europeans smile at the fact that American Presidents have no idea whom to call in Europe if there is an emergency; Europe, it seems, has too many presidents and chairpersons. Europeans themselves are equally fuzzy about who does what, but since they are not just disengaged outsiders, but subjects of European Union governance, they rarely smile. For them, the EU's fuzziness means a dilution of political authority and a curtailment of democratic self-government, none of which is anodyne. More often than not they tend to turn away from what looks like mind-boggling European complexity, toward answers found within their respective Member States; many are indifferent to the EU or, more, Euro-skeptic.

The large number of presidents – and the accompanying large number of institutions – is indicative of the Union's institutional complexity, which in turn reflects the complexity of what the Union does and how it tries to accomplish it. The EU has created both a single market in Europe and an ever-deepening political integration between Member States. Some of its institutions are autonomous and independent of Member State influence, others represent the Member States' voices at the Union level. Some are directly elected, others are not. Some decide, others advise. Together they create a huge body of law beyond the constitutive treaties. Some decisions (on external trade, competition policy, agriculture, fisheries, or the common currency, the Euro) are made exclusively at the EU level, which means Member States are prohibited from acting unilaterally. The Union is also heavily involved in areas such as environmental policy, regional policy, occupational health and safety, cross-border crime, transport, and research and development. It plays a supportive role on issues that, while predominantly dealt with by Member State governments, have cross-border impact, such as social policy, foreign policy, defence, taxation, health care, or spatial planning. Few policy areas are left exclusively to the Member

States, and they typically involve local issues such as housing, crime on the streets, and areas close to national identity such as culture and primary and secondary education. In all areas with Union involvement, legislation is implemented and executed mostly by the Member States, which requires monitoring and controlling each Member State to ensure their compliance. The Union therefore has an intricate system of legal review in place.

II. REGULATION, CONSTITUTIONALISATION, AND EFFECTIVENESS

The Union's primary method of agenda-setting, decision-making, and implementing of policies is with the law. Law, after all, is a system of representation and a tool of self-government. We elect our national representatives to have them translate our political preferences into decisions, and they do so by making law. Law is at the heart of democratic action.

The EU is no different. Its laws and institutions play, to some extent, a very similar role to that of national law and its institutions. Much of what the Union does is 'regulation', and much of its regulatory law is aimed at market integration and mitigating the negative impacts of economic activity. More recently, the EU has also been increasingly involved in regulating issues not directly related to economic activities, such as immigration, political asylum, and police cooperation in criminal matters, as part of its shift from economic community to political community.

Another prominent part of Union law concerns setting up its own institutions, processes, and values. We can call this domain of Union law 'constitutionalisation'. While the Treaties do not use the term 'constitution' – an attempt to ratify a 'Constitutional Treaty' in 2005 failed due to several disapproving referendums – they do serve constitutional functions. Taken together, the Treaties organise the Union's legislative, executive, and judicial branches and articulate their functions, establishing the Union's own architecture of government and guiding values.

These regulatory and constitutional functions are not unique to the Union, even though many details differ from regular political and legal experience within states. Since the Union is a hybrid organisation that combines Member State and non-Member State influence, its institutional architecture does not simply mimic the state template of division of powers accorded to legislative, executive, and judicial branches.

Their general shape, however, is not what makes them remarkable. What *is* unique is a third function, which we can call the Union's 'effectiveness' function.[2] This is a function unfamiliar to national law because it has no need for it. States occupy their own territory where they establish their sovereign law, both regulatory and constitutional. It is activated and employed by institutions and processes that are orchestrated hierarchically, able to rely on general compliance, and have a large array of enforcement mechanisms at their disposal if compliance fails. None of this is true for the European Union. It is not fully sovereign and does not have its own territory. Rather, it exists in the space where its Member States intersect. That space is a crowded one. National constitutional and regulatory norms and institutions take up room, and national sovereign power, traditions, and social meanings push up against the powers conferred on the Union. National norms are not always accommodating of EU law. EU law therefore has to find ways of making room for itself: for compliance with its commands, for the roles of its institutions, and for the social embedding of its meanings.

This is no easy feat. Public international law has tried to establish itself in that same space for centuries now, and has at best reached a tenuous position. Union law has been much more successful. Member State compliance with Union law has the same source as an individual complying with the laws of any given state – an automatic habit of obedience. That alone looks like a miracle to which I will return (see Chapters four and five). It is, of course, not a miracle, but the result of legal strategies which allow EU law to coopt and, if that fails, even trump national law. These strategies show that EU law possesses a distinctly relational dimension – a hybrid, bridge-like character – which sets it apart from national law on the one hand, and from international law on the other. Consequently, the Union's constitutional order is unique in its composite, compound quality.

All this happens in order to manage the considerable interdependence between the Member States.[3] That management rests upon the idea that most problems of transnational nature can be better solved on a transnational plane rather than within the confines of national sovereignty. Hence, the Union's perspective is usually one of unity. It privileges centralised decision-making and, thus, uniformity and sameness

[2] The Court of Justice of the European Union has, for decades, used the French term '*effet utile*' as one of the guiding principles in its interpretation of EU law.

[3] This is one of the main themes in S Weatherill, *Law and Values in the European Union*, Oxford, Oxford University Press 2016.

over difference. Member States often have different views, favouring autonomous decision-making within their own systems of political representation and legitimacy. Beyond that desire for autonomy, however, their positions are seldom unified. The 27 Member States often have so little in common that it is hard for them to formulate any kind of shared position. Their traditions, cultures, economies, society-wide beliefs and institutional set-ups are wildly diverse. There are also multiple cleavages between groups of Member States: large versus small, east versus west, north versus south, old versus new, rich versus poor, external Union border versus no external Union border, Euro versus no Euro as currency, coordinated versus liberal market economies. Taken together, this makes 28 different perspectives on what the European Union is and what it should do (27 Member State perspectives and one Union perspective), all backed by their own good logic, by self-confident institutions, and by powerful political and economic interests.

III. THE MAJOR THEMES OF THIS BOOK

It is within, and because of, these contending positions that several themes have developed, interacted, and shaped the EU over time, which this book will explore. These themes range from issues of democratic self-government and legitimacy via the vertical (between Union and Member States) and the horizontal (between Union institutions) distribution of powers to questions of political identity. Most of them relate back to some aspect of the underlying fundamental question of how power is distributed, balanced, and justified between the Union and its Member States. We will follow these recurring themes throughout this book where they will arise in many contexts and guises.

A. Balancing Power between the Union and its Member States

The first theme is about competences, and addresses the shifting power balance between Union and Member States head-on. Unlike states, the Union has limited competences: those competences that the Member States conferred upon it in the founding Treaties. The Union does what it does because the Member States have unanimously agreed to authorise its action. Should the Union act outside its Treaty mandate, its actions would lack legitimate authority and rob Member States of regulatory autonomy. The protection of Member State competences is therefore of the highest political and constitutional significance. And yet it appears as if competences keep drifting from the Member States towards the Union to a degree that 'there simply is no nucleus of sovereignty that the Member States can invoke, as such, against the Community'.[4] As we will see, the main reason is that Union institutions read grants of competence in a robust way. In doing this, they profit from the lack of red lines in the Treaties, which allows them to make the most of bare-bones competences. The Union's Court of Justice has not often intervened on behalf of Member States' competences. As a consequence, Union competences appear to self-extend. Member States are left increasingly frustrated with their shrinking regulatory ambit, and the maintenance of a politically acceptable balance between Union and national competences is threatened.

B. Balancing Power between Union Institutions

A second, related theme is the growing supranationalisation of formerly national powers within the Union's system of governance. The shift within the (vertical) balancing of Union and Member States' competences re-emerges at the Union level. There, powers and competences are (horizontally) balanced between different Union institutions. Some of them are completely independent from Member State influence (like the Commission); others speak on behalf of the Member States and consist of Member States' ministers (the Council) or even the heads of Member States (the European Council). Union institutions that are insulated from direct Member State influence are called 'supranational', as they voice the collective interest of the EU and appear like the 'conscience' of integration in that they protect values and interests beyond the purely national horizon. Union institutions that channel Member State influence are called 'intergovernmental', as they relay Member State positions to the Union sphere through the mouths of powerful Member State representatives; in doing this, they resemble international organisations (like the UN or the WTO) in orthodox international law. The Union's institutional configuration, with both supranational and intergovernmental bodies, echoes the more general struggle to balance power between Union interests and Member State

[4] Writing as early as in 1990: K Lenaerts, 'Constitutionalism and the Many Faces of Federalism', (1990) 38 *American Journal of Comparative Law* 205, at 220.

interests. The reason for this tension derives from the many different procedures available for resolving a given issue, each with different levels of Member State autonomy and EU involvement. If the Union enacts a law (which, in 'Union-speak', is called either Directive or Regulation), the applicable procedure will vary according to what the material policy area is. In most areas, Member States have agreed to share power with supranational institutions, and even leave them the lion's share of power. In other areas they are less cooperative. When they felt a policy area to be close to the heart of their national sovereignty – like the power of the purse, taxation, and the power of the sword, criminal law – they have concocted procedures that decrease supranational involvement, for instance by limiting the number of supranational institutions involved (the European Parliament will not be involved, say) or by downplaying supranational influence (the Commission, say, will not have a monopoly on setting the agenda since the Member States are allowed to produce the first draft of legislation).

Competences and procedures are laid down in the founding Treaties, so all seems well and clear. Alas, as in life, rules go only so far in providing clarity and peace. Most power plays take place within, rather than outside of, the normative frame, and the same is true here. Both supranational and intergovernmental institutions use the rules to their advantage to maximise their own influence. Therefore, while Union competences are limited, they are not static. They seem to self-extend in what has been called a 'competence creep',[5] which makes them easily the most contested theme in European integration, both in the vertical sense of balancing Member State and Union powers, and in the horizontal sense of the intergovernmental/supranational divide.

C. Strengthening Democratic Accountability

A third theme is the gap in democratic legitimacy as a problem for European governance. On the one hand, international organisations are rarely even to the slightest extent democratic. On the other hand, the Union is no ordinary international organisation. In ever-increasing fields, the EU is involved in regulation that directly touches upon the core of

[5] S Weatherill, 'Competence Creep and Competence Control', (2004) 23 *Yearbook of European Law* 1.

national powers, civil liberties, and economic and non-economic policy choices. In domestic political systems, these are matters that require robust democratic accountability, control, and legitimacy. We would therefore expect democratic bodies to do these things, not independent agencies. Why should it be different at the Union level?

It is, though. The Commission – the closest thing to a Union 'government' – cannot be voted out of office and is only partially accountable to the European Parliament. The European Parliament *does* enjoy democratic legitimacy because it is the only Union institution that is directly elected. However, it massively over-represents smaller Member States (similarly to the US Senate), has lesser powers than national parliaments, and voter turn-out is embarrassingly low. Furthering the non-democratic nature of the EU, the Council decides in an often non-transparent, even secretive manner, and is not subject to direct accountability by either national parliaments or the European Parliament. Such gaps in democratic legitimacy are owed to the fact that the Union needs to square national self-determination with supranational integration, and democracy with efficiency. But the fact remains that the Union system of government, on the whole, does not live up to ideal standards of democracy, nor even to the standards of other political systems.

Even if it did meet such standards, the democracy problem would not go away. The creation of a European political structure with direct legal effect within Member States does not leave Member States' political structures untouched, but rather distorts their domestic balance of powers. Above all, the executive branch is empowered at the expense of the legislative branch; the European Parliament is no adequate substitute for the diminished role of national parliaments and the judicial branch is weakened since the Court of Justice of the EU has distinctly different methods, interests, and sensibilities from its national counterparts.

Democracy in the Union is, therefore, multidimensional – a matter of interpenetration, complementarity, and intermingling. The upshot is that reforming the Union system of government, for example, by empowering the European Parliament even further, is not only not enough, but it may also be a democratic problem. Most Member State citizens would probably not appreciate a European Parliament with powers equal to national parliaments, because their political home, and their democratic identity, has not (yet?) migrated from the Member State to the Union.

D. Forging European Political Identity

This brings us to a fourth theme that resurfaces at every corner in many guises: the lack of European political identity. It is a truism that the Union and the nation-state are (and are meant to be) different forms of political community which command very different imaginations, beliefs, and loyalties. The Member States are located at the thicker end of constitutionalism, where law and political identity are thoroughly connected and sustain each other. National law, and the constitutionalism it sustains, are laden with memory and myth, not just reason and interest. This is what makes them 'ours'. National law exerts strong normative pull, not because it rests on some foundational consensus or because it threatens to coerce, but because it expresses the will of the sovereign. In any democratic regime, the citizens themselves become part of that sovereign.[6] Law at the Member State level, then, is not simply about the promise of order, but about identity. As such, it is highly political in a constitutive sense, and dangerous.

The Union labours at the thinner end of constitutionalism. Its law lacks the components that are constitutive of individual and collective identity in nation-states. Conceived as a contract and as a project guided by enlightened rationality, the Union epitomises the project of rule-based rationality. This is a problem of social legitimacy just as much as it is a problem of law, because social legitimacy is linked to the Union's legal texts: they were never effective at constructing an imaginative fabric that allows the European polity to inscribe its own identity onto the identity of its citizens. Union texts constitute a single market which erases history, identity, and individuality. They do not constitute a collective self, and therefore fail in appearing authentically 'ours'. In European integration, then, there is a disconnect between authority and legitimacy.

E. Bridging Gaps: Law vs Politics, Market vs Values, Hierarchy vs Dialogue

All four themes interact with each other and produce a litany of sub-themes that will continuously resurface in this book. One (mostly related to the theme of democracy) is the law vs politics divide. Law has been the

[6] PW Kahn, *The Reign of Law*, New Haven CT, Yale University Press 1997.

basic motor of supranationalism; indeed, early integration flew under the democratic radar and went under the label of 'integration by stealth'. What about law's instrumental character today? Is the legal paradigm exhausted? Should it be, and should Europe be searching for its own political imagination?

Another sub-theme (mostly related to the theme of vertical competences) is the divide between the market on the one hand, and political, social, or cultural values on the other. Single market regulation is still the lion's share of Union output, but does it trounce non-economic differences? To some extent it must, so that the single market can be sustained as a level playing-field. But where precisely is the boundary? After all, markets are not just about money, but deal with salient political and cultural questions.

Yet another sub-theme (mostly related to the overarching theme of complementarity and intermingling) is the dialogic nature of choices in both politics and law. In the Union, law is not interpreted and enunciated in hierarchical relationships but through ad hoc, changing, and unpredictable relationships. Member State courts on all levels 'talk' directly to the Union's Court of Justice by asking for the Court's interpretation of certain Union law provisions, and the European Court 'responds' with judgments. The Court's answer will depend on who asks (is it a lower tax court or a constitutional court?), on what the judicial sensibilities are (is it a Spanish administrative court, which wants to see a state of the art wording-oriented method of legal interpretation, or is it the French Supreme Court, which wants detailed policy arguments?), and on what the legal environment (is, perhaps, the German Constitutional Court watching, with a long-standing disagreement over competence questions, waiting to pounce and vacate a European Court decision?) and political environment (are Member State governments alarmed over immigration or monetary crises?) is.

These themes will present themselves frequently, be it in the context of institutional, procedural, or substantive questions of law and governance. It is my hope that by tracing these themes through this volume, the reader will get a 'feel' for the issues that make the Union the fascinating political and legal experiment that it is, and that at the same time often plague it.

1

Constitutionalism and the European Union

I. THE AMBIGUOUS STATE OF EUROPEAN UNION CONSTITUTIONALISM

THE UNION CAME into being as a creature of international law. Its Member States established it via international treaties, and still today, those international treaties (though frequently amended) form the basic documents of its legal order. But the concepts drawn from the toolbox of public international law appear increasingly outdated with respect to the European Union, which has expanded its substantive reach and its institutional prerogatives to a level that is unparalleled in international relations. It seems less and less meaningful to call the Union, with its many federal features, an international organisation.[1] More than three decades ago, most scholars therefore turned toward constitutionalism as the leading paradigm to describe, analyse, and critique European integration.[2] Constitutionalism seems to best capture what is special about the process of European integration: the EU has evolved, in critical aspects, from a community founded on international law into a union governed by a constitution. The Court of Justice calls the Union legal order 'a new kind of legal order, the nature of which is

[1] For an attempt to salvage the paradigm of international law to describe the Union, see B de Witte, 'The European Union as an International Legal Experiment', in G de Búrca and JHH Weiler (eds), *The Worlds of European Constitutionalism*, Cambridge, Cambridge University Press 2012, 19.

[2] For an early and influential formulation of this position see E Stein, 'Lawyers, Judges, and the Making of a Transnational Constitution', (1981) 75 *American Journal of International Law* 1. A decade later, constitutionalism had become the leading paradigm, see the classical text by JHH Weiler, 'The Transformation of Europe', (1991) 100 *Yale Law Journal* 2403. Another decade later, the constitutionalist account was already canonized mainstream, see, for instance, P Craig, 'Constitutions, Constitutionalism, and the European Union', (2001) 7 *European Law Journal* 125.

peculiar to the EU, its own *constitutional* framework and founding principles, a particularly sophisticated institutional structure and a full set of legal rules to ensure its operation' (emphasis added).[3]

The mere fact, however, that there is now a widely shared vocabulary which revolves around the concept of 'constitution', and that everyone reads the founding and development of the Union as a narrative of gradual constitutionalisation, does not reflect a consensus about what exactly that means or entails. It is perhaps the association of constitutions with their natural habitat of the nation-state that gives people pause when they speak of the EU's constitutional credentials. Those credentials often seem like some form of 'constitutionalism-lite' or '"as if" constitutionalism'.[4] Something seems amiss, and that 'something' influences the way the Union is perceived in public. The citizens of France and the Netherlands, for example, voted down the Constitutional Treaty in 2005, and the only way to rescue much-needed institutional reforms was to purge the Treaty of Lisbon of all constitutional rhetoric (see Chapter two).

Much of this 'tentative' use of constitutionalism has to do with its rudimentary form in Europe. The Union possesses only a few elements of statehood, and therefore diverges from the state model. For some, this situation is simply not worthy of a written constitution. For others, the prospect of a European constitution is disturbing because it threatens to render less relevant, or even replace, national constitutions, and thus to dissolve the nation-state in the European Union like sugar in coffee, even though most Europeans still identify the nation-state as their political home. The result is that European constitutionalism, like an operating system, hums in the background of European integration and governs its institutions and processes, while at the same time it has become a point of major political, and at times legal, contestation.

II. STATE CONSTITUTIONALISM AND UNION CONSTITUTIONALISM

Whether or not the Union legal order can be adequately conceptualised as a constitution hinges on what we mean by 'constitutionalism'.

[3] Opinion 2/13 *Accession to the ECHR II*, EU:C:2014:2454, para 158. Referring to the Treaties, the Court used the term 'constitutional charter' as early as 1986, Case 294/83 *Parti écologiste 'Les Verts' v European Parliament*, EU:C:1986:166, para 23.

[4] The first term is from N Walker, 'The European Union's Unresolved Constitution', in M Rosenfeld and A Sajó (eds), *The Oxford Handbook of Comparative Constitutional Law*, Oxford, Oxford University Press 2012, 1185, the second from P Lindseth, 'The Perils of "As If" Constitutionalism', (2016) 22 *European Law Journal* 696.

Within the modern liberal imagination, constitutionalism is anchored in national legal orders. But is the semantic paradigm of a centuries-old, history-laden theory and practice the appropriate framework for understanding the novel and protean entity that is the European Union? Is the constitutional imagination of the modern state the relevant template to conceive of the EU polity?

To be sure, the state *has* left a heavy imprint on the way we imagine constitutionalism. The way we think about constitutional rules follows the model of the nation-state, which sets the paradigm for both the form (such as separation of powers) and the content (such as the rule of law and human rights) of constitutionalism. The state tradition therefore provides a cue for recognising constitutional law – or for not recognising it, like in the contested case of international law.[5]

For the European Union, the powerful legacy of state constitutionalism has mixed implications. On the one hand, it provides a template for developing the Union as a discrete polity which adapts its constitutional doctrines and structures from state constitutional law. Much of this is polity-indifferent, and therefore similar in form and content. Hence, we find in the European Union features of classic state constitutionalism, such as the doctrines of direct effect of its law and, as befits all constitutional law, of primacy (see Chapter four). We also have extensive human rights protection (see Chapter seven) and a differentiated system of judicial remedies and enforcement (see Chapter five). These facets of EU law bolster the narrative of a Union legal order that has evolved from a set of legal arrangements binding upon sovereign states into a legal regime conferring judicially enforceable rights and obligations on all legal persons and entities, public and private, within the sphere of application of EU law. For many, this is the very definition of constitutionalisation.

On the other hand, the statist paradigm challenges the constitutional understanding of the EU polity. The reason is that constitutionalism is only partly indifferent to the polity it organises. In important respects, constitutions are polity-specific. While there are some aspects to constitutionalism that possess universal or moral resonance and are therefore recurrent across a wide range of polities, such as individual rights, we actually understand most aspects of a given constitution as configurative of the *particular* polity. Indeed, despite the family resemblance and shared traits, many things about Union constitutionalism and state

[5] See, for instance, J Habermas, 'The Constitutionalization of International Law and the Legitimation Problems of a Constitution for World Society', (2008) 15 *Constellations* 444.

constitutionalism are entirely different. Clearly, this is because the Union is simply not a state, and therefore lacks crucial features of states.

The first missing element is legal in nature and can be summarised as sovereign legal power. States exhibit one supreme ordering authority for the polity, which does not defer to any other internal or external authority. The European Union lacks this exclusivity of final authority; its Member States tenaciously hold on to their status as 'masters of the Treaties'.

A second feature which states have, but the Union lacks, is political in nature. It is the idea that public authority is the product of a constitutional power (a *pouvoir constituant*) residing in 'We the People'. 'We the People' is neither the population at the time of the Founding, nor is it the current population. It is not a historical fact, but rather an imagined source of sovereignty that has spoken the state into existence and lends it legitimacy. It allows citizens to conceive of themselves as part of a collective that both comprises and legitimates the state. The Union, however, has no such source, historical or imagined. It originates from an international treaty ratified by sovereign nation-states.

Finally, a third feature missing at Union level is socio-cultural in nature. We may call it primary political identity, conceived of as the idea that citizenship establishes the general associative bond through which political beliefs and commitments are articulated and negotiated. While the Union does have 'Union citizenship',[6] which the Court of Justice of the European Union (CJEU) emphatically calls 'the fundamental status of nationals of the Member States',[7] many Union citizens are indifferent towards 'their' Union citizenship. The Commission bemoans, on a regular basis, that Europeans feel alienated from the Union, that they have disappointed expectations, and that there is a widening gulf between the Union and the citizens it purports to serve. The political home of individual and collective identity in Europe is still, and perhaps increasingly, the Member States, not the EU.

Because the Union must exist alongside and in relation to states which still claim these three features associated with the modern state for themselves, the EU does not possess any of them, at least not in the fullest sense.[8] Lacking these legal, political, and socio-cultural attributes, the

[6] Arts 20–25 TFEU.

[7] Since Case C-184/99 *Grzelczyk v Centre public d'aide sociale d'Ottignies-Louvain-la-Neuve*, EU:C:2001:458.

[8] N Walker, 'The European Union's Unresolved Constitution', in M Rosenfeld and A Sajó (eds), *The Oxford Handbook of Comparative Constitutional Law*, Oxford, Oxford University Press 2012, 1185.

Union appears to operate on the thinner end of the spectrum of constitutional development. The state constitutionalism template makes the EU seem like a lesser constitutional creature, full of deficiencies and functional equivalents compared to 'the real thing'. That, however, is only one way of understanding the EU's story. If we look beyond the state constitutionalism template, we can understand the Union as not just based upon the model of the state (with deficient results), but as something entirely different. Lawyers call the EU's constitutional structure '*sui generis*', which means 'a species of its own'. The blend of constitutionalism specific to the Union, then, need not be a space of absence, but rather a space of alternative visions, of new (and perhaps exciting) political meaning, and therefore of unique possibilities.

III. THE UNION CONTEXT OF CONSTITUTIONALISM

What does it mean to look at the organisation and practice of European integration through the lens of constitutionalism? How does the typical constitutional model fare when we map it onto the Union's operational landscape, and how does the absence of those three elements of law, politics, and culture – sovereign legal power, *pouvoir constituant*, and political identity – show? A comprehensive answer requires an understanding of the Union's non-linear history, its institutional set-up, and the peculiar role that law plays in the process of integration, which the rest of this book will provide. However, at this point we can already expect European Union constitutionalism to diverge from the state template of constitutionalism in a number of ways.

First, the very foundations of EU constitutionalism are far from settled. We know what we see when we look at the state. When we look at the European Union, we may feel like we are looking at the inkblot of a Rorschach test. There is considerable uncertainty and disagreement regarding the fundamental questions of what the Union is and what precisely the point of it is: What is the Union for? Is it essentially a successful trading bloc, which would imply that its constitutional features serve the overarching purpose of facilitating the free circulation of production factors? Or is it more than that, perhaps even a proto-federalist entity, which would imply that its constitutional features reach far beyond the market? A proto-federalist conception would require consideration of values beyond those of market-exchange as well, and these values would need to somehow be balanced. States do not have to grapple with such questions: no one asks what the point of a state is, and what it is for.

Second, the EU relates to other polities in different ways than do states. It is not a fully sovereign counterpart with a territory and a population of its own, but rather occupies the space where states intersect. Neil Walker brings this unusual dynamic to life beautifully by calling this space a 'crowded space' of overlapping boundaries.[9] Both the Union and its Member States inhabit that space. The relationship between the Union and Member States, therefore, is one of complementarity and intermingling. Most of the time, such intermingling leads to collaboration. Sometimes, however, it reveals competing or incommensurable values and leads to political power struggles featuring assertions of exclusivity, demarcation, and fence-building. The Union's existence in this crowded space undoubtedly affects multiple dimensions of EU constitutionalism, mostly because its lack of strict hierarchies sets it apart from state constitutionalism.

Third, the logic of interpenetration extends to the inner workings of the Union. Unlike states, which possess an institutional structure that contributes to the polity as a whole, the Union possesses an institutional structure that is hybrid, composite, and compound. Union institutions emphasise bridging between different polities rather than privileging unity. Union constitutionalism, therefore, differs from state constitutionalism with respect to how the Union operates, both in terms of who acts and how they act (see Chapter two). This difference is not merely institutional or procedural; it extends to questions of representation and legitimation. While state constitutionalism can organise itself around the principle of representing the inner unity of the polity, Union constitutionalism has no such representative claim to base itself upon. Rather, like a prism, it fragments unity through the necessary representation of multiple polities and interests, unable to decisively favour any one of them over the others. This makes it much harder for the EU to construct anything more than a tenuous 'narrative' of 'us'. Union constitutionalism is therefore not embedded in a feeling of unity among the people living within the EU. Without such a sense of a collective whole, it is difficult to determine on whose behalf Union institutions actually speak. This problem of representation shades into a problem of legitimacy. The authority of national political systems comes from their democratic mandate. Much of the Union's authority, however, comes from its claim that integration is necessary and needs to 'get done'. It is not easy to reconcile these two different modes of legitimacy, or to balance them.

[9] Ibid, 1193.

We can expect Union constitutionalism to be a mode of mediating such conflicts.

Fourth, within the 'crowded space' of European integration, the Union operates with a restricted policy horizon. It cannot simply turn its attention to whatever policy problem it deems deserving of a solution. While states set their own limits to their jurisdictional reach, the EU is limited by the confines of the powers that the Member States have transferred to them. It possesses narrower powers than states, and its jurisdiction is only partial. The Union's constitutionalism, therefore, is restricted with respect to what the Union can do, both in terms of powers (lawyers prefer the term competences) and in terms of procedures (see Chapter three). Such restrictions are sometimes hard to accept, since the problems need to be solved regardless of what the Union's policy horizon is. Consequently, Member States are often willing to expand that horizon by transferring more competences to the Union, and Union institutions make robust use of the powers they have. Despite not setting its own agenda, Union constitutionalism is in a process of constant expansion.

Fifth, locating the Union's constitutionalism at the thinner end of the constitutional spectrum reveals it as 'unsettled'. It is confined to a space crowded by long-standing Member State constitutions and is thus besieged by the historical weight and the contemporary power of nation-state sovereignty. At the same time, it is the paradigmatic example for global constitutionalism, and thus those with hopes for further international integration beyond the nation-state press it to further integrate itself with the Member States besieging it. This has a dual effect. On the one hand, EU constitutionalism is, and will remain, inherently disputed and contested. In this it is different from state constitutionalism, which is a settled legal and political form (even though much within that form is, of course, contested). On the other hand, EU constitutionalism is something that is always developing, incipient, and inchoate. Its constitutional status is an eternal 'not quite yet'; process, as one observer remarked, is everything.[10] In this, too, it differs from state constitutionalism, which – while there may always be times of adaption or consolidation – we generally experience as a settled state of affairs. Both aspects point not towards what the Union does, or how it does what it does, but what it means. These are, in other words, aspects of a constitutional imagination specific to the European Union. Much of it reflects on the theme of democracy because that imagination is about how we, as citizens,

[10] I Ward, *A Critical Introduction to European Law*, Cambridge, Cambridge University Press, 3rd edn 2009, 83.

conceive of self-government, and it also goes to questions of political identity.

Finally, the complementary character of the Union polity ensures that it can only assert itself if the Union makes its voice heard and passes effective measures. The boxed-in character of the Union makes this a difficult mission. International law is, in this respect, a cautionary tale. Because it inhabits the crowded space between sovereign nation-states, international law is routinely ignored if national interests point in a different direction than its injunctions provide. The Union's bridging mechanisms require additional punch if they want to avoid international law's fate and be effective even when EU measures collide with Member State interests. The collaborative relationship between the Union and its members, therefore, sometimes turns into a competitive relationship. Much of that competition is a legal one and translates into the question of what the relationship is between Union law and Member State law, specifically which law – that of the Union or that of the individual Member States – should take precedence when a conflict is identified. Union law has developed considerable punch. In terms of procedure, judicial remedies succeed in establishing the rule of law (see Chapter five). In terms of substance, Union law is directly effective within Member States and takes precedence over domestic law (see Chapter four).

In sum, we can expect European Union constitutionalism to be much more volatile than the traditional national constitutional template. While it is true that the role of law is central to structuring European integration, and that EU law 'wins' when we are faced with an incompatibility of Union law and national law, that law rests on the unsettled ground concomitant with EU constitutionalism. Its foundations are unclear because we cannot be sure what it is for. Its representational claim is fractured because it cannot represent a polity as a unified whole. Its legitimacy is uncertain because it is not embedded in a narrative of 'us'. Its reach is ambiguous because it is both restricted and expanding. And its resilience is uncertain because it is hemmed in by national forms of constitutionalism within its Member States. These features make Union constitutionalism the dynamic and fascinating creature that it is, but they also give rise to tensions in European integration that will reappear throughout this book. It is doubtful whether there can be definitive answers to the political, legal, and cultural questions that these tensions raise. But understanding European constitutionalism in a way that is sensitive to both the law and to its political, economic and cultural context will provide significant insight into what European integration is about, how it works, and what its limits are. As we move through these themes, we will see that much of the EU's constitutionalism is the path-dependent result of political developments (see Chapter two), extensions of its institutional (see Chapter three) and procedural (see Chapter four) structure, which rely heavily on law and the courts (see Chapter five), creating ramifications in the Union's policies, above all the single market (see Chapter six), as well as in the position of citizens (see Chapter seven).

FURTHER READING

Avbelj M (ed), *The Future of EU Constitutionalism*, Oxford, Hart Publishing 2023.

De Búrca G and Weiler JHH (eds), *The Worlds of European Constitutionalism*, Cambridge, Cambridge University Press 2012.

Walker N, 'The European Union's Unresolved Constitution', in M Rosenfeld and A Sajó (eds), *The Oxford Handbook of Comparative Constitutional Law*, Oxford, Oxford University Press 2012, 1185.

Weiler JHH, *The Constitution of Europe*, Cambridge, Cambridge University Press 1999.

2

Constitutionalism and European Integration History

I. HISTORY AND EUROPEAN CONSTITUTIONALISM

WHILE CONSTITUTIONALISM EXHIBITS features that we can understand as independent of a specific political community, such as fundamental rights, separation of powers and the rule of law, it also allows for the peculiarities of a particular polity to unfold, casting them into a constitutional form. These peculiarities unfold over time, and it is here where history plays a significant role. For example, historical analysis can explain the emergence of the polity's distinct institutional and procedural set-up, and can trace the changes within this structure.

European Union constitutionalism is particularly dynamic and volatile (see Chapter one). Consequently, the Union's arrangement of institutions, procedures, and powers has always been in flux. New institutions are created, old ones are given more or less power; procedures are abandoned or reinvented; the balance of power between the actors is constantly changing and depends heavily upon the political, economic, and social context of its integration with European countries. It matters a great deal whether a nationalist government is elected to power in France, whether the Union has to contend with a financial, refugee or pandemic crisis, whether a large national economy is heavily over-indebted, or whether new Member States are admitted. The Union's constitutional architecture and praxis have always reflected the shifts in the geography of its political landscape, and the tides of economic upswings and downswings. History translates into Union constitutionalism more directly and more forcefully than into settled state constitutionalism. We cannot understand, or critically evaluate, EU constitutionalism without understanding its history of integration with European states.

II. INTERGOVERNMENTALISM AND SUPRANATIONALISM: THE FOUNDING PERIOD

A. Europe after 1945

The idea of a European union has reverberated with decision-makers on the European continent throughout Europe's long history. Leaders from the time of imperial Rome through to modern leaders like Napoleon and Hitler have seen a European union as a way of extending their realm of power. Much of that history is therefore horrifyingly violent. Others imagined European union as a triumph over narrow state interests, but those were mostly philosophers rather than decision-makers.[1] When the first half of the twentieth century – with two World Wars emanating from European soil, countless dead, and the economy (together with pretty much everything else) in ruins – brought home the terrible consequences of nationalism, the time seemed ripe to leave that legacy behind and turn to the philosophers' ideas.

For a brief moment, this is what appeared to transpire. The 'European Movement', comprising thousands of individuals in many European countries, felt deeply about the appeal of a European union. Agreement on how to get there was, however, scant, and the movement was torn between fervent federalists and those who did not doubt the legitimacy of their nation-states. It led to the establishment of the Council of Europe in 1949, an intergovernmental organisation which fell far short of integration and sapped much energy from the European Movement. Yet by 1950, European union was not off the table due to a threefold constellation of idealism, strategic concerns, and national interests.

As to idealism, many of the decision-makers were long-standing federalists with idealistic inspirations. All sides felt the need to overcome the extremes of nationalism and the national economic protectionism of the years between World War I and World War II. Decision-makers were anxious to avoid the mistakes that were made after World War I. The Treaty of Versailles had fuelled resentment, suffered from enforcement problems, and been too static when reacting to changing circumstances. Rather than striving to put their boot on Germany's neck following World War II, it was agreed that it would be safer to embrace Germany and enmesh it in a tight system of cooperation.

[1] D Dinan, *Europe Recast: A History of European Union*, Basingstoke, Palgrave Macmillan, 2nd edn 2014, 31.

As for strategic concerns, the emerging Cold War formed an important background for early European integration. While the first impulse in rebuilding Europe was to ward off the possible resurgence of a threat from Germany, this defensive posture soon transformed into a reaction against military and economic threats from the Soviet Union. In 1948, the United Kingdom, France and the Benelux countries (Belgium, The Netherlands and Luxembourg) entered into the Treaty of Brussels, a military cooperation treaty directed against Germany. Only one year later, Stalin was instead seen as the real threat. This shift in focus resulted in the formation of NATO and extending the Western European defence project to include the United States, which strongly backed a united Europe as a bulwark against Soviet communism. The US also enacted a massive aid project for Europe known as Marshall Aid, which they also saw as a way to facilitate European integration. To implement Marshall Aid distribution, the Organisation for European Economic Cooperation (OEEC) was founded in 1948 and led to growing interdependence among European economic systems. Western Europe, then, was populated by a dense network of international organisations (Treaty of Brussels, OEEC, Council of Europe, NATO). With the hardening of the Cold War, it seemed imperative to include a revitalising German economy in the project to integrate Europe. The US therefore forced French foreign policy to change and accept the swift creation of the Federal Republic of Germany in 1949. To gain support from the still wary French elites, coal and steel production in the Ruhrgebiet – a densely populated region at the river Ruhr between Düsseldorf and Dortmund – was placed under the 'International Authority for the Ruhr' in 1949, which was controlled by France, the Benelux countries, the UK and the US. West Germans were very unhappy with the Authority. Further aligning German and French national interests required the creation of a different institutional framework, which would become the European Coal and Steel Community (ECSC), a 'latecomer'[2] among the Western European international organisations and the nucleus of today's European Union.

B. The Schuman Plan 1950

On 9 May 1950, French Foreign Minister, Robert Schuman, presented a proposal that, at first blush, does not seem like much, but would become

[2] KK Patel, 'European Regional Integration from the Twentieth to the Twenty-first Century', in R Coman et al (eds), *Governance and Politics in the Post-Crisis European Union*, Cambridge, Cambridge University Press 2020, 35, at 36.

'something akin to a European Declaration of Independence in its vision and blueprint'.[3] Schuman suggested that France and Germany should pool their coal and steel resources pursuant to an international agreement under which supervisory power was given to an independent body named the High Authority. While named after Schuman, the Schuman Declaration (or plan) was actually the ambitious brainchild of Schuman's right-hand man, diplomat and European federalist Jean Monnet. Its ultimate goal was peace, as the first sentence of the Declaration made clear: 'World peace cannot be safeguarded without the making of creative efforts proportionate to the dangers which threaten it.' The creative effort should ultimately point to a 'united Europe': 'A united Europe was not achieved and we had war.' That goal could only be achieved, said Schuman, through the 'elimination of the age-old opposition of France and Germany'.

That, however, was easier said than done. How do you eliminate 'age-old opposition' in 1950, only a handful of years after the savagery of German occupation, after the holocaust, and after the horrors of World War II? Other international instruments, among them the Charter of the United Nations and the Council of Europe, used lofty rhetoric of friendship, forgiveness, and redemption, which must have sounded hollow in the ears of those whose memory of what Germans had done was still fresh. It would take decades for revulsion and animosity to subside.

Conversely, the Schuman Declaration does not speak of friendship, forgiveness or redemption, and not even of solidarity. Rather, it announced that Europe 'will be built through concrete achievements which first create a de facto solidarity.' Concrete achievements are the opposite of grand plans, on the one hand, and of mere words, on the other. Grand plans, such as the 'United States of Europe', were not on the table, and so the Schuman Declaration flatly rejects them, including the American model: 'Europe will not be made all at once, or according to a single plan.' It would be small and incremental steps that would build Europe, and they would be concrete investments rather than grand words.

The concrete investment of the Schuman plan was a narrow focus on sectoral integration: the shared administration only of coal and steel resources. Monnet and Schuman blended vision, symbolism, and pragmatic national interest. Coal and steel were highly symbolic. First, coal

[3] JHH Weiler, 'Deciphering the Political and Legal DNA of European Integration', in J Dickson and P Eleftheriadis (eds), *Philosophical Foundations of European Union Law*, Oxford, Oxford University Press 2012, 137, at 146.

and steel were needed to forge weapons. The Declaration therefore envisioned a future where 'any war between France and Germany becomes not merely unthinkable, but materially impossible.' Second, joint Allied control of coal and steel production in the Ruhrgebiet was intensely disliked by Germans and equally intensely backed by the French government. Both the Ruhrgebiet and the Saarland, the two most important heavy industry areas in Germany, had been sites for heated contestation between the two countries. Third, coal and steel were the major resources needed to rebuild Europe from the ashes of World War II. Despite their symbolic value and strategic importance, the pooling of coal and steel supplies did not, in the eyes of Schuman and Monnet, eclipse French national interests – on the contrary. Monnet's recovery plan for France (he was head of the French General [Economic] Planning Commission (*Commissariat général du Plan*)) involved expanding steel-producing capacity. That, however, was a problem due to a shortage of coal; French industry was heavily dependent on supplies of coking coal from the Ruhrgebiet.[4] It was highly pragmatic thinking on Monnet's part to combine the first step towards European integration and peaceful German-Franco relations with an idea of how to ensure continued French access to coal.

C. Embracing the Monnet Method: The European Coal and Steel Community (ECSC) 1951–52

On the German side, Chancellor Konrad Adenauer eagerly accepted the Schuman plan. The reasons were, again, both idealistic and pragmatic. Adenauer, like many of the founding fathers of European integration, was a Roman Catholic from a border region who had suffered under Nazi rule. He was firmly committed to Franco-German reconciliation and European integration. At the same time, like Schuman and Monnet, he had the national interests of his country at heart. First, Germany was left a pariah nation after the War. The Schuman plan was a chance to regain international acceptance. Second, Germany was also left divided into two separate states, the Federal Republic of Germany (FRG) and the German Democratic Republic (GDR). Adenauer feared (correctly) that the GDR would be dominated by the Soviet Union. A fervent

[4] S Bulmer et al, *Politics in the European Union*, Oxford, Oxford University Press, 5th edn 2020, at 99.

anti-communist, he was anxious to establish a strong Western, capitalist orientation for the FRG, and, to accomplish that, needed to bind it to the West politically, economically, and strategically. Third, the Schuman plan was a way to remove Allied control of the Ruhrgebiet and to forestall further plans to dismantle its industrial infrastructure.

The Schuman plan was, from the outset, devised for additional European nations to join. The Benelux countries did not need convincing. They had already formed a customs union of their own and immediately saw the advantages they would accrue in an even wider and liberalised market. Squeezed into the northwest corner of Europe by their two large neighbours, they shared heavily interdependent border regions, and therefore had a vital interest in anything that promised peace between them. Italy also joined, even though it was not part of the same industrial region as the other five countries. It was governed by premier Alcide de Gasperi, another Roman Catholic, Christian Democrat, border-region European idealist. Like Adenauer he wanted to rebuild his country's reputation; like Germany, Italy was on the front line of the emerging Cold War (it shared a border with communist Yugoslavia) and had a Communist party popular enough to win elections. European integration would tie the country to the West. De Gasperi also saw a chance to overcome Italy's long-standing economic weaknesses; it was the poorest of the six countries, and liberalisation would turn that around (indeed, a decade later, Italy was among the most advanced economies in Europe).

The glaring absence was, of course, the United Kingdom. British rejection of the invitation to join was not altogether surprising. The UK had never been occupied or defeated; nationalism had not been discredited by fascism (as it had in Germany, Italy, and Vichy France); and the British economy seemed, at the time, far stronger than the economies on the continent. The UK was still an empire and felt like a world power with global strategic and economic responsibilities and interests. British coal supply was also secure since its Labour government had just succeeded in nationalising the British coal and steel industries.

The motives of the founding members are a window on an enduring theme in European integration. While Member States cede sovereign rights to the Union in order to pool powers and share the making of previously autonomous decisions, they do so for common goals as much as for their own national interests. Shared sovereignty, variable boundaries, composite identity, compound governance, and fragmented democracy are all possible as long as the nation-state supplies the Union with its own form of legitimacy. Calculations of what individual Member States get out of the Union are not necessarily churlish, but part of a complicated legitimacy mix within the hybrid creature of the Union. The UK is a case in point: to this day, the UK has been deeply torn over whether or not it belongs in Europe.

The supranational/intergovernmental division of powers – a central issue within the Union system of governance – has its origins in the Schuman plan. The plan's truly revolutionary move was to place coal and steel production under the administration of a High Authority with supranational powers: 'The Authority's decisions will be enforceable in France, Germany and other member countries.' The decisive word here is 'in'. Unlike international law, which is binding 'on' states, the High Authority's power was to pierce the 'corporate veil' of the Member States and have direct effect within each country, just like national laws do. We will see later that this is one of the hallmarks of supranationalism (see Chapter four).

Only a month after Schuman's presentation of the plan, negotiations started in Paris, with France, Germany, Italy, and the Benelux countries, on drafting the Treaty of Paris, the founding document of the European Coal and Steel Community (ECSC). Signed in 1951 and enacted in 1952, the Treaty of Paris established a single market in coal and steel and had four principal institutions. The High Authority, composed of nine appointees who were entirely independent from Member States, was the main executive institution, with decision-making powers directly effective within Member States. A Council, composed of representatives from each government, had only limited decision-making power but rather a consultative role. An Assembly, composed of delegates from national parliaments, had advisory powers. A Court of Justice, with nine judges, acted as the ECSC's judiciary. While the remit of the ECSC was narrow and the common market for coal and steel itself never played a huge role in the history of European integration, its institutional set-up was revolutionary and paved the way towards broader integration.

D. Grand Plans Collapsing: The Failed European Defence Community (EDC) and European Political Community (EPC) 1954

While today it is obvious that moving directly from a Europe of nation-states to a fully integrated union is neither possible nor desirable, this was not so clear in the early 1950s. There were three contending positions as to what should happen to Europe. The first were integrationists who were aiming for a European Federation. The second position sought to protect national sovereignty and aimed for classical treaty-guided cooperation of sovereign governments sharing the same goals (peace and prosperity). The third was the camp of pragmatic problem-solvers, like Jean Monnet, who were sympathetic towards supranationalism but ready to compromise on their way there. Although the Treaty of Paris had been a success of Monnet's approach, federalists now pursued more ambitious goals and made plans to create a European army.

While the US needed European states to step up their defence contributions against the Soviets, and therefore wanted Germany to rebuild its army, for France, German rearmament was unthinkable. French premier René Pleven, and Monnet together proposed a compromise of pooling another resource in common: soldiers. German soldiers would wear European uniforms and not be under sole German command; they proposed creating the European Defence Community (EDC), whose institutional decision-making would be modelled after the ECSC. The problem was that unlike the clear shared interests underlying a common market for coal and steel, there was no sense of a common foreign policy, which rendered a common army superfluous. To address that problem, another supranational organisation, a European Political Community (EPC) was now planned, which they hoped would add political guidance and a democratic dimension. Federalists seized upon the political momentum towards integration and drafted a treaty that would have gone far beyond Pleven and Monnet's plans, creating a comprehensive European federation, with a two-tier European Parliament (one chamber directly elected, one chamber a Senate of members of Member States' parliaments), a European Executive Council, a Council of National Ministers, and a Court of Justice. The EPC, which would have joined the European Convention for the Protection of Human Rights and Fundamental Freedoms (ECHR), would have moved Europe from a space where sovereign nation-states cooperated to an institutional structure akin to a federation.

The Federalists' plans proved to be too much and too fast. Successive French governments did not ratify the treaties, which dealt them their fatal blow. Germany rearmed pursuant to a different international treaty called the 'Western European Union' (WEU), which was an extended version of the Brussels Treaty with Germany and the UK added, and then joined NATO in 1955. The lesson governments learned from the failure of the EDC and EPC was that radical federalism did not work and that Monnet's incrementalist strategy – which came to be known as the *méthode Monnet* – was more likely to succeed.

E. Back to Monnet: Euratom and the European Economic Community (EEC) 1957

Decision-makers regrouped and went back to sectoral integration, especially in economic (rather than highly political) fields such as transport and nuclear power. The idea of a common market – a single market where goods, services, workers and capital could circulate freely across a level playing-field of Member States' territory without barriers – resurfaced as integration's raison d'être. Negotiations on how to deepen European integration ended with the decision to establish two further supranational communities, the European Atomic Energy Community (EAEC, or Euratom) and the European Economic Community (EEC). Both Treaties were signed in Rome on 25 March 1957, were ratified by all Member States, and entered into force on 1 January 1958. Members were the original six states; again, the UK did not want to have anything to do with the common market.

Whereas Euratom was slow and unproductive, the EEC was instantly successful. Its aim was highly ambitious: to progressively establish a single (or common, or internal) market within the territory of its Member States. Not only were barriers to trade – like tariffs, quotas, and discriminatory taxation – to be eliminated, but also a common external tariff was to be established. Its objective was to merge the Member State markets into one single market, avoiding any artificial partition along national lines. This requires, as I will explain later (see Chapter six), both far-reaching deregulatory measures (like the prohibition of non-tariff barriers across all aspects of production) and broad legislation which harmonises Member States' regulatory regimes in a multitude of policy areas. A highly efficient system of government was needed to accomplish such a Herculean task.

The Treaty of Rome's institutional architecture was partly a continuation of the ECSC experience and partly something novel. The Parliamentary Assembly (soon to be called the European Parliament) and the Court of Justice were shared with the ECSC. The EEC had, however, a separate Council of Ministers composed of a representative of each Member State at the ministerial level, and a separate Commission with members who were independent of direct Member State influence. The Council was to represent Member States' national interests, whereas the Commission was to represent the Community interest. The Council and the Commission were supported by a bureaucracy of as many as 3,000 civil servants, a number that would grow in coming years. These institutions of each of the communities were merged in 1965 through the Treaty of Brussels (or 'Merger Treaty') and henceforth shared by all three communities (the ECSC, the EEC, and Euratom).

The subsequent step of allocating the functions and power of these institutions was just as important to their success as establishing them in the first place: Who would legislate? Who would hold executive powers? Here, one of the most persistent themes of this book emerges. For meaningful integration to work, Member States must cede certain sovereign powers to institutions at the European level. Some of these institutions are independent (such as the Commission), while others channel national interests onto the European plane (such as the Council). Even when powers are transferred to Brussels, there will still be a struggle over how much influence Member States retain (intergovernmentalism) and how much influence independent Community institutions will gain (supranationalism).

As we will see in many places in this book, this struggle usually ends in compromise and power-sharing, and it did here as well. Legislative power went mainly to the Council, but the Commission received the exclusive right to get the ball rolling and propose legislation. Executive power, too, was divided between the Commission and the Council. While I will explain the details later (see Chapters three and four), the delicate balance of intergovernmentalism and supranationalism began with the Treaty of Rome.

In this context, another theme, recurrent in this book, arises: the question of democratic legitimacy. Compared to the ill-fated EPC, the EEC placed no trust in parliamentary decision-making. The Parliamentary Assembly, renamed the European Parliament (EP) in 1962, was almost powerless, with a bare right to be consulted in only a few policy areas. But establishing a single market goes to the core of Member State identity and needs robust democratic legitimacy. The previous solutions – legitimacy through national influence in the Council, plus a dose of independent expertise and technocracy from the Commission – would be insufficient. To this day, the Union struggles over solutions to this problem.

F. From Progress to Political Crisis: The 1960s

(i) Economic Success

Economic integration within the EEC made rapid and impressive progress. It hugely expanded its contribution to world trade, and industrial production increased 70 per cent from the previous decade.[5] The elimination of customs duties was completed three years earlier than planned. At the same time, the Common Agricultural Policy (CAP) was created. A highly dirigiste policy, it guaranteed minimum prices for agricultural products and supported farmers financially. These two developments may seem at odds with each other, but they are not. France, the chief architect behind (and principal beneficiary of) the CAP and wary of open competition in a single market, linked the two issues; progress in integrating markets had to be bought with progress in regulating agriculture.

(ii) Legal Revolution

In the legal arena, the Court of Justice in Luxembourg changed the nature of European law forever. In a string of landmark decisions (which I will explain in detail, see Chapter four) throughout the 1960s and early 1970s, the Court took the Treaty of Rome out of the realm of classical international law and ushered in a new age of 'constitutionalisation'. First, it accorded European law 'direct effect'. Individuals could now use EU law provisions and enforce them as rights in their national courts against their Member States. Member States could no longer simply violate their European law obligations, because European law could now act as the law of the land. This was a sharp deviation from orthodox international law. Secondly, the Court decided that European law enjoys 'primacy', or supremacy, over national law. Every European norm trumps every national norm. This bolstered their ruling on direct effect: individuals could now invoke European law against Member States, and they would always prevail when there was a discrepancy between EU and national law. Thirdly, the Court held that competences would be implied in favour of the EEC when necessary to serve its legitimate ends. This inverts orthodox international law doctrine, which states that typically, treaties must be interpreted in a way that encroaches as little as possible on national sovereignty. Finally, the Court read human rights into the Treaty of Rome despite the fact that the Treaty was utterly silent on that issue. Taken together, these doctrines have earned the Court the adjective 'heroic'[6] and ushered European legal studies into its current paradigm of constitutionalism.

[5] I Kershaw, *The Global Age: Europe 1950–2017*, London, Penguin 2018, 161.

[6] JHH Weiler, 'The Transformation of Europe', (1991) 100 *Yale Law Journal* 2403, at 2428.

(iii) EFTA and the UK

The economic success of the EEC led European nation-states that were not members to create an economic organisation of their own. The UK, Denmark, Sweden, Norway, Austria, Switzerland, and Portugal established the European Free Trade Association (EFTA). As the name spells out, EFTA was exclusively concerned with creating a free trade area (and the removal of barriers to cross-border trade), not with melding Member State markets into a common one. Political integration in EFTA was therefore much looser, and the national sovereignty of its members much more protected. This looser integration was reflected in EFTA's institutional architecture, which was significantly less supranational than the EEC's.

EFTA did little to help the UK fight its now deteriorating economic performance. As ties to the Commonwealth faded and the 'special relationship' with the US turned more and more one-sided, the EEC market rapidly overtook Britain's. In 1961, the UK therefore reconsidered its stance toward the EEC and applied for membership. At that time, however, Charles de Gaulle, an ardent nationalist, was President in France and vetoed British entry (something he repeated when the UK reapplied in 1967). He feared that Britain's presence in the EEC would damage relations between the Franco-German leadership, distrusted the UK's 'special relationship' with the United States, and was afraid the UK might alter dynamics in the CAP.

(iv) The 'Empty Chair' Crisis 1965

The existence of the CAP provided de Gaulle with an opportunity to seriously slow down supranational processes in the EEC. Fixed prices and subsidies are expensive, and its financing came under pressure. This coincided with two other developments. The Treaty's fixed timetable mandated a change in the Council's mode of decision-making, moving from unanimous to qualified majority voting (which meant France lost its veto and could be outvoted) in some areas which affected agriculture. Additionally, the Commission proposed to increase supranational involvement in the budget. These developments together pointed towards significantly less individual Member State influence and further supranationalism. De Gaulle fervently objected. When the discussion deadlocked, he imposed a French boycott of all Council meetings, which basically ground the EEC to a halt. De Gaulle's boycott, later dubbed the 'empty chair crisis', lasted seven months and was a major setback for European integration.

The empty chair crisis is one of the first instances of our recurring theme that the supranational/intergovernmental divide can create consequential tensions between Member States and the EU. Who holds the strings when push comes to shove? De Gaulle made it clear that Member States control the pace of integration, or, more accurately, a single Member State does. Without formally retaining a veto, de Gaulle still successfully exercised veto power. The empty chair crisis ended with an uneasy settlement between France and the other five Member States, called the 'Luxembourg Compromise' or the 'Luxembourg Accord'. It allowed for individual Member States to veto Council decisions on matters of 'very important national interest', which was intentionally left undefined. In other words, regardless of whether the Treaty prescribed qualified majority voting as the method of the Council's decision-making, a lone Member State could always demand the decision require a unanimous vote. The Council was stuck with every Member State retaining its veto, whatever the formal law – a state of affairs which lasted almost another 20 years.

This was a resounding victory for intergovernmentalism. The Commission found itself severely weakened as Member State interests gained the upper hand. In this period, the EU's agenda was increasingly controlled by informal conversations between the heads of state and government of the Member States (which later developed into an official institution of its own, the EU's European Council). The shift in the balance of power between the EU and Member States made it harder and harder to successfully carry out legislative negotiations, for every negotiation was now conducted under the shadow of a derailing veto. The Council was increasingly blocked, and the single market became more and more a chimera. The European Communities (as they were called since the Merger Treaty 1965–67) went into gridlock.

G. From Political to Economic Crisis: The Early 1970s

De Gaulle left office in 1969, and the UK was finally able to join in 1973, along with Denmark and Ireland. (Norway did not join because of a Norwegian referendum against it.) This brought the European Communities from six to nine members, and from six to nine vetoes in the Council. None of the three newcomers were shy in advancing their national interests, and voted accordingly. The UK, especially, continued its 'semi-detached stance'[7] and did not really view itself as part of Europe. Its ancient legal, constitutional and institutional traditions, its geography as an island at the edge of Europe, and its historical attachment to the affairs of its overseas empire rather than of the European continent, meant that politicians and population alike retained a certain sense of distinctiveness. With every Member State pursuing its own particularist interests in the Council, and the Luxembourg Accord's unanimity rule in place, the Council accumulated a huge backlog of legislation meant to address problems within the Council's purview.

Amid political paralysis, an economic crisis ensued. The oil crisis of the early 1970s hit when OPEC imposed an oil embargo by cutting oil production by 25 per cent and raising oil prices for sales to Western oil companies by 70 per cent. The price of oil quadrupled, with an enormous impact on European economies that were heavily dependent on oil. The oil crisis exacerbated problems in a European economy already shaken by a turbulent international economic environment. The post-war US economic hegemony had eroded to the extent that President Nixon ended the convertibility of US dollars into gold in 1971, collapsing the post-War international monetary system. It was the first severe recession since before World War II and led to stagnation later called 'Eurosclerosis'. Facing a remade economic world order, the Community would have to reinvent itself; its founding period was over.

H. Taking Stock: The Equilibrium of Supranationalism and Intergovernmentalism in the Founding Period

It is important to understand how, during the founding period, the struggle between supranationalism and intergovernmentalism played out. On the one hand, supranationalism, while a noble ideal, seemed to have succumbed to pressure from national interests. Member States became increasingly involved and influential. Decision-making reverted to the rules of orthodox international law because, despite what the Treaty prescribed, Member States retreated from majority voting and reverted to de facto unanimity in the Council. The powers of the Commission, the most supranational institution in international organisation architecture in the world, declined. The heads of state and government of

[7] I Kershaw, *The Global Age: Europe 1950–2017*, London, Penguin 2018, 165.

the Member States, acting as the 'European Council', took control of the political agenda. Autonomous European policy-making declined in concomitance with the weight of supranational institutions and supranational features in intergovernmental institutions.

On the other hand, with its doctrines of direct effect, supremacy, implied powers, and human rights, the Court of Justice had steered the judicial component of the European Communities away from intergovernmentalism. Its legal order now had all the hallmarks of a proto-federalist one. Transnational law was enforced by individuals against their own states in national courts.

These two developments seem contradictory, but they are two sides of the same coin. The devolution of supranationalism happened in the political field (where decisions and laws are made) and can be called 'decisional intergovernmentalism'. The strengthening of supranationalism happened in the legal field (where law is applied and enforced) and can be called 'normative supranationalism'.[8] Their inverse rise and fall are connected. As a starting point, consider two models of control over an organisation. In the first model, you control decision-making and make sure there is not a single provision you disapprove of. If you succeed – if you approve of all the rules – you do not mind hard law enforcement, because you can be sure that you approve of whatever is being enforced. In the second model, you do not control decision-making, and thus do not approve of every norm in existence, but you have the power to obstruct enforcement of those norms you disapprove of against yourself. If you have that power, you do not mind losing control over the process of law-making.

The Community, in its foundational period, followed the first model. Each Member State retained the power of veto in the Council and therefore succeeded in being 100 per cent in control of the law-making process. Therefore, Member States were able to accept the hardening of the law enforcement process through judge-made doctrines of direct effect and primacy of European law. In fact, they not only accepted these doctrines, but welcomed them. The power of veto means difficult and tortuous negotiations in the Council. Once those result in a successful agreement, however, Member States now *want* the result enforced through muscular legal institutions. This relationship goes in both directions; because of the hardening of law enforcement through the Court of Justice, Member

[8] The nexus has been systematised by JHH Weiler, 'The Community System: The Dual Character of Supranationalism', (1981) 1 *Yearbook of European Law* 267, at 281.

States have a strong incentive to retain control over the law-making process. This incentive was on full display in the Luxembourg Accord: the incentive was strong enough to defy Treaty norms about majority voting. Intergovernmentalism in the political sphere and supranationalism in the legal sphere, then, condition each other. They are not antidotes but represent a balancing of Community and Member States, of centre and margin, and of whole and part. It is an equilibrium.[9]

III. THE NEW SUPRANATIONALISM: THE ROAD TO EUROPEAN UNION

A. Stagnation and Expansion: Mid-1970s to Early 1980s

British, Danish and Irish accession did not yield long-term momentum. On the contrary, Denmark and, above all, the UK became recalcitrant partners in integration, which intensified under Margret Thatcher beginning in 1979. The oil crisis was followed by a larger economic crisis in Europe, and although it was the result of wider trends in international political economy, the Member States did not find a common position in foreign affairs. The Community remained in limbo, with the Council largely blocked. Community objectives were left unfulfilled, and progress was very slow.

The Community received a jolt when a small wave of democratisation swept across Europe in the mid-1970s. Greece's military dictatorship fell, a revolution overthrew the right-wing regime in Portugal, and Spain's longtime dictator, Franco, died. All three newly democratic governments filed applications for membership of the EC and all three applications were accepted, for both democratic and strategic reasons. It was generally assumed that EC membership, which was conditional on having a democratic government, would provide a bulwark against resurgences of authoritarianism, keep intranational anti-capitalist groups at bay, and dissuade Member States from reorientating towards the Eastern bloc. Greece joined in 1981; Spain and Portugal followed suit in 1986.

This 'Southern enlargement' had a huge impact on the Community. Since all three countries ultimately stabilised as democracies, the Community strengthened its own democratic credentials. Politically, the new members

[9] JHH Weiler, 'Community, Member States and European Integration: Is the Law Relevant?', (1982) 21 *Journal of Common Market Studies* 39, at 47.

shifted the EC's orientation toward a stronger Mediterranean focus to policy. While the southern enlargement was politically advantageous for the EC, it was economically doubtful whether the three national economies were ready to join and compete on equal terms. Demand for larger structural funds (which are meant to support poorer regions in Europe) rose considerably. Institutionally, the number of members – 12 members meant 12 veto players – and their growing economic and political heterogeneity led to even greater blockage in the Council.

It was a steep price for maintaining the equilibrium between intergovernmentalism and supranationalism. Institutionally, there was much demand for a reform of decision-making procedures, but due to lack of agreement nothing materialised. Politically, the EC could not deal with a host of pressing issues. Appetite for new projects dried up as the costs of enlargement went up and more diverse interests had to be accommodated. Widening the Community came at the price of deepening its tensions. Economically, Member States mostly dealt with the fallout of the recession, especially rising unemployment, on their own. The single market seemed further away than ever because harmonisation failed. Legally, one of the most problematic developments, also a major theme in this book, began to show: 'competence creep' from the Member States to the Community.

In principle, the Community operates within a limited set of competences defined in the Treaty. It cannot regulate or legislate for what it wants (like state legislatures) but always needs a firm legal authorisation by the Member States in the Treaty to do so. Should Union institutions act beyond their Treaty mandate, they would unambiguously lack legitimate authority for the action taken and rob Member States of their regulatory autonomy. This, however, is precisely what seemed to begin happening: competences and powers appeared to be drifting towards Brussels. The reasons are varied, and I will explain the details below (see Chapter four). Competence creep is of the highest political, legal, and constitutional significance. Politically, Member States were increasingly frustrated with their shrinking regulatory ambit. Legally, it led to a growing fear that Member State legal orders and the Community legal order might clash if Member State courts decided to take matters into their own hands and declare Community abuse of competences unconstitutional. Constitutionally, competence creep subverts the Community's foundations, which is the consensual but limited grant of competence by the Member States. Member State courts would start to reject fundamental constitutional doctrines, like primacy, if competence creep did not stop.

B. The New Supranationalism: The Single European Act (SEA) 1986–87

In response to this malaise, many high-level reports suggested a strengthening of supranational institutions and procedures. In 1984, the Commission, under the dynamic leadership of its new President, Jacques Delors, convinced the Member States to set themselves the target of removing remaining barriers to trade, and completing the single market by 1992 (the '1992 programme'). While this sounded like a restatement of an old objective, it was a watershed moment. Member States agreed on a promising common goal and were ready to do what it took to get there. Part of the impetus was the sluggish development of the European economies, which stood in stark contrast to the Japanese and the US economies.

Again it seemed as if the Monnet method had won the day: rather than a grand scheme of general goals and comprehensive institutional reforms, it was a list of roughly 300 separate measures, written in technocratic, even exhausting detail, that eventually garnered the support from all Member States.[10] Among those measures was the proposal to switch the mode of decision-making in the Council from unanimity to qualified majority voting in single market-related harmonisation matters. In 1985, the European Council agreed on these measures and on the timetable that came with them because they were deemed necessary to reach their shared goals. A new amendment treaty was drawn up, the 1986 Single European Act (SEA), which entered into effect in 1987.

The SEA revitalised the Community in several ways. First, both the target of the single market and its due date provided the Community with a renewed sense of purpose. Second, it had immediate practical consequences in its removal of various barriers to trade. Third, since a single market is such a wide-ranging undertaking, numerous new policy areas came into view as topics the Community would need to involve itself in (protection of health and safety at work, protection of the environment, research and development, social policy, and even some coordination of foreign policy). Fourth, the SEA's introduction of qualified majority voting for single market measures had far-reaching impact. It expedited the legislative process in Brussels, which now took up much

[10] 'Completing the Internal Market' – White Paper from the Commission to the European Council, COM(85) 310 final (14 June 1985). A White Paper is a discussion document from the European Commission that presents specific proposals for EU action.

less time and became immensely more efficient. There was one crucial downside to all this, however: exacerbating the competence problem. The creep of competences to Brussels had started earlier, but since the blocked Council had not been able to act on them, it had not impacted much. Unblocking the legislative process now made them a salient issue. The Commission, in its revived role as agenda-setter, proposed countless measures in policy areas that Member States had never dreamed of surrendering to the Community.

C. The Shattered Equilibrium of Supranationalism and Intergovernmentalism

The lasting impact of instituting qualified majority voting in the Council lay in its upsetting the previous equilibrium between intergovernmentalism and supranationalism. The intergovernmental/supranational balance had been that by retaining their individual veto, the Member States remained firmly in control of decision-making. While controlling law-making, they did not mind extensive law enforcement by the European Court. That control, however, was lost with the SEA. With the veto gone, Member States could now be outvoted and lost their individual grip on law-making.

At the same time, they did not regain control of law enforcement. The Court's doctrines of direct effect and primacy were firmly in place, and individuals were busily suing Member States for breach of European law. European law could not be ignored with impunity.

With the SEA, Member States lost individual control of how European integration unfolded. For the first time in history, they were now bound by norms they had not necessarily agreed to, nor were they in a position to prevent enforcement of such norms against them. Intergovernmentalism lost out.

This was more than merely a shift in the existing balance of power away from the Member States towards the Community institutions. It unleashed a problem of explaining the EC's democratic legitimacy which still remains largely unsolved. The first part of this problem was the broad exercise of power afforded to Member State executive branches. In the Council, members of national executive branches turn into members of the European legislative branch where they can escape, to a large degree, parliamentary accountability to their own state. While this was not a new problem, the SEA's obviation of national legislative channels catalysed executives' enactment of legislation to an unforeseen extent, both in quantity (many more legislative acts) and quality (a significantly wider scope of policies).

The second part of the democratic problem goes deeper and connects with the rise of anti-EU feelings today. The SEA's new supranationalism shoved the issue of legislative legitimacy into the spotlight, eliciting a multitude of difficult questions. Why should, say, Denmark be held to law that it did not want, but which was forced upon it by a coalition of foreign states? What precisely binds Denmark to such 'foreign'-made law? Is there a legitimate legislative process in Brussels? Is the European Union's population a 'European people' whose representatives in Brussels have a legitimate right to legislate for all? Is majoritarianism a legitimate part of a European democratic process, and is it possible to apply the notion of democracy, which has historically evolved solely within state constitutionalism, to European decision-making processes?

These questions about democracy seamlessly extended to questions of collective identity, another major theme of this book. If 'we' are, first and foremost, Europeans, distinctions between 'us' and 'them' within Europe break down, and majoritarian decision-making is nothing more than daily bread. If 'we', however, are Danish, French, German, Polish, or Hungarian, questions about legitimacy linger and require plausible responses to concerns about both democratic procedures and inner justification. The SEA has led European integration on a path that forces Europeans to engage in serious soul-searching, requiring them to find out who they really are, and who they want to be.

D. The Road to European Union: The Maastricht Treaty 1992–93

The 1992 programme was a huge success, both politically and economically. By the target date, almost every measure the Commission had identified was achieved. A wave of investment and business activity ensued, emboldening the Commission to press on. It soon set its sights on monetary union and pushed the idea of a single currency controlled by a European Central Bank. In spite of British opposition, Member States in 1989 agreed to set up an intergovernmental conference (IGC) – which is a meeting of representatives of the Member States to discuss and decide on revisions to the Treaties – to prepare for Treaty amendments on monetary union.

When the communist bloc collapsed and the Iron Curtain came down shortly after, German Chancellor Helmut Kohl seized the opportunity to go down in history as the man who made reunification possible. At the same time, he needed to allay concerns about a possible German hegemon in the middle of Europe. Therefore, he signalled his desire for continuity in Germany's relationship to the Community by pressing for deeper integration to bind Germany ever more tightly with supranational co-operation.[11] As a result, a second IGC, on political union, was convened to run alongside the one on monetary union. Both worked throughout 1991 to prepare the Maastricht Treaty which created the 'European Union'. The UK accepted the Treaty despite its many institutional changes, but only after it had made sure that a chapter on social policy was removed and that it could opt out of monetary union and retain usage of the Pound.

(i) Policy and Institutional Changes

The biggest single policy initiative in the Treaty was monetary union, termed 'Economic and Monetary Union' (EMU). Introducing a new currency, and abolishing old currencies, is of course a hugely complex matter, and Member States had different economic stakes. Since monetary union works only if there is economic convergence, some feared painful structural adjustments. Others feared monetary destabilisation and inflation. The result was, as usual, a compromise. On the one hand, the EU would provide for strict convergence criteria for prospective members of monetary union (such as ceilings on budget deficits). It would also create a strong, independent European Central Bank (ECB). On the other hand, the Union combined lax enforcement mechanisms with broad Member State control over economic policy.

The biggest change the Maastricht Treaty made to the Treaty of Rome was a new Treaty architecture. It reorganised European activities into three areas, or 'pillars', of the new European Union.

The first pillar, by far the most important, included the whole European Community (as well as Euratom and ECSC). Its policy responsibilities were centred around managing the single market, including competition law and external trade, and all related policies, such as environmental, cohesion, consumer protection, and agricultural policies. Its decision-making mode was decidedly supranational. The most important institutional change in this pillar, besides establishing the ECB, was

[11] JJ Anderson, 'The European Union, the Soviet Union, and the End of the Cold War', in D Dinan (ed), *Origins and Evolution of the European Union*, Oxford, Oxford University Press, 2nd edn 2014, 255, at 266.

its empowerment of the European Parliament in a legislative role which, in some matters, became almost the equal of the Council.

The second pillar dealt with 'Common Foreign and Security Policy' (CFSP). Since the Member States saw foreign and security policy as the core of their sovereignty, they did not cede competences in this area to European institutions and cancelled all supranational control. CFSP became an intergovernmental pillar which only imposed weak obligations on Member States, mainly to inform and coordinate through institutions representing state interests (such as the Council and the European Council).

The third pillar was called 'Justice and Home Affairs' (JHA). It dealt with policies such as asylum and immigration and included new mechanisms of cooperation between Member State courts (judicial cooperation) in civil (for example family law or the law of succession) and criminal matters. Like the CFSP, these were subjects close to what Member States defined as sovereign powers, which they were unwilling to give up to supranational modes of decision-making, implementation, and control. The governance mode here was therefore a mixture between the first (supranational) and the second (strictly intergovernmental) pillars.

(ii) Assessment

The Maastricht Treaty left observers ambivalent. Despite its impressive architectural changes and the inclusion of new policy areas, it did not resolve any of the pressing constitutional problems of European integration – problems that trouble the Union to this day.

First, concerns about the EU's relationship to democracy and legitimacy went unassuaged. While the European Parliament had gained more powers, it was still a far cry from national parliaments and, importantly, did not enjoy a convincing amount of social legitimacy. Voter turnout at the first European elections was embarrassingly low and has only continued to sink.

Second, competence creep was not stopped, which led to growing frustration among Member States and made a clash between the CJEU and Member State constitutional courts more likely. Indeed, arguably the strongest Member State constitutional court, the German Federal Constitutional Court, vowed to watch over the European exercise of its competences and threatened to undermine European law supremacy.[12]

[12] BVerfG, 12 October 1993, 89 BVerfGE 155 – *Maastricht Treaty* (translation at: https://iow.eui.eu/wp-content/uploads/sites/18/2013/04/06-Von-Bogdandy-German-Federal-Constitutional-Court.pdf).

Finally, the Maastricht Treaty added the worry that the idea of a European identity would be undermined by growing fragmentation. The pillar structure produced a confusing mix of intergovernmentalism and supranationalism, EMU and CFSP allowed for opt-outs, and social policy found its way into a separate treaty outside the Union framework. Maastricht Treaty norms therefore did not apply to all Member States alike, and this created fear of a possible precedent for a 'Europe à la carte' where Member States could engage in cherry-picking.

Public reaction to the Maastricht Treaty was unfavourable. In France, the Treaty passed a referendum only by the narrowest of margins, in Denmark it passed only at the second attempt. Germans, who loved their Deutsche Mark and the price stability that came with it, withdrew much of their support for European integration. Rather than a symbol of European unity, the new currency (the euro) risked enflaming nationalist sentiments. A revision of Maastricht was already on the horizon.

IV. THE NEW INTERGOVERNMENTALISM: TOWARDS TODAY'S UNION

A. A String of Dissatisfying Treaty Amendments: From the Mid-1990s to the Early 2000s

The Union grew to 15 Member States when three former EFTA countries – Austria, Finland and Sweden – joined in 1995. They did so for two reasons. First, the EC's single market had enormous economic pull. Foreign investment went to the single market rather than to EFTA states. Even big companies from EFTA countries, such as Volvo from Sweden, relocated to the EC. Second, all three countries had been neutral during the Cold War, and membership in the Union, with its CFSP, seemed incompatible with neutrality. This changed with the collapse of the Eastern bloc.[13]

(i) The Amsterdam Treaty 1999

The collapse of the Eastern bloc also meant that many Eastern European countries applied for membership. All Member States paid lip service to a major Eastern enlargement of the Union, but with unequal conviction. Germany and the UK were strongly in favour: Germany for security

[13] Bulmer et al (n 4), 503–4.

reasons, and the UK liked the prospect of a bigger market and anticipated that widening the Union meant it would be harder for the EU to deepen its influence into Member State affairs. France and the Mediterranean Member States accepted enlargement but worried about the shift of attention, money, and power away from the South towards the East.

In 1996, Member States convened an IGC to review how the Treaty was working. One important aspect under review was EMU with its uneasy compromise between hard rules and lax enforcement; another was JHA with its unwieldy decision-making process; and yet another was the CFSP which had disgraced itself during the Yugoslav civil wars. Above all, the Union already had 15 Member States, which had to be accommodated within institutions designed for six. With at least 10 more Member States ready to join, which would bring the total number to 25, and even more hoping to do so, institutional and procedural reform was absolutely essential.

The IGC produced slim results, and the Treaty that resulted from it, the 1997 Treaty of Amsterdam, produced only modest reform.[14] It was not insignificant though. First, it reviewed pillars two and three. In pillar two, the CFSP, the Amsterdam Treaty created the post of High Representative in order to give European foreign and security policy a face and more coherence. It also slimmed down pillar three, JHA, by moving most policies under its purview into the 'normal' supranational decision-making mode within the first EC pillar, thus reducing fragmentation and refocusing pillar three on police and judicial cooperation in criminal matters. Second, the Treaty added policies and provisions that tried to communicate to the population that it had its citizens' interests at heart. The Treaty gave the EU's fundamental rights commitment a more prominent place, introduced a chapter on employment policy, strengthened transparency and subsidiarity, and enhanced competences in consumer and environmental protection. Third, the Treaty replaced unanimity in the Council with qualified majority voting in some areas and gave the European Parliament more powers.

However, all of the pressing issues, such as the size of the Commission and the European Parliament, the nature and details of qualified majority voting, and the institutional framework for a Union of at least 25 members were deferred to a later date. Institutional reform fell short, which meant that even before the ink on the Amsterdam Treaty had dried, everyone knew that a new Treaty would need to be drawn up.

[14] P Craig, 'Development of the EU', in C Barnard and S Peers (eds), *European Union Law*, Oxford, Oxford University Press, 3rd edn 2020, 10, at 24.

(ii) The Nice Treaty 2001

In the late '90s, Eastern enlargement took centre stage. In 1998, accession negotiations began with Poland, Estonia, Slovenia, Hungary, the Czech Republic, and Cyprus; in 1999, with Bulgaria, Latvia, Lithuania, Malta, Slovakia, and Romania. The challenges were enormous. Admitting so many Central and Eastern European countries, who had only recently undergone a transformation from command economies to market economies, would be a formidable undertaking. How could they be accommodated without watering down integration? On a deeper level, if a shared political identity is, in some way, a condition of legitimate exercise of public power, what exactly do Swedes and Bulgarians, Poles and Portuguese, or Germans and Cypriots have in common? The problem of European identity, a recurrent theme in this book, became more glaring.

It was perhaps the monumental nature of the task that set decision-makers against each other. During the longest European Council meeting in the history of European integration, in Nice at the end of 2000, the heads of state and government haggled over the extension of qualified majority voting to more areas, the weighting of votes, and the size of the Commission and the European Parliament. As Desmond Dinan succinctly puts it, 'rarely had national leaders devoted so much time to so few issues with so little to show for their efforts.'[15] The size of the Commission was to be reduced in stages, but Ireland managed to later reverse that decision when the resulting Treaty of Nice did not pass the Irish referendum. Ireland was subsequently allowed to renegotiate some of the terms, just as Denmark had a few years before. The size of Parliament was capped but it was still enormous (well over 700 MEPs). Veto rights were removed from almost half of the Treaty articles where they still applied, but persisted in important areas of national interest.

What Nice will be remembered for, though, is the proclamation of the 'Charter of Fundamental Rights of the European Union'. The Charter was the Union's first written bill of rights, and it had been drafted not by an IGC but by a body termed 'Convention', with a process deliberately created with more transparency (citizens and interest groups could follow it and feed it with suggestions) and democratic legitimacy (representatives from all Member State parliaments and from the European Parliament were added to the usual representatives from Member State governments). The Nice summit did not, however, make the Charter legally binding, leaving that for later.

[15] Dinan (n 1), 270.

While the 2001 Treaty of Nice paved the way towards comprehensive institutional reform, it did not itself arrive there. There was a palpable concern to prevent further competence creep, an increasing emphasis on intergovernmentalism, and hence a weakening of, or at least a new role for, institutions like the Commission.[16] Like the previous rounds of Treaty amendments, the Nice Treaty did not settle fundamental issues concerning democracy, legitimacy, competences, and political identity. More negotiations, and more Treaty amendments, would be needed.

(iii) The Failed Constitutional Treaty 2004

Aware of the difficulty of their task, Member States set in motion a deliberative process over the 'Future of Europe'. Rather than leaving the debate to another IGC behind closed doors, they drew on the 'Convention' format that had led to the Charter of Fundamental Rights. The reason was the problem of democratic legitimacy which had taken centre stage after the SEA. Member State governments were confronted with it each time they amended the Treaties, and national electorates were reluctant to accept the changes. It appeared as if there was a growing gap between public opinion and the elites, and negative referendum outcomes made public opinion impossible to ignore. The 'Constitutional Convention' was meant to secure legitimacy and make integration more inclusive and transparent. Despite these efforts, media and popular attention was low. This left seasoned government representatives to dominate the Convention, and the skillful and experienced Valéry Giscard d'Estaing – as former French Prime Minister and MEP, practically the epitome of a self-selecting Euro-elite – steered the Convention towards a Draft Constitutional Treaty.[17]

The Convention developed its own constitutional vision of the Treaty. The draft used unabashedly constitutional language previously reserved to nation-state political systems ('constitution', 'European laws' etc), and although it did not explicitly mention the word 'federalism', the Treaty had strong undertones of federalist values. It had a primacy clause for Union law, a motto, a flag, an anthem, and a Europe Day.

Public opinion responded very unfavourably. Referenda in France and the Netherlands rejected the Constitutional Treaty by comfortable

[16] Bulmer et al (n 4), 169.

[17] C Church and D Phinnemore, 'Carrying the EU Forward: The Era of Lisbon', in M Cini and N Pérez-Solórzano Borragán (eds), *European Union Politics*, Oxford, Oxford University Press, 7th edn 2022, 29, at 32.

margins (more than 60 per cent of the Dutch voters said no). Much of popular rejection had its roots in general dissatisfaction with unemployment, social welfare difficulties, and globalisation.[18] But the referenda proved that people were not convinced that a constitutionalised, federal Union, replete with its own symbolism, was the right answer. The European Council, in a state of shock and with no 'plan B', thought it best to pause for a 'period of reflection'.

This was a sensible decision for a couple of reasons. First, Member States were divided on how to proceed, and Eurosceptic voices dominated national conversations. Second, with 25 members and three more almost in, institutional reforms seemed more important than ever. Eastern enlargement was close to complete. By 1 May 2004, eight Central and Eastern European countries (the Czech Republic, Estonia, Hungary, Latvia, Lithuania, Poland, Slovakia, and Slovenia) as well as Cyprus and Malta had joined the Union, bringing the number of Member States to 25. Two more eastern countries, Bulgaria and Romania, took longer to satisfy accession criteria, and joined three years later in 2007. Croatia was also a credible candidate that made good progress (it would join in 2013).

B. The Treaty of Lisbon 2007

When Germany took over the Council presidency by rotation in January 2007, it produced a road map for how to proceed. It convinced the other Member States that the institutional reforms made in the Constitutional Treaty were inevitable. A new IGC was launched, worked quickly to sort out some loose ends, and produced a new treaty, the Treaty of Lisbon, which was signed in 2007 and entered into force in 2009. It adopted the bulk of the Constitutional Treaty's reform provisions while dropping the constitutional terminology and anything else that might be reminiscent of a European superstate. It has not been amended since and is the current legal framework for the European Union.

While the Lisbon Treaty finally delivered much-needed reform, the process itself highlighted the continuing tension between democracy and expertise. Given that democratic legitimacy implies taking the result of a referendum seriously, it seemed at least ironic that the rejected Constitutional Treaty was relabelled and repackaged so it could escape

[18] R Dehousse, 'The Unmaking of a Constitution: Lessons from the European Referenda', (2006) 13 *Constellations* 151.

popular vote in those countries that had held referendums and rejected it, and was pushed through in very little time. Many saw this as elitist or cynical; the whole episode did nothing to help the legitimacy of the European Union.

Institutionally, the Lisbon Treaty collapsed the three pillars into one common institutional structure, now called the 'European Union', which replaced and succeeded the European Community (which disappeared). This was certainly more transparent than the Maastricht pillar architecture. There were (and still are) now two Treaties in effect. The first is the 'Treaty on European Union' (TEU) with provisions on values and objectives, core provisions on the main institutions of the Union, and the Union's foreign and security policy. The second is the 'Treaty on the Functioning of the European Union' (TFEU). It is the renamed and reformed EC Treaty, with detailed provisions on the single market, the Union's policies, and the Union institutions and their processes and procedures. Both treaties have the same legal standing. Remnants of the former pillars are, however, still there. What used to be pillar three (cooperation in criminal matters) was moved into the TFEU, in a Treaty chapter called the 'Area of Freedom, Security and Justice' (AFSJ). Some of its decision-making rules are still quite different from the 'normal' supranational decision-making for much of the rest of the Union. The same is true for former pillar two: the CFSP was moved into the TEU, and its rules are still almost exclusively intergovernmental.

The TEU and TFEU, as established by the Lisbon Treaty, are the rules that are in force today, and control what the Union does and how it does it. While I will explain their details in the contexts where they matter, I will simply point here to a few key structural elements.

First, the Treaty placed special emphasis on fundamental rights. It has a basic provision on human rights.[19] Also, the Charter of Fundamental Rights of the European Union was made legally binding, with the same legal value as the TEU and the TFEU.

Second, Member States were eager to demonstrate that they were the ones who held the reins. They focused on Union competences, stressed their limits, categorised them, and included, for the first time, a provision that laid down a procedure should a Member State wish to withdraw from the Union. Unexpectedly, 10 years later that procedure became the legal basis for the UK to leave.[20] All these provisions were reactions to competence creep and designed to strengthen the role of national democracies within the Union construct.

[19] Art 6 TEU.
[20] Art 50 TEU.

Third, the ordinary legislative procedure was established as the default legislative process for most policy areas, strengthening supranational decision-making and empowering the European Parliament in particular. Member States have, however, retained a veto, or some other form of emergency brake, for policies they see as unduly encroaching upon their sovereignty, such as tax harmonisation, CFSP, social security, and criminal matters.

Finally, the Treaty of Lisbon left the tension between supranationalism and intergovernmentalism unresolved. While the Treaty was the culmination of a long period of constitutional consolidation (even if the word, 'constitution', was not explicitly used) and unrelenting expansion of Union activity, Member States and their citizens remained determined to retain some control of the integration process. In many areas they succeeded, since the Treaty allowed for policy-making through intensified policy coordination among Member States rather than through choices and decisions made by supranational institutions. Formally, the European Council and the Council gained more influence. Informally, Member State representatives at all levels increasingly convened in gatherings like breakfast meetings or fireside chats where they predetermined formal meeting outcomes. More often than not, this put Member States in the driver seat.[21]

V. CRISIS MODE: THE LAST 20 YEARS

The Treaty has continued to function reasonably well even while the Union, and with it many other parts of the world, entered multiple crises soon after ratification. A series of overlapping crises – the financial crisis, Brexit, populist Eurosceptic challenges, immigration, and the COVID-19 pandemic – have dominated Union business since 2010.

A. The Financial Crisis

In 2009, it became apparent that Greek government statistics had concealed the true extent of its budget deficit. Greece had escaped serious supervision because, due to EMU's incomplete architecture, Union

[21] D Hodson and U Puetter, 'The European Union in disequilibrium: new intergovernmentalism, postfunctionalism and integration theory in the post-Maastricht period', (2019) 26 *Journal of European Public Policy* 1153.

control over Member States' budgetary policy was weak. Rating agencies downgraded Greece's creditworthiness; Greece was now in danger of defaulting on its debts, which would have collapsed the value of the euro. Member States and Union institutions now had to consider bailing out Greece. With its credit ranking downgraded and its problems with repaying its debt, Greece triggered worries about other Member States' budgetary health (for example Italy's), and serious downward pressure on the euro followed. Since Greece's debt crisis compounded with its banking crisis, there was now a strong likelihood the crisis would spread beyond Greece to countries whose banking sectors were exposed to the housing bubble which had just burst. Indeed, a wave of further credit downgrades rolled through Europe, hitting, among others, Spain, Italy, and even France which was stripped of its triple-A rating. More countries, particularly Ireland, Portugal, Spain, and Cyprus required large support sums.

In response, the EU reformed EMU. After a sluggish beginning, mainly owing to German opposition, and a series of 'measures which are not wholly conventional'[22] undertaken to bail out the debtor countries without violating the Treaty's no-bailout clause, the ECB was ready to assume the role of lender of last resort vis-à-vis Member States to save the euro. Rescue packages, however, came with severe austerity conditions, putting in place a system of fiscal retrenchments and welfare reform of unprecedented breadth. The political consequences were enormous. Demonstrations and strikes turned violent. Governments collapsed across Europe, as did trust in political parties and political institutions, domestic and European. The social consequences of the mandated austerity measures were staggering. Youth unemployment rose to 50 per cent in Greece and Spain. Public health declined because a quarter of Greeks did not have any health insurance. The number of Greeks living at risk of poverty rose from 19 per cent in 2008 to 45 per cent in 2013 while social benefits declined by 25 per cent between 2009 and 2012.[23] The Union's social legitimacy crumbled because people in the states impacted by austerity measures saw those measures either as technocratic dictatorship by independent institutions without democratic accountability (such as the Commission, ECB, and IMF) or as punishment imposed on the poorer South by the richer Northern Member

[22] Advocate General Kokott in her Opinion in Case C-370/12 *Pringle v Government of Ireland and Others*, EU:C:2012:675, para 1.

[23] D Chalmers, G Davies and G Monti, *European Union Law*, Cambridge, Cambridge University Press, 4th edn 2019, 41.

States. Indeed, democratic and even constitutional politics in those states were marginalised.[24] The plunge in trust and social legitimacy led to the rise of populism in many Member States.

B. The Refugee Crisis

The refugee crisis unfolded from the backdrop of increased migration due to the fallout from the 'Arab Spring' uprisings. Many refugees attempted treacherous crossings by sea, across the Mediterranean between Turkey and Greece or between North Africa and Italy. Increasing numbers of people have reached Europe (particularly since 2013 with a spike in 2015), but many died during the journey. Union and Member States were barely up to the challenge. The single market and its system of effectively borderless travel meant that refugees could move from Greece or Italy to countries that were richer, had a more permissive attitude vis-à-vis refugees, and had an already substantial migrant population, like Germany or Sweden. Many refugees sought to claim asylum in those countries. However, this flew in the face of one of the key pillars of the Union's asylum governance (the 'Dublin Regulation') which specifies that an asylum application needs to be made and processed at the point of entry into the Union. Enforcing this regulation put enormous pressure on Italy and Greece, who could not handle the task of processing the sudden influx of migrants in an orderly, timely, and dignified manner. After all, both countries had also been hit hard by the financial crisis.

Member States reacted in very different manners. Italy and Greece called for financial support and help in relocating refugees. German Chancellor, Angela Merkel, unilaterally suspended the Dublin Regulation for a while in order to let refugees in, regardless of their point of entry. Hungarian populist Prime Minister, Viktor Orbán, did the opposite; he made sure refugees on their way to Germany would not pass through Hungary, by completing a wall along its southern border with Serbia. Others (including, after some time, Germany) instigated controls at their borders to monitor and regulate the flow of migrants. Freedom of movement of persons, a cornerstone of the European single market, was in danger of breaking down. States at the periphery of Europe encouraged asylum seekers to move on; richer states and transit states erected barriers and controls precisely to keep that from happening. The Commission

[24] Ibid.

repeatedly pressed for collective responses and tried for mandatory relocation schemes, but to no avail.

With harrowing pictures of dead children on beaches and of thousands of refugees in overcrowded camps, Europe faced a crisis of values. How serious was Europe about human rights and humanism? What does talk of an 'ever-closer Union' and 'solidarity' mean if, in reality, Member States did not help each other? The number of migrants finally went down due to a controversial agreement with Turkey, which promised to close the border, but the crisis of values did not go away. Critics remarked that the 'dirty deal' with President Erdogan, who had turned Turkey into an authoritarian regime, laid bare Europe's duplicity and hypocrisy.

C. The Populist Challenge

Liberal values were also at stake in the rise of national authoritarianism within some Member States. In 2010, Viktor Orbán's Fidesz party achieved a landslide electoral victory in Hungary and retained a comfortable majority in 2014, 2018, and 2022. In Poland, the Law and Justice Party (PiS) under the leadership of Jaroslaw Kaczyński won the 2015 elections and was re-elected in 2019. Fuelled by the euro crisis and the refugee crisis, both governments had stated their ambition to steer their countries away from liberalism. Motivated by illiberal, and sometimes ethnic, nationalism and by hostility to migration and minorities, they began a series of changes to their constitutions, limited free media outlets, and weakened the power and independence of the judiciary, a process called 'democratic backsliding'.

The Union was faced with the novel dilemma of Member States abandoning the values of the Union, including respect for democracy, the rule of law, pluralism, justice, and solidarity.[25] Article 49 of the Treaty on European Union declares that only states that respect these values and are committed to promoting them may be admitted to the Union. While it is easy to keep illiberal states out of the Union, it is another matter entirely to impose sanctions on states that are already members and then turn illiberal. The Treaty provision tailored as a response to serious and persistent breaches of EU values[26] requires unanimity. Unsurprisingly, Poland and Hungary pledged they would block such sanctions against

[25] Art 2 TEU.
[26] Art 7 TEU.

the other. A new 'rule of law mechanism' providing for a process of dialogue and reports was put in place, but it did little to end the rule of law crisis.

Initially, the Union did little and was criticised for its passivity. Then the Commission started to bring cases against Hungary and Poland to the Court of Justice of the European Union, which ruled against them. Both countries changed some of their controversial policies, but neither did so comprehensively or substantially. In response, the EU established financial incentives to reverse democratic backsliding. A regulation informally known as the 'Rule of Law Conditionality Regulation', for instance, made respect for the rule of law a condition for Member States to claim funds from the EU budget.[27] The Commission and the Council froze funds of more than €100 billion, which prompted more reform. PiS rule in Poland has since come to an end, paving the way for restoring democracy there (which turns out to be far from easy), but the situation remains extremely tricky. Both illiberal governments have enjoyed overwhelming public support in their countries, and the same public backs their countries' Union membership. Exit, in other words, is not a possible resolution. The surge in populism has already damaged the Union's constitutional architecture in that both countries have openly defied CJEU judgments and undermined constitutional doctrines. With more populist parties on the rise in other Member States, the problem is unlikely to go away any time soon.

D. Brexit

In 2016, after an extraordinary political gamble by then Premier, David Cameron, and a bitter, often resentful and untruthful referendum campaign, the UK narrowly voted to withdraw from the Union. The outcome of the referendum presented a considerable shock to most onlookers. The country was split down the middle, with the poor, the old and those without a university education most likely to vote 'leave', and opposition to migration and multiculturalism being the principal drivers. The affluent, those under 45 years old, and those with a university education were most likely to vote 'remain'.

Negotiations were extremely difficult, mostly because of the border between Northern Ireland and the Republic of Ireland and the haggle

[27] Regulation (EU, Euratom) 2020/2092 of 16 December 2020, OJ L 433 I/1.

over future UK–EU relations. Whereas UK negotiators were not well prepared, the Union managed to speak with one voice and to protect its single market. The Union's united front stemmed from the existential nature of the challenge Brexit posed to the Union. For the first time in the history of European integration, exit had proven a viable alternative to reform. The Union faced the real possibility of a domino effect, especially from Member States with right-wing or left-wing populist governments or leanings.

However, not every British 'leave' vote was a populist one. Some of the criticism levelled at the Union had a grain of truth to it, even if the 'us versus them' rhetoric and the 'foreign judges' campaign chose language that was hyperbolic and simplified things dramatically. But such is the nature of political campaigns, and dramatic, reductive messaging does not mean that there was no truth in the claim that European integration significantly limits national regulatory autonomy. It is one of the consistent themes of this book that Union governance alters national democratic processes, mostly by empowering the executive branch at the expense of the legislature, and that it reduces judicial control by national courts. There are many compensations, but they are not, in nature, democratic. It is not that far-fetched to reframe this dynamic as a curtailing of democratic self-government, and it would be a mistake to dismiss demands for a more democratically accountable Union as objectionably populist.

E. The COVID-19 Pandemic

In 2020, the COVID-19 pandemic hit the world, and Europe. The first response of Member States was not to act together in solidarity, but to look after their own. Imposing export bans on medical grade goods in short supply, and introducing border restrictions was, perhaps, a natural reaction to the deadly and contagious pathogen. But the Member States' reactions did little to strengthen belief in the ubiquitous rhetoric invoking 'European values', and challenged the core project of integration: the single market.

Union reaction was therefore swift, even though the Union has scant competences in health. Health is a policy area where states have been reluctant to cede powers. The Union therefore used powers focused on its authority over the single market and fiscal powers.

First, using its single market competences (which are numerous, see Chapter six), the Commission threatened Treaty infringement proceedings against Member States, reiterated the importance of the free movement of goods to combatting the pandemic, called for solidarity between Member States, and framed the single market as the best way to get there. Its arguments shifted political attention away from regarding the pandemic as an issue of national public health and reframed the necessary response as one of European public health, all-the-while threatening legal proceedings against non-compliant Member States.[28]

Second, the Commission intervened in the market for pharmaceutical products, again using its single market powers. It negotiated agreements with vaccine producers and concluded advance purchase agreements on behalf of interested Member States. That strategy was beset with supply and rollout problems, some of them the fault of Member States.[29]

Third, the Union used its fiscal powers and its ability to mobilise funds to support Member States. One response was to temporarily suspend EMU limits on national deficits and debt. Another was to make huge sums of money available to the Member States. The most important instrument was the 'Recovery and Resilience Facility', established in the context of an amended long-term EU budget with a recovery package of €750 billion in grants and loans (known as 'Next Generation EU', NGEU). The size of this package alone was enormous enough to raise eyebrows, and Member States, for the first time in integration history, granted the Commission a mandate to issue such a high amount of debt on the international capital markets on behalf of the Member States. While this was (in the words of the European Council) in response to the 'unparalleled economic challenge' of the pandemic, and thus a one-time event, the joint issuance of common debt bonds through the Commission opened Pandora's box. Southern Member States immediately declared this to be the model for the future, and the Commission, in 2022, proposed to issue new EU debt to cover Ukraine's short-term financial needs. Unsurprisingly, this is politically fraught terrain and strongly contested.

Both the total size of lending and the joint issuance of debt bonds signal a shift in the Union's raison d'être. It is no longer mainly about increasing GDP through the efficiency of the single market (where the Union acts as a law-maker) and maintaining the common currency (where it acts as a policeman over Member State budgets and banks), but about security through fiscal solidarity (where it acts as a lender).

[28] E Brooks et al, 'COVID-19 and EU Health Policy', in M Cini and N Pérez-Solórzano Borragán (n 17), 421, at 429.

[29] Ibid, 430.

Indeed, the COVID-19 pandemic focused the EU on healthcare, social assistance, mitigation of unemployment risks, and industrial recovery – matters that are central to the welfare state.[30]

F. Crises as Self-Reinforcing Cycles?

Much of the EU's management of the aforementioned crises shares important characteristics in form, substance, and effect. Formally, its emergency measures are usually undertaken at the last minute by institutions that enjoy, at best, mediocre democratic legitimacy, are not engaged in much consultation, and are relatively indifferent to popular support. Substantively, such measures are highly intrusive. Their effect is to sideline domestic democratic procedures, which leads to the popular impression of being disempowered by far-away technocrats. Since these Union measures are often accompanied by an 'emergency discourse' that denies the existence of alternative political action, the demand for alternatives is satisfied, rhetorically, by populist movements. Populism stakes much of its appeal on criticising self-referential elites, and the Union's crisis management is an ideal target for them. The result is a European Union that appears to undermine democratic self-government, damage the underlying values of democracy and freedom, and threaten the constitutional and cultural identities of Member States. This leaves the Union between a rock and a hard place. It can go back to a model of integration where it acts without democratic input and relies solely on output legitimacy, or it can bear the costs of inaction. Both responses provoke nationalist backlash which, in turn, facilitates Union emergency action.[31]

VI. CONSTITUTIONAL CHALLENGES

Despite the changing tides of economic swings and political shifts in post-War European history, the trajectory of the Union's development is remarkably linear. It started as an international organisation

[30] P Genschel and M Jachtenfuchs, 'Postfunctionalism Reversed: Solidarity and Rebordering during the COVID-19 Pandemic', (2021) 28 *Journal of European Public Policy* 350.

[31] C Kreuder-Sonnen, 'An Authoritarian Turn in Europe and European Studies?', (2018) 25 *Journal of European Public Policy* 452.

that managed a small part of the 'crowded space' between its Member States and, through ambitious institutional, procedural, and doctrinal measures, extended its ambit ever further, reaching ever deeper into politically salient affairs. It now seems primed to take on matters associated with the modern welfare state. In all this, the Union was uniquely effective. Effectiveness, however, came with a price. Consolidating the Union's constitutional system meant destabilising national constitutional systems, especially with regard to democratic self-government. Broadening the scope of Union powers meant decreasing national regulatory autonomy. While in the past, Member States were generally supportive of European integration, they have become more ambivalent. As the shaky democratic credentials of the Union have moved centre stage, Member States' permissive consensus has reverted into a constraining consensus. This makes it difficult to find the unanimous agreement that is necessary to amend the Treaties. The upshot is that Member States are caught in an uneasy tension. On the one hand, they are anxious to keep integration strong so they can weather future crises, continue to reap economic benefits (the UK's economic difficulties after Brexit are a cautionary tale), and find Europe's geopolitical place in a world where strongmen and new superpowers unapologetically redraw maps (the cautionary tale here is Ukraine). On the other hand, they are just as anxious to protect their national interests as ever and remain firmly in charge of what direction the Union is about to take. This keeps old constitutional challenges alive and aggravates them: How to distribute power between Union and Member States and balance supranationalism and intergovernmentalism? How to produce legitimacy to counter growing popular discontent towards Europe? These challenges linger on within a context of centrifugal forces. Materially, the gap between wealthy northern and continental Member States and struggling Member States in the south and the east has grown and increased the need for social solidarity. Socially, the disagreements over cultural issues (gender, religion etc) and liberal democracy have further exacerbated tensions. The next chapters will explain the institutional and procedural toolkit which allows the Union and its Member States to approach and confront these challenges.

FURTHER READING

Dinan D, *Europe Recast: A History of the European Union*, Basingstoke, Palgrave Macmillan, 2nd edn 2014.

Dinan D (ed), *Origins and Evolution of the European Union*, Oxford, Oxford University Press, 2nd edn 2014.
Milward AS, *The European Rescue of the Nation-State*, London, Routledge, 2nd edn 2000.
Patel KK, *Project Europe: A History*, Cambridge, Cambridge University Press 2020.
van Middelaar L, *The Passage to Europe: How a Continent Became a Union*, New Haven CT, Yale University Press 2013.

3

Institutions and Power

I. CONSTITUTIONALISM AND THE UNION'S INSTITUTIONS

THE EUROPEAN UNION'S system of governance has a bad reputation. It is often depicted as a tremendously bloated bureaucracy that wastes taxpayers' money, engages in obscure political squabbles, and is stacked with faceless functionaries applying rigid rules far removed from the citizens. This is a tabloid cliché. What is true, however, is that its processes are highly complex and it does offer a low level of accountability. The result of the more nuanced truth thus remains a worrying distance between EU officials and citizens.

The Union's institutional configuration is necessarily complex because it reflects the unusual nature of EU constitutionalism. Recall that the Union has neither sovereign territory nor a population of its own and must instead inhabit the 'crowded space' between its Member States. Its constitutionalism is therefore hybrid and composite, and works to ensure collaboration, cooperation, and mutual respect between the Union and its members (see Chapter one). Without effective collaboration, integration would dissipate. For instance, the Union does not have its own police force or administrative machinery on the ground, but instead relies on the compliance of Member State administrations to implement its laws. It therefore has to take Member State interests into account when it makes law or policy. Consequently, its governance apparatus needs to have inbuilt mechanisms that incorporate national interests into its decision-making process, either through specific institutions (such as the Council) or through the representation of national voices in hybrid procedures. These mechanisms, and the resulting influence of Member States, vary depending on the policy area in question. Policy-making in cross-border trade in goods, for example, is decidedly less aggravating to the tensions we have discussed around identity, democracy, and national sovereignty than in foreign and defence policy, and therefore features a more prominent role for supranational institutions. Complexity, then, is the concomitant feature of EU constitutionalism.

Specifically, the Union's institutional complexity undercuts what may be the defining idea of institutional design within state constitutionalism: separation of powers. The national constitutional template divides authority between institutions so that they may check each other. EU constitutionalism, however, places a premium on facilitating institutional cooperation. Its defining feature is not distributing power to legislative, executive, and judicial branches, but balancing the interests of individual Member States and those of the Union as a whole. To be sure, Union institutions do in part mirror domestic bodies, and a traditional separation of powers is not entirely missing. However, the main institutional balancing in the Union takes place not between its own branches, but between the Union and its constituent parts.

Just as the complexity of Union institutions is the logical outcome of the peculiar nature of EU constitutionalism, so too is their low level of accountability. Union institutions are limited to only the powers that Member States have transferred to them (see Chapters one and four). Those powers are granted so that the EU institutions may realise specific goals articulated in the Treaties. Their mission is therefore much more goal-oriented than that of national institutions, and their legitimacy is tied more intimately to how effectively they realise those goals. That basis for Union constitutionalism shifts its institutional focus away from 'input legitimacy' (accountability, for instance through democratic elections) and thus gives far more attention to its 'output legitimacy' (effectiveness in achieving goals). Indeed, since democratic processes are rarely efficient and often cumbersome, Union institutions have a weak link to them precisely *in order to* ensure that they are better able to deliver on their goals.

The downside is obvious. First, measuring legitimacy by the ability to produce higher quality collective goods for European citizens alone makes Union institutions vulnerable to the vicissitudes of political and economic circumstances. Second, if voters cannot determine who is accountable for what, they will feel that European integration is a trade-off in terms of self-government. Third, low accountability means low sensitivity to citizens' concerns because unaccountable institutions do not design policy outcomes with public opinion in mind. Low sensitivity, in turn, is unresponsive to the rise of Eurosceptic sentiment, and may even have caused it.

The Union's institutional set-up therefore involves a balance, not only between Union and Member State interests, but also between efficacy and democracy. That balance varies between policy fields, is highly contested, and differs from what the state template of constitutionalism suggests.

II. THE EU INSTITUTIONAL FRAMEWORK

The Union's main political institutions are the European Parliament, the European Council, the Council, and the European Commission. The denomination of most of them – 'Council', 'European Council', and 'Commission' – indicates that the Union is indeed built upon novel institutional foundations, though terms like 'Parliament' suggest some continuity with state experience.

At both the legislative and executive levels, one body representing Union interests and another representing national interests are bound together. This institutional configuration is the result of a dilemma the founders faced, and the compromise they achieved. If the Member States want to pursue a common policy in certain fields, should they either go down a well-trodden path and do it through bargaining and negotiations between governments? Or should they try something new and place the policy in the hands of a largely independent institution which makes all the decisions? On the one hand, the classical intergovernmental way would lead to processes of laborious bargaining and produce results governed by the lowest common denominator. On the other hand, the supranational way would dramatically reduce national regulatory autonomy and minimise democratic legitimacy.

Jean Monnet's idea, in 1951, was to place decisions about coal and steel under the power of a supranational institution (see Chapter two). From the sidelines, British Prime Minister, Clement Attlee, attacked this institution as 'an irresponsible body appointed by nobody and responsible to no one'.[1] The Dutch, too, were suspicious and resisted leaving national governments without tight control over Community power. Monnet backed down and agreed to get Member States' governments involved. The initial institutional configuration of European integration was thus born: a supranational authority and Member States' governments in the driving seat, plus some judicial and a little parliamentary control.

Thus, the Treaty of Paris created the innovative High Authority (what we now know as the Commission) and gave it an institutional counterpart, the Council. Whereas the Commission was independent and had European interests in mind, the Council was composed of Member State

[1] Quoted in L van Middelaar, *The Passage to Europe: How a Continent Became a Union*, New Haven CT, Yale University Press 2013, 43.

ministers and had national interests in mind. The two institutions shared the power to legislate, in that the Commission alone had the power to *propose* policies and legal acts, whereas the Council had the power to *decide* based on these proposals (known then as 'the Commission proposes, the Council disposes'). This interplay between institutions representing the European general interest and institutions representing national interests still forms the essence of what has become known as the 'Community method'. The *Pas de deux* of Commission and Council was later altered through the empowerment of the European Parliament (or EP) and the addition of the European Council (the heads of state and government). Each gained more power over time, the EP because of growing concerns about democratic legitimacy, the European Council because of growing concerns about Union efficiency. The basic institutional configuration however – institutions representing the general European interest (Commission and Parliament) paired with institutions representing the interests of the Member States (Council and European Council) – has survived to this day.

III. THE COMMISSION

Among the Union's political institutions, the Commission is arguably the most interesting, and perhaps also the most controversial. For the first time in history, a separate executive body with significant powers and its own political leadership has been set up at the centre of an international institution.

A. What it does

Article 17(1) TEU underscores that the Commission 'shall promote the general interest of the Union and take appropriate initiatives to that end' and continues to list the Commission's powers. They fall into three categories: policy elaboration, policy implementation and management, and enforcement.

The most important role of the Commission is that of an agenda-setter. In nearly all areas (except the CFSP and some areas of police cooperation), it has the sole right to develop policy proposals. Almost nothing can be done unless the Commission proposes and initiates legislation for it. This includes negotiating international trade and cooperation agreements.

Once Union law and policy are in place, it falls to the Commission to implement them. Often, the Union legislator (Council and Parliament) lays down broad principles and leaves the technical details to the Commission. The Commission then elaborates 'delegated' or 'implementing' rules, sometimes in cooperation with regulatory agencies created for that purpose. The Commission also 'manages' policies. Among these, two stand out. One is competition policy since the Commission is the competition authority for the single market, including powers to vet and veto mergers. The other is the Union budget since the Commission has the power not merely to propose the draft budget but also to ensure that Union funds are invested wisely. Its role, then, is to turn broad legislation into concrete rules to regulate complex tasks.

Finally, the Commission acts as guardian of the Treaties and deals with non-compliance. It monitors the correct application of Union law in the EU and its correct implementation in the Member States. It can send warnings, impose fines, and bring cases before the Court of Justice (see Chapter five). It can also penalise Member States that run up excessive budget deficits. Its responsibility is to prosecute Member States whose violation of Union rules threatens the effectiveness of European integration.

These powers make the Commission the core executive of the Union, although its tasks go beyond what executive powers do in any given political system. They are not far short of powers enjoyed by national governments, at least in many economic fields. In other fields, however, the Commission's power is limited in comparison with national government executives. It does not, for example, wield powers over armed forces, foreign policy, or the nomination of judges.

The Commission uses its powers astutely and in combination. For instance, it relies on its privileged position with the Court of Justice to foster case law in areas where it wishes to push its legislative agenda through. In a strategy aptly called 'lesser evil', the Commission poses a dilemma by initiating legal proceedings against Member States in Luxembourg, thus threatening unpredictable outcomes through judge-made case law and legal uncertainty. Governments can avoid the worst-case scenario of an adverse court ruling by agreeing to a compromise in the Council. The strategy changes the options Member States can decide between. Instead of deciding whether they prefer a common European policy to their national prerogative, they must weigh whether they prefer a common policy to regulation through case law. Most governments choose the former. In another strategy called 'divide and conquer', the Commission uses the infringement procedure in Luxembourg to initiate domestic changes in some Member States, thus breaking down opposition in the Council and winning allies. It targets key governments within the blocking minority in the Council, which are then likely to switch sides and support the Commission proposal for policy change.[2]

Much of the Commission's strong position within, and huge influence on, the Union's political process is a result of its agenda-setting role. Not much can happen without the Commission deciding to make a proposal, which then shapes the ensuing political debate. Furthermore, the Commission is also a veto player. It can withdraw a proposal at any time, particularly if it is not happy with the changes that the Council and Parliament, the Union's co-legislators, agree upon. Therefore, Council and Parliament cannot simply ignore the Commission's viewpoint after the proposal has been made; the threat of withdrawal gives the Commission significant influence on the subsequent debates and, ultimately, the outcome (see Chapter four). It is, so to speak, the third, non-official co-legislator.

B. How it is Organised

The Commission is a hybrid creature, and the name refers to two bodies. Its most prominent facet is the political 'College' of 27 Commissioners, which provides supranational leadership. But the Commission is also a powerful permanent bureaucracy.

(i) Commission Bureaucracy

The Commission bureaucracy employs some 30,000 officials based in Brussels. They are recruited through competitive examination; unlike other international bodies, the Commission does not rely on Member States to appoint them. They are spread across more than 40 Directorate-Generals (DGs) and special services that cover an array of policy sectors, such as competition, agriculture, or the environment. These DGs and services are the equivalent of national ministries. They operate in a similar fashion. Portfolios vary in importance, depending mostly on how important the policy field covered by the DG is and how much power

[2] These strategies are described in detail, with many examples, by SK Schmidt, *The European Court of Justice and the Policy Process: The Shadow of Case Law*, Oxford, Oxford University Press 2018, 100–06.

the Union enjoys in that field. In some fields, like competition policy or agriculture, the Union has both legislative and executive powers and is largely independent from Member States; DG Competition and DG Agriculture are, therefore, powerful DGs. In other fields, like education or culture, Member States have retained many powers for themselves; DG Education, Youth, Sport and Culture is correspondingly less powerful (and naturally less coveted among Commissioners and civil servants as a workplace).

The number of approximately 30,000 officials seems high for an international organisation, and it is habitually invoked by Eurosceptics to denounce the Commission as a bureaucratic monster. Relative to national or regional administrative bodies, however, 30,000 civil servants is a small number for an administration that organises a polity of 450 million citizens. By way of comparison, Munich, a German city with 1.5 million citizens, has an administration of well over 50,000 employees. One of the reasons for the Commission's relatively small size is that Union law is largely applied at the national level, and the Union relies on national administrations to implement EU law. Cities like Munich, conversely, employ people who handle quotidian tasks like building and policing streets and litter-picking. For instance, even though veterinary inspections at the EU border are regulated by Union law, it is national civil servants of the border states who conduct them. This is different from many federal states, including the US, which use their own federal agencies rather than State officials 'on the ground', and is the effect of the Union's constitutional position in the crowded space between Member States. It provides bridging mechanisms and manages interdependence through interpenetration, but it does not set up competing implementation structures.

(ii) College of Commissioners

The College of Commissioners acts as the highest decision-making body within the Commission; it is its face and its powerhouse. Each Commissioner, one from every Member State, is nominated by the head of state or government of their country, like a national minister. Yet, members of the Commission are 'completely independent' and may 'neither seek nor take instructions from any Government',[3] and 'Member States shall respect their independence and shall not seek to

[3] Art 17(3) TEU.

influence them'.[4] These strictures turn members of the College from national politicians into independent office-holders because the Commission, in its role as an honest broker between Member State interests and as enforcer of Union law, needs to be seen as a neutral actor. Every Commissioner has a portfolio, all of which naturally differ in their profile and desirability, leading to controversy around portfolio assignments. The number of Commissioners has increased over the years as more Member States were added, growing from six to 27. This presses the decision-making process to its limits, but still Member States decided to stick with one Commissioner per country. This seems surprising, considering that instructions from national governments, or other attempts to influence the independent Commissioners, are ruled out by the Treaties in the strongest terms. The reason is that Member States – especially smaller ones who do not have much power in other Union institutions – still defend what they perceive to be their national interests in the Commission. Commissioners are independent, but they do not lose their national identity. There is still a sense of legitimacy in having 'our' Commissioner who speaks 'our' language and appears before television cameras. While blatant partisan bias is rare and Commissioners justify their activities in the European general interest, Commissioners' behaviour and decisions are, in one way or another, inevitably influenced by their national affiliations.[5] And they should be: Commissioners bring valuable national sensitivities to the Brussels table, and they also act as envoys for communicating and explaining Union decisions to national constituencies.

(iii) Commission President

The College of Commissioners is chaired by the Commission President who is responsible for the overall policy coordination and who allocates the portfolios among the Commissioners (with the exception of the foreign policy portfolio, which is reserved for the High Representative of the Union for Foreign Affairs and Security Policies).[6] The President has a key role in the Commission: he or she can reshuffle the Commission and force Commissioners to resign. These powers are similar to those of national prime ministers. The analogy does not fully hold though: there

[4] Art 245 TFEU.
[5] R Thomson, 'National Actors in International Organizations: The Case of the European Commission', (2008) 41 *Comparative Political Studies* 169.
[6] Art 17(6) TEU.

has never been a major reshuffle and the Commission President has no veto power over anything. Moreover, since Commissioners are chosen by their national governments, they are not all members of the same political party, so there is no guarantee of a close ideological fit with each other or with the President. Still, the President does have major influence over the rest of the Commission, and over the Union political process in general. Certain Presidents (for instance, Jacques Delors 1985–94) have used this influence to great effect (see Chapter two).[7]

Historically, the Commission President and the Commissioners were appointed 'by common accord' of the Member States' governments. Member States simply accepted whoever was nominated as Commissioner by the other governments. Commissioners were (and still are) national senior cabinet members; the Commission Presidents have almost all been, since 1995, sitting prime ministers in their national governments. Due to concerns about the Commission's legitimacy, the role of the European Parliament in the appointment process has considerably increased over the years. Since the Commission President wields so much influence, the appointment process has turned quite contentious, resulting in big spats in 2014 and 2019.

The President is elected by the European Parliament on a proposal by the European Council (the heads of state and government), which is obliged to take into account the results of the elections to the European Parliament.[8] The first step in the process – which prior to 2014 was the decisive one – is thus undertaken by the heads of Member States in the European Council. Their priority is to find a President of impeccable competence who can command the confidence of national governments. In 2014, however, Parliament tried to subvert the usual order of this process. The largest parties decided in advance who their preferred candidates for Commission President were, and had them explicitly campaign in the European Parliament election campaign as candidates of their parties (*Spitzenkandidaten*) for that post. Obviously, this imitated national election processes where voters know that the political party they vote for will determine who becomes prime minister. Parliament did so to assert its own democratic credentials. Just as obviously, this

[7] H Kassim, 'The Presidents and the Presidency of the European Commission', in E Jones et al (eds), *The Oxford Handbook of the European Union*, Oxford, Oxford University Press 2012, ch 16; on Commission Presidents who did *not* use their powers effectively, see D Dinan, 'Famous Non-Performers: Franco Malfatti, Gaston Thorn, and Jacques Santer', ibid, ch 17.

[8] Art 17(7) TEU.

came at the expense of the powers of the European Council, with heads of state and government expected to acquiesce in the European Parliament's choice. Predictably, the European Council was not happy about this change, but yielded in the face of pressure from Parliament, Commission, and much of the media (who loved the idea that back-door negotiations would be replaced by a democratic process), and the candidate of the winning party, Jean-Claude Juncker, was indeed nominated and then elected.

Five years later, in the 2019 elections, the EP tried to entrench the *Spitzenkandidaten* process, again interpreting the Lisbon Treaty's vague rules to mean that the European Council would have to elect the nominee of the Parliament party with the most seats as Commission President. For this election cycle, it would have been conservative European People's Party chair, Manfred Weber. He had forged an impressive career in the EP but had never held high political office in Germany and had no executive experience. The European Council flatly refused to nominate him. After long consultations, the European Council and the European Parliament compromised on the conservative German Ursula von der Leyen, a former minister in Angela Merkel's cabinet. The *Spitzenkandidaten* process seemed dead in the water; the European Council had asserted its power. In 2024, though, it has retained influence over the Commission President's selection because the conservative European People's Party nominated incumbent President von der Leyen as *Spitzenkandidat*, thus securing European Council consent early on.

C. Democratic Credentials

The Commission draws its legitimacy from its reputation as an honest broker between Member States, and from its expertise. Many believe that these considerations do not make it sufficiently democratically accountable given the great deal of power it has. Indeed, the Commission is at the centre of the Union's decade-old dilemma of input and output legitimacy. On the one hand, more accountability might impair its performance as an effective problem-solver, since accountability risks compromising the Commission's independence. On the other hand, more effectiveness makes it harder to integrate it into a democratic decision-making process in Brussels.

The Commission itself reacts to this dilemma by playing to both sides when needed. In response to the charge of insufficient accountability, it insists that it assumes the role of a technocratic management body that consists of impartial experts and does no more than hold Member States to their Treaty commitments. In response to the charge of insufficient effectiveness, it assumes the role of a highly political decision-making body that consists of seasoned politicians pursuing the European common good. The Commission, in a virtuoso manner, oscillates between the opposing ends of an executive's role: that of the managerial function of the independent agency and that of the political function of a true government. While in the Union, citizens do not elect the Commission President, and cannot even vote the Commission out of office, the Commission nonetheless has long harboured the wish to be a true Union government and to wield powers more akin to a federalist system. Member States, however, will not permit it, for fear of further loss of political control.

D. Promoter of the General Interest of the EU

Being something of the 'conscience' of European integration, the Commission has traditionally been seen as *the* supranational voice of the collective interest within the European Union.[9] More recently, however, it has faced strong competitors for that role, notably the European Parliament, which can more persuasively claim to represent Europe's citizens as it is the only institution within the Union's government that is directly elected. The European Council too has collective European interests at heart, even though it is not part of the Union's supranational structure but still a clearly intergovernmental body. Even the Council is not, as we will see, insensitive to European collective interests. This mounts pressure on the Commission to justify its strong position given its undemocratic nature. The *Spitzenkandidaten* process was the immediate result of that pressure, as it promised to lend at least some democratic credibility to the Commission President. The Member States' resistance to it circles back to one of the major themes in this book: What is the acceptable balance between supranationalism and intergovernmentalism? The uncertain nature of the *Spitzenkandidaten* process is yet another sign of Member States' unwillingness to let go of more sovereign rights and tendency towards a 'new intergovernmentalism' (see Chapter two).

[9] Art 17(1) TEU.

IV. THE COUNCIL

As it stands today, the Council consists of a representative from each Member State at the ministerial level.[10] The Council therefore speaks on behalf of the Member States. Instructions from Member States are not forbidden like they are in the Commission. On the contrary, relaying Member State positions to the Union sphere through the mouths of national ministers is precisely the point of the Council. It is one of the main Union institutions – in fact, it is the primary decision-making body, although today it shares this role to a large degree with the European Parliament – and yet it is dominated by national interests. Formally a Union institution, the Council seems a rogue institution in conflict with Union values, and is therefore eyed by other Union actors with a degree of suspicion: Isn't it subverting the supranational Union method through intergovernmental bargaining that the Union is supposed to render obsolete? The inner world of the Treaty, says an observer, overlaps with the intermediate circle of members.[11] Constitutionally, this is the logic of an interlocking, interpenetrating, and hybrid polity working itself through in the Union's institutional set-up.

A. What it does

Article 16(1) TEU describes the tasks of the Council as follows:

'The Council shall, jointly with the European Parliament, exercise legislative and budgetary functions. It shall carry out policy-making and coordinating functions as laid down in the Treaties'.

This is rather vague, especially the latter part. The reason is that the Council – being the voice of the Member States in the Union's system of government – takes on many functions, both legislative and executive, in almost all spheres of Union decision-making. It is the Union institution that is furthest removed from the state institutional template of separation of powers.

The Council acts as a legislator and jointly controls the EU budget. It shares this legislative role to a large extent with the European Parliament. In the ordinary legislative procedure (which makes up the

[10] Art 16(2) TEU.
[11] van Middelaar (n 1) 29.

lion's share of legislation), it is the EP's exact equal; in special legislative procedures (say, tax harmonisation) it is more powerful than the European Parliament (see Chapter four). To a certain extent, the Council is comparable to the upper chamber of a bicameral legislative system, particularly comparable to Germany and the US, where membership of that chamber is directly linked to membership of one of the constituent polities. It is this power in the legislative process – the Council has to say 'yes' before any law can be adopted – that is particularly significant and leads to the perception that the Council is the principal law-maker.

The Council also has a prominent executive role. First, it coordinates and, in some cases, polices Member States' policies in certain fields (such as economic and fiscal policy, education, culture, youth and sport, employment policy). For instance, it can rule that Member States which have the euro as a common currency are running excessive budget deficits and impose significant fines if state violations persist. Second, the Council frames the Union's Common Foreign and Security Policy (working closely with the European Council and the High Representative who, besides being a Commission Vice-President, presides over the Foreign Affairs Council[12]) and makes the decisions necessary to define and implement it based upon the strategic lines supplied by the European Council. Third, it concludes international agreements negotiated by the Commission with non-Union countries and international organisations (working closely with the European Parliament). Fourth, the Council is the most important institution involved in the highly political process of appointing high-ranking Union personnel. Fifth, it can take other Union institutions before the Court of Justice for failure to comply with EU law. Finally, the Council prepares European Council meetings and ensures their follow-up.

As Article 16(1) TEU stipulates, the Council's functions are extensive and multifaceted, ranging across the Treaties ('policy-making and coordinating functions as laid down in the Treaties'). The reason is that the Council is a site of intense negotiation – sometimes of grim disagreement, but mostly of building trust and consensus. Since Member States want to see their voices represented and heard at all stages of Union decision-making and policy-making, the Council has its fingers in practically every competence pie.

[12] Art 18(3) and (4) TEU.

Because of its composite carousel-like structure, the Council has been called an institutional chameleon.[13] It changes colour in response to institutional needs. While it was designed as, and still is, the political decision-making centre at *Union* level, its members have been elected, or appointed by those directly elected, at the *national* level. Ministers are always part of the executive branch, but in the Council they enjoy both formal and substantive legislative power, either autonomous of or shared with the European Parliament. The Council changes colour when switching from its legislative to its executive role, such as in foreign policy, where it adopts conclusions, recommendations, decisions, and sanctions on a wide range of issues,[14] and in asylum and immigration policy, where it still enjoys a prominent role.[15] The role of the Council in non-legislative and operational decisions has grown greatly throughout the waves of institutional reform. It is this blurring of the boundaries between legislative and executive tasks – wearing different hats in fast succession during its meetings – that makes the Council chameleonic.

B. How it is Organised

(i) Council Formations

Unlike the Commission, the Council has no fixed source of membership. It consists of 'a representative of each Member State at ministerial level, who may commit the government of the Member State in question and casts its vote'.[16] What position that exactly is depends on whom the Member State government sends. That decision is influenced by election results, party allegiances, and the subject matter under discussion in Brussels. Indeed, different configurations in the Council evolve depending on what subject matter is under consideration. If decisions on agricultural subsidies were being considered, governments would send their minister for agriculture; when the Council focused on the budget, they would send their finance minister. Therefore, the Council has various formations (today, 10), with the General Affairs Council, the Foreign

[13] H Wallace, 'The Council: An Institutional Chameleon', (2002) 15 *Governance* 325.

[14] Arts 26(2), 28(1)(2) and 29 TEU.

[15] Art 76(b) TFEU, eg, is an exception to the Commission monopoly as it hands the power of legislative initiative to a quarter of the Member States.

[16] Art 16(2) TEU.

Affairs Council (presided over by the High Representative of the EU for Foreign Affairs and Security Policy) and the Council of Economic and Finance Ministers (ECOFIN) being the key formations. Each formation has its own organisational culture, legislative agenda, and pace. This makes the Council not a single institution, but really several parallel institutions: in one guise or another, it is continually in session although its members do not live or work in Brussels since they are, first and foremost, ministers in their own countries.

(ii) COREPER and Working Groups

The ministers are just the tip of the iceberg in a system that involves many more layers, and many more national officials. The Council is aided by a Secretariat of nearly 3,000 officials. The workhorse of the Council is a network of about 150 standing expert working groups. They serve as a clearing house for issues that are technical and not very controversial, and as a warning system in case such issues turn out to be more controversial than previously thought. The working groups are coordinated by what is probably the most important part of the Council – COREPER, which is short for the French version of 'Committee of Permanent Representatives'. Permanent representatives are diplomats, the ambassadors from the Member States to the Union. They are formally charged with preparing their ministers' Council meetings, but in reality wield significantly more power. They meet at least weekly (ministers meet at most monthly) and negotiate across the entire gamut of Union affairs. The vast majority of all Council decisions – more than four out of five – are settled in substance during these weekly meetings, before ministers even get involved. COREPER has no formal decision-making power; everything must still be approved by the Council's ministerial members before enactment. It is, however, one of the most important de facto decision-making bodies of the Union and has been singled out as 'Europe's real power center'.[17] COREPER diplomats usually enjoy long tenure, live in Brussels, and are socialised into a common system of problem-solving. They develop long-standing personal relationships characterised by mutual trust, the willingness to help each other out, and the sense of what is a fair solution acceptable

[17] Then Portuguese Prime Minister, António Costa, at the beginning of Portugal's Council presidency in 2021, quoted in J Lewis, 'The European Council and the Council of the European Union', in M Cini and N Pérez-Solórzano Borragán (eds), *European Union Politics*, Oxford, Oxford University Press, 6th edn 2019, 155, at 164.

to everyone in the room. There is, unsurprisingly, a code of confidentiality that isolates COREPER from both public attention and from purely national interests. In German political parlance, their official designation is '*ständige Vertreter*' (permanent representatives), but they are often referred to, jokingly, as '*ständige Verräter*' (permanent traitors).

The Council, therefore, is less a single, unitary body, and more 'a composite of national officials working at different levels of political seniority and policy specialization' involving roughly 60,000 national officials in hundreds of meetings every month. It embeds Member State governments into a 'networked club of collective decision-making that deeply penetrates into the national capitals and domestic politics' of the Member States.[18]

(iii) Council Presidency

The Council is chaired by a minister of the Member State that holds the rotating Council presidency. Member States take turns for six months each. The rotation is meant as a power equaliser, giving small Member States the same chance to influence the agenda as big members. The presidency carries formidable logistical duties, mostly scheduling and chairing an endless set of meetings, negotiating with the European Parliament, and solving disputes between Member States (especially along the usual battle lines north vs south, east vs west, big vs small, euro vs no euro, external border vs no external border etc). Small Member States strain under this workload, but a system of 'trio rotation' – an 18-month work programme organised by three Member States, taking turns every six months – alleviates that burden and enhances continuity and coordination within the presidency. Although arduous, the presidency is highly coveted as it allows individual Member States, within limits, to order the Council agenda and advance their own strategic priorities. At times, these limits are tested. When Hungary took over the rotating Council presidency in July 2024, for example, populist Prime Minister Viktor Orbán immediately went on renegade diplomatic missions to Kyiv, Moscow, and Beijing, all within one week, declaring that he had come as an emissary from the EU. Member States were irritated, Brussels fumed and protested, COREPER voiced clear political disapproval, and there was even talk of cutting Hungary's presidency short.

[18] Lewis (n 17), at 155.

(iv) Decision-Making

Is the Council a classical intergovernmental body, akin to so many other political institutions in international organisations? Yes and no. Its nature depends not just on its membership but also on which decision-making procedure it is following. Some policy areas deemed politically sensitive, like taxation, are governed by unanimity voting. The ambit requiring unanimous voting, however, is constantly shrinking. Most areas now are governed by qualified majority voting, QMV (which is defined as at least 55 per cent of the Member States, comprising at least 15 of them and representing at least 65 per cent of the population of the Union[19]). QMV entails that while the Council is home to Member State interests, it is, in nine out of 10 cases, not home to a Member State veto. Member States can out-manoeuvre each other, but they can no longer – as they could under the unanimity rule – control the policy outcome.

The need to build coalitions to either be part of the qualified majority or to forge a blocking minority puts the weighting of votes centre-stage. The weight of Member State votes is probably the most contested question in the history of European integration; repeatedly, intergovernmental conferences ended in disaster for lack of consensus on how to weight and balance votes once new Member States joined and the vote weights had to be recalibrated. The current formula, introduced in the Lisbon Treaty, seeks a delicate balance between preserving individual national voices and reflecting the different Member State sizes. It rewards Member States with larger populations more than previous formulations did, the winner previously being Germany, and the loser being Poland. After Brexit and the new power mix in the Council, however, Poland's position was strengthened.

Despite QMV, the Council is characterised by a distinct culture of consensus. Member State governments do everything in their power to reach a satisfactory solution for all and tend towards informal unanimity even where passage via QMV is possible. Part of the reason may be that states that have a veto are inclined to have a heightened sense of self-interest and look for matching concessions, whereas states that do not have a veto know they can be outvoted, are less protective of their partisan interests, and look to construct common solutions (except in politically

[19] Art 16(4) TEU. An additional clause requires at least four Member States to form a blocking minority – a safeguard against hypothetical big-state coalitions since any three of the biggest four (Germany, France, Italy, and Spain) represent more than 35% of the population.

truly salient matters).[20] As we will see in Chapter four, another part of the Council's emphasis on reaching consensus, at least in legislative matters, is the negotiating power of the Commission. The Commission manages to push the Member States in the Council so far towards consensus that the percentage of votes in favour, under QMV and unanimity, are identical, although one would have expected that, under QMV, Member States would voice their dissent more often.

This makes the Council less of a forum for 'hard-headed bargaining' than intergovernmentalists expect it to be. Rather, as both a defender of national interests and the collective system of decision-making at the heart of the Union, the Council blurs the distinction between intergovernmentalism and supranationalism. It is only in highly salient policy areas – for instance, fiscal policy during the financial crisis – that the Council's consensus culture breaks down, that bargaining success is defined in terms of how the outcome serves the national interest, and that the Council becomes the site of a potentially divisive form of politics that risks undermining the common European good.

V. THE EUROPEAN COUNCIL

The European Council is not to be confused with the Council, which is the Union's central decision-making institution, or with the Council of Europe, which is a different international organisation altogether. It brings together the heads of state and government of the EU's Member States – not those who have mere ceremonial roles, but those who lead governments and determine the direction of Member State politics. Clearly, it is the most powerful site of representation for national interests in the EU.

A. What it does

The Treaties understate the European Council's real powers. According to Article 15(1) of the TEU, the European Council 'shall provide the Union with the necessary impetus for its development and shall define the general political directions and priorities thereof. It shall not exercise

[20] D Naurin, 'Most Common When Least Important: Deliberation in the European Union Council of Ministers', (2010) 40 *British Journal of Political Science* 31.

legislative functions'. In practice, no other Union body can match the political authority of the European Council. The European Council therefore acts as a sort of 'board of directors' and supplies political and strategic guidance. Its most significant power, then, is agenda-setting. While it does not legislate, it does dictate the EU's general direction, and more or less tells the other institutions what to do and where their priorities lie. As the principal agenda-setter, the European Council provides political guidelines which the Commission then follows through more detailed legislative proposals.

The European Council also makes key decisions concerning the Union and its Members. One such decision involves the question of whether any Member States have seriously breached the values of the EU; another is to set the criteria a state wishing to join the Union must meet. It even has a central role in amending the Treaties, thus acting as a guardian of the overall architecture of the Union. Finally, choosing the right people for important positions ranks among the most crucial and sensitive decisions in the Union, and many cases are delegated to the European Council. It makes appointments to other Union institutions, often in tandem with them. It appoints, for example, the President of the Commission, the High Representative for Foreign Affairs and Security Policy, and the Executive Board of the European Central Bank.

Due to its political power, the European Council is well-suited to resolving issues which have reached an impasse within the Council of Ministers. In some particularly sensitive fields, such as aspects of social security systems or fundamental aspects of criminal justice systems, the Treaty specifically allows Member States to refer a legislative proposal to the European Council for resolution ('brake procedures'). Informally, Member States can always bump up matters to the European Council if the issue is too controversial to be resolved in the Council.

Finally, the European Council has a prominent role in the CFSP, where it identifies strategic objectives and sets out guidelines, and more generally acts as a forum for Member States to consult each other.

B. How it is Organised

The European Council's roots lie in the occasional informal gatherings among the heads of state and government which became routinised in the early 1970s. The empty chair crisis had caused a loss of confidence in the Commission (see Chapter two), and Member States felt a different motor was needed to drive the Community forward. Initially, the informal meetings without formal decisions allowed the European Council as much flexibility as possible. However, with 27 Member States, this format eventually became unsustainable, and the meetings were officially integrated into the Treaties as a distinct institution. The European Council now meets at least four times per year and has an elected President (rather than a rotating presidency) whose role is to mediate between Member States and to keep communication channels open with the Commission and the Parliament. That is easier said than done. The European Council's agenda-setting role sets it at odds with the Commission, which claims similar prerogatives. The bitter rivalry between then European Council President, Charles Michel, and Commission President, Ursula von der Leyen, from 2019 to 2024 was a long-running embarrassment for the Union.

Both the President of the European Council and the Commission President are members of the European Council, and the High Representative for Foreign Affairs and Security Policy takes part in its work. However, only the heads of state and government get to cast a vote. Decisions are usually made by consensus. European Council meetings still go by the name of 'summit' and are as high-profile as they are furtive.

Being the 'queen bee' of the Union,[21] the European Council wields unique power. This is helpful for agenda-setting, resolving impasses, and establishing credible commitments that have to be honoured domestically. At the same time, however, the Council's power runs afoul of the EU's frequent self-advertisements as a 'Union of law' (see Chapter five). Over-optimism and an atmosphere of cooperation in the European Council (reinforced by media expectations that every summit will achieve some spectacular result) sometimes lead the European Council to over-reach into spheres that belong to other institutions. Horizontally, although prohibited from legislating, the European Council often specifies details and deadlines that should be set by the Commission, the Council, or Parliament. Vertically, although restricted to Union competences, the European Council extends its agenda-setting power into areas that should be left to individual Member States. It is difficult to see how legal and political checks in place would realistically constrain the European Council. The European Council's actions are technically subject to review by the Court of Justice, but it is hard to imagine the

[21] D Curtin, *Executive Power of the European Union: Law, Practices, and the Living Constitution*, Oxford, Oxford University Press 2009, 72.

Court striking down a decision by the 27 heads of state and government. The European Council also must submit reports to the European Parliament, but it is an open question how seriously the European Council would take any critical parliamentary reviews.

Recent years have seen a European Council frequently and directly involved in aspects of day-to-day Union and euro area decision-making. The financial crisis was a catalyst for closer coordination than ever before; the European Council met at an unprecedented frequency during that time. It worked out all major institutional reforms during the crises, which were far-reaching and cut deeply into domestic politics. Throughout the crisis, it insisted on finalising all financial aid decisions itself, leaving only implementation to the Eurogroup, and provided detailed instructions for other institutional actors, notably the Commission and the ECOFIN Council. Indeed, the European Council has arguably become the new centre of political gravity within the Union. This kind of 'new intergovernmentalism'[22] in the Union shifts the locus of power back to cooperative bargaining between the Member States. In such a dynamic, a Member State's size and wealth determines much of that Member State's influence in the European Council. These asymmetries in power naturally affect negotiations. In the context of the still largely informal, intergovernmental bargaining style within the European Council, larger Member States are more successful since they can utilise these asymmetries more extensively than in the supranational framework of the Union method. As a result, the powerful members are the dominant actors when forging policy initiatives or responding to crises. Germany and France have especially shaped the European Council's path during the COVID and financial crises, with smaller Member States relegated to the margins. The European Council's consensus culture appears, therefore, sometimes as a culture of forced rather than real consensus.[23]

VI. THE EUROPEAN PARLIAMENT

The European Parliament (EP) has evolved more than any other Union institution. It has transformed from a marginal, mainly consultative Assembly composed of representatives from Member States' parliaments

[22] U Puetter, *The European Council and the Council: New Intergovernmentalism and Institutional Change*, Oxford, Oxford University Press 2014.

[23] M Dawson and F de Witte, *EU Law and Governance*, Cambridge, Cambridge University Press 2022, 34.

into a (mostly) true co-legislator whose representatives are directly elected by all Union citizens. While the gradual but significant empowerment of the EP has parliamentarised the Union's political system and deepened integration, the EP is still a far cry from national parliaments and faces challenges as to its representative function.

A. What it does

Article 14(1) TEU stipulates:

> The European Parliament shall, jointly with the Council, exercise legislative and budgetary functions. It shall exercise functions of political control and consultation as laid down in the Treaties. It shall elect the President of the Commission.

These are all functions and powers associated with parliamentarism: law-making, budgetary power, and powers over the executive.

With regard to law-making, the EP's powers have considerably strengthened over time. Originally, it had no more power than the right to be consulted, and only if the Treaties so specified. The 1992–93 Maastricht Treaty introduced a legislative procedure which made the EP something of a co-equal partner to the Council in a limited number of policy areas. The current Lisbon Treaty extends those areas significantly in what is now called the 'ordinary legislative procedure' (OLP).[24] It is used in about 90 per cent of legislation. Under the OLP, the EP has the power to negotiate joint texts with the Council and enjoys the power of veto (more on OLP in Chapter four). Even with these considerable expansions of authority, the EP's legislative powers are weaker than those of national parliaments. First, the EP is constrained by the limited powers Member States have ceded to the Union. Unlike national parliaments, it cannot simply act whenever it identifies a political problem. Second, it has no monopoly on adoption, but shares that power with the Council. Third, the EP has no power of legislative initiative;[25] that power lies with the Commission. Fourth, the OLP is not the only legislative procedure. In some sensitive areas, the EP is still either merely consulted (for example, taxation) or only has the power to veto a proposal – they cannot even

[24] Art 294 TFEU.

[25] All it can do is request the Commission to submit a proposal, Art 225 TFEU. The Commission, however, is not obliged to follow that request, and even if it does follow it, it has freedom over the contents of its proposal.

amend it (for example, new legislation on combating discrimination). These 'special legislative procedures' weaken the EP's legislative powers considerably.

The EP has a central role in determining the EU's budget, but here too that role is shared with the Council and the Commission. Union budget rules are complex. The five-year multi-annual framework for Union expenditure sets annual ceilings. The annual budgets are then set every year, and have to comply with the multi-annual framework. For the adoption of the multi-annual framework, the EP has (only) the power of consent. For the adoption of the annual budget, the EP submits a draft budget according to a legislative procedure similar to the OLP, which gives the EP the right to both amend and veto. Unlike national parliaments, then, the EP lacks complete control over both revenue and expenditure.

As to powers over the executive, the EP enjoys some powers of appointment and dismissal over the Commission. It must approve the President of the Commission after he or she has been nominated by the European Council. Once the President has been accepted, the EP must also approve those whom the Commission President and heads of state have nominated as members of the College of Commissioners.[26] The EP has tried to leverage these powers extensively. As mentioned above, it has tried to pressure the European Council to always accept the candidate for Commission President of the EP party that secured the most votes in the European elections (*Spitzenkandidatensystem*), but this gambit has partly failed. The EP also has the power to subject all prospective Commissioners to extensive questioning before it gives or denies its assent. In addition, the EP has the power to censure the Commission as a whole and require the entire body's resignation,[27] which has never happened, though one Commission resigned in 1999 following the threat of such a motion of censure.

While these are substantial powers, they are less expansive than what parliamentary systems usually provide to state legislatures. We expect executive power to be derived from the legislature, which appoints the executive and sets conditions for the way it exercises its powers. The EP cannot do either of these things. The link between the EP and the executive is weaker than in domestic systems. The EP does not need to support the Commission in order for its continued existence as parliaments do,

[26] Art 17(7) TEU.
[27] Art 17(8) TEU, Art 234 TFEU.

since the Commission's dissolution will not result in snap elections to the EP. As a consequence, there is no 'majority party' and no 'opposition party'. There are political groups of MEPs who are members of similar political parties in different Member States (conservative, social-democratic, liberal, green, etc) who work together in shifting alliances on a case-by-case basis when deciding whether to support a Commission proposal. These party groupings have huge incentives to cooperate because of the inner workings of the ordinary legislative procedure. The number of near unanimous votes in the EP is striking.[28]

B. How it is Organised

(i) Elections and Daily Work

The EP is unique in that, since 1979, it is the only EU institution that is directly elected. European elections take place every five years and are synchronised with the appointment of the new Commission. They are organised nationally, sometimes even on different days. There are no genuinely transnational political parties. In Parliament, the representatives do not sit in national blocs and do not vote along Member State lines; rather, they are organised in groupings, loosely arranged according to political ideology. The largest grouping at present is the centre-right, the second largest the centre-left; they often work together constructively. Fractious groupings on the left and right are more common than in national parliaments; until recently they were still peripheral. The 2024 elections, however, have resulted in major gains for far-right forces.

The EP today has 720 members, who convene in Brussels (three weeks out of four) and Strasbourg (four days per month). France will not compromise on being the EP's second seat. Obliged to divide its activities between these two cities, the EP has serious image problems, since this arrangement is exceedingly expensive and makes the EP look like a travelling circus.

The EP normally votes by simple majority. Its proceedings are presided over by a President who enforces its rules of procedure and represents the EP in European Council meetings. Much of the EP's day-to-day work is carried out in committees which reflect, by and large,

[28] See, for instance, S Hix, A Kreppel and A Noury, 'The Party System in the European Parliament: Collusive or Competitive?', (2003) 41 *Journal of Common Market Studies* 309.

the tasks of Commissioners and Directorates-General and the Council configurations, which sometimes lead to turf wars similar to those in the Commission.

(ii) Representation

Representation is 'digressively proportional' to make sure smaller Member States have a voice too. This means that although smaller Member States have fewer MEPs than larger Member States, their citizens are better represented per capita. Germany, for instance, with a population of almost 85 million, has 96 MEPs; Malta, with a population of approximately 0.5 million, still has six MEPs. Germany's population is proportionally far greater than this split of MEP numbers would suggest. One German MEP represents roughly 885,000 German citizens, whereas one Maltese MEP represents fewer than 9,000 Maltese citizens. The relative influence of the Maltese MEP is 10 times higher than that of the German MEP. Little wonder that this has been criticised – by, among others, the influential German Federal Constitutional Court[29] – because it goes against the idea that the vote of each citizen has equal weight. The weighing of seats does not seem to have too drastically impeded the influence of larger Member States, however. German MEPs dominate the political groupings and hold key positions in all important EP committees.

(iii) Empowerment and Democratisation

The EP narrative of popular empowerment and direct election can be told as a story of democratisation and federalisation. Member States did more than merely compensate for the loss of national parliamentary power. They coordinated the steady extension of Union competences and the rise of QMV in the Council – both the most important themes that animate Treaty revision – with a dose of direct representation, thus bolstering the Council's claim to indirect representation. Many see a directly elected EP as a step towards a more federal system of government.

But what can look like democratisation, and what the EP itself, blessed with a healthy ego, presents as a heroic tale of its uphill battles

[29] BVerfG, 30 June 2009, 123 BVerfGE 267, paras 280–89 – *Lissabon* (translation at http://bit.ly/3KTy6me).

against Member States for increased democratic decision-making, can also be told as a history of building the house from its roof down.[30] European Parliament was no triumph of bottom-up process; it was yet another example of top-down imposition. First, Member States established an Assembly of indirectly elected parliamentarians in 1952, which renamed itself a Parliament in 1958. Only more than 20 years later was it given a constituency: the first direct elections were held in 1979 and have since taken place every five years. It took another 13 years before those voters were proclaimed to be political citizens, when the Maastricht Treaty introduced the category of 'Union citizenship'. Finally, another 12 years later, in 2004, those citizens were handed constituent power, when important Member States held national referendums on the Constitutional Treaty (rather than ratifying it through national parliaments). The Treaty was met with a firm 'no' from the French and the Dutch populations and would have met with further resistance had the ratification process not been abandoned then (see Chapter two). Much of the disquiet among citizens was about the fact that something called a 'constitution' was on offer. What would be left of national constitutions?

It is a variant of this concern that informs much of the public's sentiment towards the European Parliament: What will be left of national parliaments? European citizens ask themselves who, in fact, is their 'true' representative – their European, or their national MP? The answer hinges on who they see themselves as – European or national citizens. The legitimacy of a claim to representation depends on the identity of the represented; representation reflects who we are. The questions concerning individual and collective identity that have haunted the Union since its inception are particularly visible with respect to the EP and its claim to speak in the name of 'the people'. The simple fact is that most people in Europe do not think of themselves as first and foremost European. Instead, they find their primary sense of political allegiance within the state of which they are a citizen.

The EP's representational claim is therefore tenuous, and it shows. While the strongest argument for its direct election had been that it would bring the voice of European citizens into the heart of Europe's government, thereby increasing the legitimacy of the Union as a whole, turnout in European elections has steadily fallen. The more powerful

[30] van Middelaar (n 1), 276.

the European Parliament has become, the less interested the voters are. Turnout has varied between Member States, but it is much lower than for national elections across the board. It continuously fell from 63 per cent in 1979 to under 43 per cent in 2014. After a vigorous campaign in all Member States to encourage voting, turnout increased slightly to a little over 50 per cent in the 2019 elections, but that was no revival of interest. In 2024, turnout stagnated at around 50 per cent again.

European elections are still widely seen by the electorate and by national parties as less important than national elections. They are perceived as not affecting the question of which party or coalition governs the EU, and as not affecting the most powerful institutions of the Union, the Council and the Commission. Consequently, EP campaigns (which are organised and financed by domestic political parties) centre on the record of national governments rather than party differences on European issues. European elections function as mid-term elections in which voters punish incumbent governments and give support to protest parties.[31]

If, at most, only half of the electorate casts its vote, the legitimacy of the EP is seriously undermined. Strengthening the EP by granting it more and more powers relieves the Union's democratic deficit only if one already accepts it as an authentic voice of the European people. If, by contrast, one doubts that an international institution can represent people without there being a proper 'people', then strengthening the Parliament only exacerbates the Union's democracy and legitimacy problems. A parliament is not something that can simply be superimposed onto the political landscape in the hope that the result will be a functioning democracy. Parliaments need to be rooted in an overall democratic culture and organisation, and of that culture they are but a small, institutionalised part. They rest on structures that generate constant interaction between people and state, eg, political parties, associations, citizen movements, and communication media, which combine to make a democratic public space. European political institutions lack a corresponding public since political parties, media, and civil society are all predominantly delineated along national borders, and the European Parliament suffers from this defect visibly.

It is perhaps the insolubility of this defect that leads the EP to try and strengthen its own legitimacy through output rather than

[31] S Bulmer et al, *Politics in the European Union*, Oxford, Oxford University Press, 5th edn 2020, 288–89.

through its representational claim. It justifies much of what it does by claiming a particular sensitivity to issues that are important to citizens but overlooked by states. For instance, the EP plays an essential role in strengthening consumer protection, data protection, and non-discrimination, and the place of the individual within European integration in general.[32]

VII. CONCLUSION

Intricate institutional arrangements make the Union its own worst enemy, as they open it up to the criticism of being unresponsive and opaque. If we zoom out from the details, however, a different picture emerges. The EU's constitutional framework is informed by a blend of supranational effectiveness (secured by some degree of autonomy from partisan state interests) and intergovernmental control (exercised by the Member States' heavy involvement in the Union's daily operation). History's lesson to Europe has been that intergovernmental bargaining alone failed miserably to prevent the terrible excesses of two World Wars. Europe's response has been an ongoing commitment to a deeper form of interdependent cooperation. It has equipped institutions other than state institutions with extraordinary powers and with a certain degree of autonomy from the unilateral expression of state interests. At the same time, it has allowed Member States a huge say in the Union's daily affairs, especially in areas that are close to what states conceive of as the core functions of national sovereignty. It is this balance between the 'supranational' and the 'intergovernmental' that is not only the Union's basic working system but also what sustains Europe's unique system of constitutionalism beyond the nation-state. Institutional functions and powers have therefore been designed to represent and balance diverse interests along that supranational/intergovernmental divide.

FURTHER READING

Curtin D, *Executive Power of the European Union: Law, Practices, and the Living Constitution*, Oxford, Oxford University Press 2009.

[32] Dawson and de Witte (n 23), 37–38.

Hix S and Høyland B, *The Political System of the European Union*, London, Bloomsbury Academic, 4th edn 2022.
Hodson D, Puetter U, Saurugger S and Peterson J (eds), *The Institutions of the European Union*, Oxford, Oxford University Press, 5th edn 2022.
Kenealy D, Hadfield A, Corbett R and Peterson J, *The European Union: How Does It Work?*, Oxford, Oxford University Press, 6th edn 2022.

4

Governance and Legislation

European Union constitutionalism places a premium not on separation of powers between its own branches but on balancing power between the Union and its Member States. Its central goal is cooperation and effective collaboration between the EU and its constituent parts. We have seen how this goal maps onto the institutional landscape of the Union's system of governance (see Chapter three). The same holds true for how those institutions interact with each other. The hybrid and composite character of EU constitutionalism translates into the Union's policy processes in respect of what Union institutions can do and how they do it. The first two sections of this chapter will explain each in turn.

What any given institution can do depends on an agreement between Member States and the Union about the appropriate range of policy areas open to Union intervention. This is a question of Union competences, which section I explains. The Member States have agreed to transfer some of their sovereign powers to the Union, albeit in limited fields and with a wide variety of consequences. In some areas the Union is the exclusive decision-maker, for instance in external trade or agriculture. In other areas the Union is heavily involved through the development of comprehensive policies, for example in environmental policy. In yet other areas the Union does play a role, but its decisions are less definitive, for instance in foreign or social policy. Since the Treaties carefully spell out the degree of Union involvement permitted for a particular policy area, it appears as if the Member States, as 'masters of the Treaties', are in control of the width and depth of Union activity. That is only partially true. The Union's institutions have the interpretative latitude to use these provisions for their own purposes, and it is far from easy for Member States to correct those practices. A shared understanding of the ambit of Union powers requires, at the very least, the channelling of national views into the Union's policy-making process without damaging the European nature of that process. Competences are an intricate exercise in power-sharing and finding the appropriate balance between national and Union interests. As this section will explain, it is through interpreting competences that many tensions arise and EU constitutionalism is put under great strain.

How the Union's institutions do what they do depends on the same delicate balance of interests, as section II explains. Here too Member State interests need representation within the Union's processes. The degree of representation is dependent on the policy area and varies from field to field. This is what makes Union policy-making such a complex and, at times, convoluted and opaque practice. The relationships between the Union's institutions rely on an intricate mix of procedures, methods, and instruments. They are densely networked, with much taking place behind closed doors and out of the spotlight. Understanding the formal procedures, then, does not mean one understands what is actually happening. The second section details the Union's legislative process and shows how Union constitutionalism has a way of working itself through in a manner that results in informal and diverse practices.

The laws that the Union's legislative process produces appear, on their surface, to share in the EU's constitutional template of power-sharing and balancing. These laws are called 'regulations' and 'directives'. Whereas regulations create a uniform standard and are directly applicable within Member States, directives need to be transposed into domestic law by domestic parliaments and seem to leave Member States much more discretion. Surprisingly, however, the effect of the Union's legislative output is much more unitising than the Treaties suggest. It was the European Court who, in the early 1960s, handed down seminal judgments that made much of EU law directly effective within the Member States (so that Member States can be bound against their wishes) and forced Member States to obsolesce their own laws, including their national constitutions where they conflicted with EU law. This legal revolution created a pan-European rule of law and brought the Union's legal order very close to what we would expect from the state template of constitutionalism. Section III of this chapter spells out the details of this arrangement.

Finally, the Union's political ambit and its procedural inner workings move it away from an economic community towards a political union. Its considerable powers raise the question of how its authority is founded on democracy (as Article 10 of the TEU claims it to be). Union institutions seek to bolster their democratic legitimacy; despite these efforts, national publics are sceptical as to the EU's democratic qualities. The Union's democratic credentials, then, will be the subject of the final section of this chapter.

I. WHAT THE UNION DOES: EU POLICIES AND COMPETENCES

A. The Ambit of the Union's Competences

The Union sets policies in many areas that directly affect the daily lives of its roughly 450 million citizens. It sets the rules for the movement of goods, services, people, and capital across the borders of the Member States; it regulates agriculture, establishes standards for the protection of workers in the workplace, of consumers, and of the environment; it conducts social policy, and even facilitates the extradition of criminal offenders from one Member State to another. It is hard to imagine a Member State making policy in complete isolation from Brussels. Some, therefore, see the Union as a superstate in the making.

(i) Transferring Power: The Principle of Conferral

That, however, is not true, because the Union does not exercise control over all policy areas. Rather, it is a selective policy-maker, and its power varies significantly depending on the policy sector. This comes as no surprise in the light of the Union's unique brand of truncated constitutionalism. As we have seen in Chapter one, the Union lacks (legal) exclusive final authority as well as (political) sovereignty. Its competences are therefore not theoretically unlimited in their reach, unlike those of states. The Union cannot simply take action in whatever area it wants whenever it wants to. Rather, it needs a legal basis in the Treaties that authorises it to act.

If there is a problem of, say, public health, the Commission cannot simply decide to propose legal acts, and the Council and the European Parliament cannot simply pass legislation they deem appropriate. Rather, they will first have to determine whether the Union is constitutionally competent to act. The answer is affirmative only if the Treaties so provide. The Treaties also stipulate *what kind* of action the Union is allowed to take – for instance, legislating on its own, coordinating and supporting Member States, consulting with Member States, etc. In the area of public health, for example, the Treaties give the Union the power to act, but only to 'complement the Member States' actions', and never to harmonise law across all Member States.[1] If the Treaties do not confer power to act upon the Union at all, that power remains with

[1] Art 168 TFEU.

the Member States.[2] EU lawyers call this the 'principle of attributed (or enumerated) powers', or the 'principle of conferral' (the latter is the term the TEU has used since 2009).[3]

The principle of conferral is of the highest constitutional significance. It is about nothing less than the control Member States exercise over the integration process, and therefore over their own self-governance. It is thus not just about the raw exercise of power, but about democracy and legitimacy as well.

(ii) Sharing Power: Competence Categories

Union competences do not, however, operate like an on/off-switch which demarcates some acts as 'permissible' and others as 'impermissible'. Rather, depending on the policy area, different competences grant the Union different powers, mandate that the Union institutions follow different procedures, or provide different decision-making rules and voting requirements. Unsurprisingly, outcomes vary – from Union rules controlling the whole policy field, via harmonisation of (some of the) Member States' rules, to the Union only being able to enact 'soft' rules such as benchmarking procedures. The crucial question then is not whether but *how far* Member States have chosen to limit their sovereign regulatory autonomy in order to benefit from collective action, and *how much* power they have delegated to the Union. Competence is not a matter of yes or no, but a matter of degree.

At one end of the spectrum, Member States may have agreed to act within the Union, that is through Union institutions, or to not act at all. This is the domain of 'exclusive' competences where autonomous Member State action has been renounced completely and once and for all. Member States cannot act at all, either unilaterally or in accord with other states, regardless of whether Union institutions have acted. It is only the Union legislator which may adopt policies and legally binding acts. EU competences are exclusive in the policy areas of the customs union, the common commercial policy, competition in internal market areas, monetary policy for those Member States who have adopted the euro as their currency, and the protection of marine biological resources.[4]

[2] Arts 4(1) and 5(2) TEU.

[3] Art 5(2) TEU: 'Under the principle of conferral, the Union shall act only within the limits of the competences conferred upon it by the Member States in the Treaties to attain the objectives set out therein. Competences not conferred upon the Union in the Treaties remain with the Member States.'

[4] Art 3(1) TFEU.

This list seems like an odd assortment, and it is. The Treaty, in 2009, simply codified all the areas where the Court of Justice of the EU had previously held Union competences to be exclusive.

At the other end of the spectrum, the Union merely facilitates Member States coordinating their national policies around common objectives and perhaps providing guidelines. The two main examples are economic policy and employment policy.[5] Equally weak are the Union's 'supporting, coordinating, and supplementary' competences with the EU providing financial incentives to support what Member States do. Here the Union may act without superseding the competences of the Member States who retain their full legislative power. There are some areas where the Union is explicitly prohibited from harmonising Member State laws and regulations. These include policies on human health, industry, culture, tourism, education, youth and sport, civil protection, and administrative cooperation.[6]

In between these two extremes, 'shared' competence is the default catch-all category. Member States agree that the Union may act to help achieve the common goals in the pertinent area. Policies under this category cover everything from the internal market, social policy, cohesion, agriculture and fisheries to the area of freedom, security and justice, the environment, consumer protection, transport, energy, public health, research, technological development, space, development cooperation, and humanitarian aid.[7] These are, as the Treaty puts it, the 'principal' areas of shared competence; the list is not exhaustive. Shared competence, therefore, is more of an umbrella term than a precisely delineated category: sharing power through police cooperation is entirely different from sharing power in the common market. While there is significant variation between the policy fields, all of them permit the Union to act via directly effective legal acts. The Union of course does not have to act; the same goes for Member States acting unilaterally. Usually, however, both may act at different times, which means that there will be many normative conflicts which need rules for peaceful adjudication. The basic rule here is that Member States shall exercise their competence to the extent that the Union has not exercised its competence.[8] In other words, Member States have to stand back when, for as long as, and to the extent that the Union is acting. This principle is called 'pre-emption'. It is tricky,

[5] Art 5 TFEU.
[6] Art 6 TFEU.
[7] See the lists in Art 4(2), (3) and (4) TFEU.
[8] Art 2(2) TFEU.

for several reasons. One is that the impression that it is clear when the Union is acting and when it should act is misleading. Scattered throughout the Treaties are competence provisions for very specific constellations in very specific policy fields, and some of them contradict the principle of pre-emption. For example, in environmental policy, Union measures are meant to set minimum rules only, which 'shall not prevent any Member State from maintaining or introducing more stringent protective measures'.[9] To understand the exact reach of a specific competence, one has to plod through provisions buried deep in the Treaty. Second, the precise scope of what is covered by Union law is often in doubt. The threshold between Union competence and Member State is unclear and shifting, depending on what exactly the Union has legislated for and how its coverage is being interpreted by political and judicial institutions.

(iii) Exercising Power: Beyond Legislation

These competences are legislative in nature. The Union, however, reaches far beyond legislative intervention. Much of EU law is framed in terms of prohibiting Member State practices. One example is single market law where Member States are not allowed to keep restrictions on cross-border trade, such as quotas, tariffs, or legislation that has the effect of hindering trade. Another example is the Union's foundational principle of prohibiting discrimination on the basis of nationality. These prohibitions define much of the ambit of Union law, but they do not involve Union legislative interventions.[10] In order to appreciate the full range of Union competences, one has to absorb the full scope of the Treaties.

(iv) Explaining Power: Building, Correcting, and Cushioning Markets

To make sense of these competences, it helps to remember that most of the powers Member States agreed to confer upon the Union are related to markets. Most build markets (especially the policies surrounding the free movement of goods, services, labour, and capital, but also competition policy); some serve to protect producers from market forces (for instance, agricultural policies); and some aim to cushion the impact

[9] Art 193 TFEU.
[10] S Weatherill, *Law and Values in the European Union*, Oxford, Oxford University Press 2016, 27.

of market forces (for example, environmental policy, consumer protection, gender equality, or occupational health and safety policies).[11] Even Union powers in the field of police and judicial cooperation in criminal matters grew from the realisation that the single market harms Member State security and therefore needed a cushioning policy.

The triad of market-building, market-correcting, and market-cushioning policies also helps to make sense of why the EU was granted specific competences.

Building markets, with its emphasis on liberalisation, requires a strong role for supranational institutions and resists Member State disruption. Competences in this domain are therefore nearly exclusive and cover an extensive range of economic policies. Prime examples are internal market policies, which extend to free movement of all factors of production, and cover areas such as transport, energy, and telecommunications.

Correcting markets is much more controversial because it has redistributive implications and is, therefore, expensive. While it is also mostly exclusive, it is much more restricted in scope. Here, the prime examples are the common agricultural policy (CAP), which is a system of subsidies and fixed prices that has always made up a sizeable part of the Union's budget, and the Union's cohesion policy, which is intended to reduce inequality among European regions and to compensate poor countries for economic integration costs. Just the cohesion policy constitutes roughly one-third of the Union's budget.

The final way in which the EU regulates markets is through cushioning markets by reducing adverse effects of integration. Doing this is mostly regulatory and needs less exclusivity; much of it is a process of power sharing between Union and Member States. Examples are environmental policy or gender equality in the workplace.[12]

(v) Distinguishing Power: Union Policy and National Policy

The need for Union policies to differ from policies made at the national level again exemplifies the extent to which the template of the nation-state is only partly useful for understanding European integration. We

[11] The classification is from A Sbragia and F Stolfi, 'Key Policies', in D Kenealy, R Corbett and J Peterson (eds), *The European Union: How Does It Work?*, Oxford, Oxford University Press, 5th edn 2018, 101, and S Bulmer et al, *Politics in the European Union*, Oxford, Oxford University Press, 5th edn 2020, 334 et seq.

[12] Kenealy et al (n 11), 118.

saw its limits with respect to institutions in Chapter three, and here too Union policies are unlike national policies with respect to money, implementation, and jurisdiction.

First, Union policies involve spending very little money, as they are regulatory rather than distributive or re-distributive (with the exceptions of the CAP and cohesion policy). National policy, in contrast, usually involves spending a lot of money.

Second, the makers of Union policy are further removed than are state policy-makers from those who execute it, and from those who are governed by it. States have institutions and processes to ensure their policies are executed quickly 'on the ground'. Union policies face many more obstacles. They often have to be transposed into national law, which means that the same Union law can look different across Member States, depending on how precise the transposition is. Because there are no Union agencies 'on the ground', the Union must rely on Member State institutions and officials for implementation. The journey from Union policy legislation to its execution simply takes much longer than with national policy.

Third, the Union's jurisdiction is much narrower than state jurisdiction. As we have seen, the Union can act only if the Member States have conferred on it the competence to do so. Many areas remain under Member State control, either because Member States are reluctant to cede their sovereign rights to the Union (usually, the powers of the sword and of the purse remain firmly in national hands, as well as policies with a strong moral or cultural dimension) or because they have conferred such powers upon the Union but have subjected their exercise to tough decision-making rules such as unanimity in the Council (taxation, for instance).

B. The Broadening of the Union's Competences

A huge part of the Union's constitutional trajectory, and of the debates surrounding its evolving nature, relates to EU competences. The reason is that they are limited but not static. Their dynamism, however, points in only one direction: a centrifugal drift away from the Member States towards the Union. While this is not a surprising development given the centuries-old experience of all federal systems, the constitutional importance of the principle of conferral would lead one to expect competences to be understood in a strict way. One would also expect that the limits of EU competence would be reliably controlled, both politically and judicially, and that any jurisdictional enlargement of Union competences would not be undertaken lightly.

(i) Competence Creep

That, however, is not the case. Starting in the 1970s, the principle of conferral eroded substantially and virtually disappeared as a constraint against Union competence creep. It appeared as if there was no core of state sovereignty that was left beyond the reach of the Union.[13] Politically, this became one of the most sensitive and contested issues in European integration, with Member States often frustrated about their unceasingly shrinking regulatory ambit. Constitutionally, the erosion of the principle of conferral subverted the foundation of the Union, which was the consensual but limited grant of competence by the Member States.[14] Legally, national courts got ready to protect Member States' competences, threatening the Court of Justice of the EU with a clash of legal orders and a disregard of Union law's primacy.

In part, the Member States themselves were responsible for competences migrating to the Union. In each of the periodic Treaty revisions, they extended the scope of EU law by adding extra competences to the list of those conferred on the Union (such as environmental protection in 1987, consumer protection in 1993, and energy policy in 2009), and by widening the scope of existing provisions. Several motives were in play each time. First, Member States bring an issue onto the EU agenda because the problem they address can only be solved at the European level. Cross-border pollution, for example, cannot be dealt with unilaterally. This motive is also the official rationale for Union action, and the Commission tries very hard to justify each of its actions by invoking the cross-border motive. Second, politically, Member State governments move issues to the Union level when they want to circumvent

[13] K Lenaerts, 'Constitutionalism and the Many Faces of Federalism', (1990) 38 *American Journal of Comparative Law* 205.

[14] The European Court of Justice, in its most famous constitutionalising decisions, *Van Gend & Loos* and *Costa v ENEL* (see Chapter 6), recognised in the 1960s how fundamental the limits of granting competence were for the nascent European constitutional order. It affirmed that the Union was 'a new legal order of international law, for the benefit of which the states have limited their sovereign rights, *albeit in limited fields*' (emphasis added), Case 26/62 NV *Algemene Transport- en Expeditie Onderneming van Gend & Loos v Netherlands Inland Revenue Administration*, EU:C:1963:1, 12; Case 6/64 *Costa v ENEL (Ente Nationale Energia Elettrica)*, EU:C:1964:66, 593. In the early 1990s, however, it updated its view, and described the Member States as having 'limited their sovereign rights, *in ever wider fields*' (emphasis added), Opinion 1/91 *European Economic Area*, EU:C:1991:490, para 21.

political opposition at home, and because it allows them to avoid blame for unpopular decisions. Third, economically, differences in regulation may have adverse consequences for the competitiveness of firms between countries, so Member State governments may try to create a level playing-field by harmonising their national laws through European regulation. Fourth, some problems seem to demand transnational solutions because there appears to be an inherent ideational value in not leaving things to individual states to decide (like decent working conditions).[15]

Consensual broadening of Union competences does not, in itself, threaten the principle of conferral or the Union's constitutional foundations. The Union might still function within limits, even if those limits are stretched wider. However, there is a distinct feeling that the limits themselves are not circumscribed and that Union competences self-extend. This phenomenon has been aptly called 'competence creep'.[16] The reason is that the Commission has proposed legislation that presses against the boundaries of the enumerated Union competences, and the Council and the European Parliament have continually accepted these capacious interpretations of Treaty articles. Union institutions have chosen far-reaching interpretations of the EU's competence bases and profited from the lack of bright lines guarding Member State functions. The Treaties set out what the Union can do, and not what the Union cannot do. Therefore, it becomes hard to identify any area that is, in principle, an area of national autonomy that is off limits to the Union. Moreover, the grants of power to the Union are often framed in terms of achieving objectives within its legitimate purview. Article 114 TFEU, for example, grants the Union the competence to adopt measures harmonising national laws in order to promote the establishment and functioning of the internal market. It is driven by its function, the completion of the common market. Rather than signalling constitutional limits, it signals the breadth of Union competences. Any national practice that impacts the project of market-making may thus trigger Union competences. Union institutions have used this in muscular ways, trespassing on competences Member States thought they had reserved for themselves.

[15] H Lelieveldt and S Princen, *The Politics of the European Union*, Cambridge, Cambridge University Press, 2nd edn 2015, 214–17.

[16] M Pollack, 'Creeping Competence: The Expanding Agenda of the European Community', (1994) 14 *Journal of Public Policy* 95; S Weatherill, 'Competence Creep and Competence Control', (2004) 23 *Yearbook of European Law* 1.

(ii) Political Reactions

Member States reacted by inserting a provision into the Treaty that addressed how Union competences should be exercised. The 'principle of subsidiarity' provides that

> in areas which do not fall within its exclusive competence, the Union shall act only if and so far as the objectives of the proposed action cannot be sufficiently achieved by the Member States, either at central level or at regional and local level, but can rather, by reason of the scale or effects of the proposed action, be better achieved at Union level.[17]

However, this principle has turned out to be next to useless because 'the problems and questions that subsidiarity addresses are not the ones that the Community is faced with'.[18] It requires the Union to refrain from acting when the goals of that action could be better achieved by the Member States. Thus, once the Union decides that a goal must be reached, the principle of subsidiarity is intended to compel the Union to ask itself how much really has to be done at the Union level to reach that goal, and how much can be left to the Member States. These stipulations are woefully inadequate for reasserting the principle of conferral. The principle of subsidiarity does not require the Union to balance Union and Member States' interests, but simply assumes that Union goals must be achieved, and asks who should do the work: Can Member States achieve the Union-determined goal equally well on their own? Subsidiarity gives Member States 'a right to employment in [Union] service, wherever they can show they are up to the task, but it does not give them a voice'.[19] Even more adversely to its intentions, the way the principle is set up in the Treaty gives it a centralising effect. The goal can always be construed as a pan-European goal, such as a common environmental policy, or the single market. Member State measures can never realise such policies equally as well as Union measures can.[20] The subsidiarity test is hopelessly ineffectual.

Another means of reining in the Union is slightly more meaningful. It is performed by national parliaments who may write reasoned opinions and intervene in the Union legislative process. This intervention – hidden

[17] Art 5(3) TEU.

[18] G Davies, 'Subsidiarity: The Wrong Idea, in the Wrong Place, at the Wrong Time', (2006) 43 *CML Rev* 63.

[19] Ibid, 68.

[20] D Chalmers, G Davies and G Monti, *European Union Law*, Cambridge, Cambridge University Press, 3rd edn 2014, 396.

in a protocol attached to the Treaty and called the 'early warning-mechanism' – is, however, subject to important limitations because of its scope and short deadlines, and thus promises more than it can deliver. A determined Union legislator can always press on with its legislative draft. There is no formal guarantee that the impact of Member State parliament intervention will be more than negligible.

(iii) Judicial Reactions

Because of the lack of political bright lines, competence creep needs to be controlled, and contained, judicially. It falls to the European Court of Justice to assume this task. The Court, however, has played the role of a catalyst rather than a guardian. In all of its jurisprudence, it has never – not once – found a Union measure to be in violation of the principle of subsidiarity. Worse, the European Court has found only one instance where an EU institution has exceeded the powers granted to the Union.[21] There is no judicial control of subsidiarity whatsoever and judicial control of competences at the Union level more generally is practically non-existent. Perhaps the reason is that, in contrast to federal states, the Union has no structures – either principles in a written constitution or mechanisms like courts – that are seen as neutral in the matter of arbitrating border disputes between the centre and the regions. The European Court of Justice is listed as a Union institution, entrusted with the tasks of the Union, and it has no legislative provision to rely on which spells out at length the importance and purposes of Member State policies. There is a structural bias, and this would seem to disqualify the Court from being a good judge in competence cases.[22]

With the European Court largely idle, Member States have grown increasingly uneasy. Their courts started to take competence review into their own hands. The German Federal Constitutional Court led the way, arguing that it was a matter of national constitutional law if Brussels robbed Germany of its powers. It therefore threatened repeatedly to declare Union legal acts which it considered outside the bounds of Union competence ultra vires (which means 'beyond the powers') and thereby inapplicable within Germany. Competence review (or ultra vires review) has developed into a serious judicial battle between the European Court of Justice and Member State constitutional courts following in

[21] Opinion 2/94 *Accession to the ECHR I*, EU:C:1996:140.
[22] Davies (n 18).

Germany's footsteps. It culminated in a German Constitutional Court order declaring an act by the European Central Bank (ECB) ultra vires and, worse, aggressively setting aside the European Court's judgment on the same matter as ultra vires because it considered it too lenient on competence control.[23] Newspapers and legal journals exploded with impassioned commentaries. When the Commission retaliated by starting infringement proceedings against Germany, the conflict heated up even more. Defenders of the German Court's ruling emphasised the EU's overreach. The recently retired President of the German Court spoke of 'collusion between the European Court and the Commission' and the German judge-rapporteur, of a 'judicial *coup d'état*'. Critics of the ruling made the judgment sound outright scandalous, and personally and unabashedly criticised its authors.[24] Much political damage was done, and trust lost. It is too early to declare a winner. But the real question is whether there can be a winner at all given how unappealing both outcomes are. When Member State courts declare Union law which they perceive as ultra vires inapplicable, they destroy the uniform application of Union law across all Member States. When they don't, competence creep remains unchecked. Both paths of action threaten the very foundations of the European constitutional construct. Member State courts are therefore caught between a rock and a hard place and have to hope that the European Court eventually steps up its competence game.

(iv) Does it Really Matter?

For students of comparative federalism, this is an all too familiar story. In all federal systems, the distribution of powers between the federal and State levels is stated in vague terms. The result is that in practice, federal and state governments enjoy concurrent rather than exclusive jurisdiction in most areas. Most constitutions share a number of features that the European Treaties possess. First, they have broad and flexible clauses which authorise federal legislation to regulate interstate commerce (in the Union, this is Article 114 TFEU). Second, they possess clauses for the adoption of legislation wherever this is 'necessary and proper' in order to

[23] BVerfG, 5 May 2020, 154 BVerfGE 17 – *Public Sector Purchase Programme (PSPP)* (translation at https://bit.ly/3KRpk8d).

[24] For quotes and citations see U Haltern, 'Revolutions, Real Contradictions, and the Method of Resolving Them: The relationship between the Court of Justice of the European Union and the German Federal Constitutional Court', (2021) 19 *I-Con* 208.

achieve fundamental federal objectives (in the Union, this is Article 352 TFEU). Third, they rely on doctrines of 'implied powers' (in the Union, this has been standing judge-made law since 1971).[25] All these features contribute significantly to undermining any principle of express conferral. In addition, virtually all federal systems experience periodic waves of centralisation and backlashes looking for rebalancing. The Union has had more than its share of centralising initiatives, but it also had periods of retrenchment, such as the Gaullist resistance to majority-voting in the Council (see Chapter two). Comparative federalists, therefore, may see competence creep in the Union not as unique or worrying, but merely as one of many instances where power oscillates uneasily between central governments and states.[26]

This brings us back to one of the major themes that animate this book. While the template of the (federal) state does provide a useful toolkit to understand policy processes in the European Union, too strict an analogisation between traditional federalism and the EU can also mislead. The Union is not a federal state and lacks crucial features that make centralisation of power acceptable to both the constituent states and the citizens. To reiterate its most important missing elements, it lacks exclusive final authority; it lacks a constitutional, non-derivative source of sovereignty like 'We the People'; and it lacks primary political identity (see Chapter one). Without these legal, political, and socio-cultural features, the EU lacks the constitutional 'thickness' that allows federal states to view power centralisation as acceptable or even advantageous and limits backlash against centralised expansion. Constituent states within federal structures concede power as the price to pay for the benefits involved in being part of a federal state.[27] In the Union, things are more complicated because the loss of Member State power leads to perceptions of serious democratic costs and even the forfeiture of self-government. Its lack of fiscal federalism – until recently the Union has not engaged in substantial fiscal transfers across state boundaries, with its budget capped at little more than one per cent of EU GDP and devoted primarily to agricultural and cohesion spending – is one of the reminders that the Union does not

[25] Case 22/70 *Commission v Council (ERTA)*, EU:C:1971:32.

[26] M Pollack, 'Theorizing EU Policy-Making', in H Wallace, M Pollack and A Young (eds), *Policy-Making in the European Union*, Oxford, Oxford University Press, 6th edn 2010, 15, at 29.

[27] On those benefits, see D Halberstam, 'Federalism: Theory, Policy, Law', in M Rosenfeld and A Sajó (eds), *The Oxford Handbook of Comparative Constitutionalism*, Oxford, Oxford University Press 2012, ch 27.

operate within a typical culture of federalism. The recent financial crisis and the EU's reaction, which saw a surge of redistributive governance, has therefore caused much contestation, antagonism, and a further deepening of the Union's crisis of legitimacy.[28] With respect to competences, it leads to a perception that Member States are the victims of power theft.

C. What the Future Might Bring

It is this perception of power theft that threatens the constitutional settlement between the Union and its Member States, which is based upon the latter self-limiting their sovereignty *in limited fields* of their choosing. It also undermines the legitimacy of Union authority in general.

Functionally, Member States are far from innocent when it comes to competence creep. Even while they are scrambling to protect some degree of regulatory autonomy, they often succumb to the temptation of transferring even more competences to the Union. The reason is mundane. In many instances, the Union is simply better at performing a particular task than the Member States acting individually. Climate change, public health, security and defence, and immigration are all exigent problems Member States face in common and are more effectively solved in common. However, problem-solving often requires highly political decisions with sufficient popular support and legitimacy. Once the Union moves into areas where policies are contested and resonate on a deeply political or cultural level, its legitimacy waivers, particularly when policy choices have distributional or re-distributional implications. There is a trade-off between superior problem-solving, where the Union succeeds, and politically legitimate problem-solving, where the Member States excel.[29] This suggests a more limited role for the Union, even in situations where it may be better positioned to solve problems. With growing politicisation and contestation of European integration among citizens, anti-integration political parties on the extreme right and left gaining strength all over Europe, and Union competences increasingly touching

[28] S Hix, 'Democratizing a Macroeconomic Union in Europe', in O Cramme and SB Hobolt (eds), *Democratic Politics in a European Union Under Stress*, Oxford, Oxford University Press 2015, 180. With the COVID-19 pandemic, however, the budget rules changed in 2020, moving further into the federalist experience (see Chapter 2).

[29] S Weatherill, *Law and Values in the European Union*, Oxford, Oxford University Press 2016, 10.

upon sensitive issues – immigration, criminal law, social and fiscal policy, and the budget – once believed to be the nucleus of state sovereignty, Member States might be well advised to revoke what has been called the 'permissive consensus' in matters of Union competence.[30]

The path to a successful equilibrium, however, is far from clear. A Lisbon Treaty amendment speaks volumes about Member States' ill-fated efforts to stop the competence creep. In two places, in identical formulation, they insisted that 'competences not conferred upon the Union in the Treaties remain with the Member States'.[31] We can practically see the Member States banging their fists on the table when they wrote this, but it mistakes the actual causes of competence creep. Union institutions are not engaged in illegal power grabs, appropriating competences all over the place where they have not been conferred by the Member States. Competence usage, rather, is a question of *interpreting* what has been conferred. Union institutions have engaged in extensive interpretations backed by the European Court, so the discharge of power by the Union is completely legal. Exhorting the Union not to exercise competences where they have not been conferred is a fruitless response.

The fact remains, however, that competence creep is possibly the most serious threat to the future of continued European integration because it corrodes its constitutional foundations. Member States' inability to deal with it effectively was a major impetus for the United Kingdom to opt for exit from the Union rather than try to reform it. With the great dissenter gone, the remaining Member States might be tempted to give in and heap more competences on the Union, simply because the number of problems that cannot be dealt with effectively at the national level increases. While that would be a grave mistake, political debate since the Brexit vote has seen Member States, eager to keep the Union together, showing signs of fatigue in the face of Union institutions (above all the Commission) urging the next decisive steps in the quest for ever-closer union. It may be that Member States' constitutional courts, prepared to counterbalance competence creep by reasserting national authority from time to time, are the last line of defence against actual or potential Union overreach. The European constitutional construct may depend on their vigilance (see Chapter five). Still, this is a precarious balancing act.

[30] See eg L Hooghe and G Marks, 'A Postfunctionalist Theory of European Integration: From Permissive Consensus to Constraining Dissensus', (2008) 39 *British Journal of Political Science* 1.

[31] Art 4(1) and Art 5(2) TEU.

The European constitutional settlement also depends on uniform application of Union law and primacy, which may be the victims of national courts' vigilance.

II. HOW THE UNION DOES WHAT IT DOES: EU LAW-MAKING

A. Variable Union Decision-Making

There is no single decision-making process in the Union. With competences unevenly distributed across policy fields, policy-making in the Union inevitably became a complex variety of methods and instruments. This procedural diversity reflects the material diversity of Union policies. The core uniform commitments around the central, common project – the single market – are achieved through strong, efficient, supranational institutions and procedures. They formulate ambitious market policies, decide on them swiftly, and ensure their implementation. The preferred instrument here is hard law. Around this core, Member States have other common projects, but they are more contentious, and are therefore controlled by more flexible methods, such as less hierarchical forms of participation and instruments other than hard law. Some of these governance modes are intergovernmental, in that Member State governments (in the Council or the European Council) pull the strings. Foreign and security policy is one such policy field. Others are 'new' forms of governance, which move away from command-and-control legislation that is imposed top-down, towards rules, best-practice modes and benchmark processes that involve those to whom the rules are applied in their shaping and application. Guidelines, recommendations, and reporting obligations – lawyers call these mechanisms 'soft law' – create an ongoing framework for cooperation and networking, and establish rules that are more easily amended over time. Often these modes of decision-making rely on a combination of 'real' legislation, soft law, and financial incentives (by both providing and withholding money). The coordination of fiscal policy and national budgets (the 'European Semester' in Euro-speak) is a policy field where hard, coercive rules give way to a mode of governance that relies on persuasion rather than force.

My focus will be on legislative decision-making, which is the most commonly used mechanism of regulatory decision-making in the Union. Union legislation produces hard law, all of it binding and judicially enforceable. This is unique in international relations: democratic legislation has traditionally been the prerogative of the state legislator. International organisations rarely make any law, and if they do it is neither democratic nor particularly effective. The Union, in contrast, produces law which is directly effective within Member States and trumps national law. It does so in a way that is relatively independent of Member State dictates. National governments do have a say – no legislative act can come into existence without the Council giving its consent – but are unable to fully control the setting of the agenda, the formulation of the policy, the deliberative process, the making of the decision, the implementation of the law, or the review and feedback process.[32] This is what makes Union legislation exceptional and interesting.

B. Legislative Procedures

The EU has numerous different legislative procedures, depending on the subject area. They vary in how much power is afforded to the European Parliament (is it merely consulted, or does legislation need its agreement to be adopted?) and whether the Council acts unanimously or with a qualified majority. By far the most important procedure today is the 'ordinary legislative procedure' (OLP). Almost nine out of ten legislative initiatives are adopted here. It is also the most supranational procedure. Set out by the lengthy and forbidding Article 294 TFEU, it seeks to find a balance between the Commission (which represents the general interest of the Union), the Council (which represents the Member States' interests), and the EP (which represents Union citizens); each institution is given a specific role. Each body influences legislation at a critical juncture to maintain broad legislative input. The Commission is granted the exclusive right to start the procedure; the Council can make decisions on the basis of qualified majority voting, and the principle of parity is maintained between the EP and the Council when they decide on the Commission's draft. Neither the EP nor the Council may adopt legislation without the other's agreement. Alongside the OLP, the Treaties provide for 'special legislative procedures'. The plural is no accident. There is no single special legislative procedure, and therefore no single provision setting out its rules. They are scattered all over the Treaties and

[32] These are the typical stages of a policy cycle, see E Best, 'Policy-making in the European Union', in M Cini and N Pérez-Solórzano Borragán (eds), *European Union Politics*, Oxford, Oxford University Press, 7th edn 2022, 236, at 238; Bulmer et al (n 11), 342–46.

must be selected from the sector-specific 'legal bases' for Union legislative action. Very often, the EP is either only consulted, or it has to give its assent for the legal act to be adopted, but it cannot amend legal acts. Just as often, the Council has to act unanimously rather than by qualified majority. Special legislative procedures are used in policy sectors where Member States are reluctant to cede too much sovereignty, such as harmonising taxation, cooperating in criminal law matters, giving more powers to the ECB, or deciding how the Union is financed. Only one in ten matters is legislated on according to a special procedure, but these are all matters of great importance.

(i) What the Treaty Says

This chapter will concentrate on the OLP. Its first stage is the agenda-setting process. The European Council is *not* involved in legislation.[33] It sets agendas in a broader way, defining the 'general political direction'. Within the general framework supplied by the European Council, it is the Commission, and only the Commission, which sets the legislative agenda. It presents an annual 'Work Programme' after prior consultation with the EP and the Council; and, crucially, it has the exclusive right of initiating legislation. It is the Commission which has the last word on whether or not to present a proposal. Without the Commission's proposal, nothing can happen. The proposal itself is elaborated after extensive stakeholder consultation and presented to the EP and the Council.

The next stages are the negotiation of the Commission's draft by the Union's two co-legislators, the EP and the Council, followed by their decision on it. They can both adopt amendments to the Commission proposal, and they both have to agree on a joint text. The agreement can happen during one of three 'readings'. When the EP issues an opinion on the Commission proposal and the Council agrees with it, a joint text can be adopted at the 'first reading'. If the Council does not agree, its position is passed back for the EP's 'second reading'. If the EP agrees with the Council, the joint text is adopted ('early second reading agreement'). If it does not because it has amendments of its own, the text goes back for the Council's second reading. If the Council agrees with the EP's amendment, the text is adopted. If it does not, a Conciliation Committee is established which works on a joint text. To become law, that text needs approval in the EP and the Council at their 'third readings'.

[33] Art 15(1) TEU.

The result of a jointly agreed upon text is a legal act, which becomes part of Union 'secondary law' (Union 'primary law' are the Treaties and the Charter of Fundamental Rights). The three most important legal (law-like) instruments are 'regulations', 'directives', and 'decisions'.[34]

Regulations are the most centralising instruments available under EU law. The Union legislator uses them whenever there is need for a uniform standard among Member States. Their hallmark is their direct applicability. They function like pan-European laws: once they enter into force, they automatically form part of the domestic legal order of each Member State. No transposition is necessary (or even permitted); national legislators are prohibited from acting within the ambit of regulations. Obviously, this is a trade-off between national sovereignty and democracy on the one hand, and legal certainty and unitary rules on the other. That trade-off makes sense in areas where uniformity is particularly important. The most common use of regulations is in the single market, which requires stable and equal market conditions to operate efficiently and fairly.

Directives are less centralising. They are binding only as to the result to be achieved but they leave the choice of form and methods, ie, some discretion, to Member State legislators. Directives are used for more politically sensitive matters where Member States want some leeway over details concerning how the directive obligations fit into their national legal order. The obligations of the directive need to be transposed into binding national law within a period specified in the directive, typically within two or three years. In contrast to regulations, directives make room for political action by national parliaments in that they establish a second step of the legislative process, converting the Union rule into national law. How much latitude national parliaments actually have depends on the directive. Some directives are detailed to a degree that is comparable to regulations (for instance, consumer protection directives); others establish minimal demands, leaving much room for manoeuvring (for example, social policy). There are always more regulations than directives.[35]

Finally, the Union can also adopt 'decisions' addressed to particular parties. Most frequently, the addressee is a Member State, but sometimes it is a private party, particularly in competition law. There are also

[34] Art 288 TFEU.

[35] OLP, 2021: 51 regulations, 4 directives; 2020: 20 regulations, 3 directives; 2019: 56 regulations, 19 directives; 2018: 21 regulations, 5 directives; 2017: 20 regulations, 3 directives. Source: EUR-Lex, web search.

decisions with no addressees, which impose general duties upon the Union as an organisational entity.

The institutional roles *seem* clearly demarcated. The Council and the EP co-legislate. Only they have the power to vote, and only they need to adopt the joint text. The Commission, by contrast, has the exclusive right to get the ball rolling. This right is protected during the process, but gradually diminishes. If the Council wants to amend the Commission proposal at the first reading, it can do so, but only unanimously.[36] If it wants to add further amendments at the second reading, the Council, again, needs unanimity if those amendments are not approved by a Commission opinion.[37] By the third reading, the Commission can barely interfere. Most importantly, it cannot vote in any of the readings. The decision itself is in the hands of the Council and the EP. The Commission therefore has no direct say in the outcome of the legislative process it initiates.

(ii) What Happens in Practice

If it were only that straightforward .... As is typical, the actual legislative process is more convoluted. The Treaty has a seemingly innocuous provision, Article 293 of the TFEU, which states:

> (1) Where, pursuant to the Treaties, the Council acts on a proposal from the Commission, it may amend that proposal only by acting unanimously ....
>
> (2) As long as the Council has not acted, the Commission may alter its proposal at any time during the procedures leading to the adoption of a Union act.

On its surface, Article 293 is merely a procedural provision about a small technicality. In reality, this article fundamentally changes the distribution of powers between the Commission, the Parliament and the Council during the legislative process. The Commission can unilaterally withdraw its proposal, for purposes either constructive or destructive. On the constructive side, if the Commission agrees to amendments proposed by the EP or the Council it can withdraw its original draft, include these amendments, and resubmit the revised draft. The upshot is that the Council, in contrast to Article 293(1) of the TFEU, will not have to act unanimously because it does not need to amend the Commission's draft.

[36] Art 293(1) TFEU.
[37] Art 294(7)(c) and (9) TFEU.

The piece of legislation is therefore much more likely to be passed. On the destructive side, the Commission may withdraw its proposal if it does not like the amendments which the EP and the Council have agreed on and the Council is able to meet the unanimity rule.

a) The Commission has a De Facto Veto

In effect, the Commission receives a de facto veto. It will be remembered that the Commission's position on amendments influences the mode of decision-making in the Council. If the Commission dislikes the direction of the amendments the EP and the Council are proposing, it will act accordingly: at the first reading, it will not alter its proposal and will not accept the amendments into the new version. At the second reading, it will deliver a negative opinion. As a consequence, in both cases, the Council will have to act unanimously. Considering the different and often directly opposed interests of Member States in the Council, it is very likely that one of the 27 Member States will use its veto. Considering the fact that the EP's position is almost invariably more integration-friendly than that of the Council, it is even more likely that the EP and the Council will not be able to agree on a joint text. This creates a surprisingly muscular position for the Commission. Although it does not formally decide on the legislative initiative, it strongly influences the outcome. Amendments which the Commission does not approve of will lead to the requirement for a unanimous vote in Council and therefore, in all likelihood, derail the legislative process. The Treaties foresaw and wanted this in order to protect the Commission initiative (which represents the general interest of the Union) from Member States watering down legislation in favour of their national interests.

The consequence is that, as a practical matter, the Commission enjoys veto power even when, against all odds, Parliament and Member States, acting unanimously in the Council, agree to amend the Commission proposal contrary to the Commission's will. Despite both the EP (the majority of directly-elected representatives of the European electorate) and the Council (27 Member States' governments acting in unison) agreeing with each other, the Commission (a body of civil servants not politically accountable) can still foil the co-legislators' plan. All the Commission needs to do is withdraw its proposal.

This is precisely what happened a few years ago. The Commission proposed a procedure for granting macro-economic financial assistance to countries having trouble paying off their short-term balance of payments; its proposal would have empowered the Commission.

Parliament and Council, in a rare show of agreement, decided, after some back and forth, not to empower the Commission but rather to keep the granting process under the control of the co-legislators. After Parliament had amended the Commission proposal accordingly, and a few hours before the Council was set to agree with Parliament unanimously (which would have meant that the amended proposal had been adopted), the Commission withdrew its proposal, derailing the whole legislative process. The Member States were furious and sued the Commission. The Court agreed that the Commission was entitled to act as it did, but only when the amendments suggested by the EP and the Council distorted the proposal in a manner which would prevent the objectives pursued by the proposal from being achieved and which, therefore, deprived it of its raison d'être.[38]

b) The Commission can Pressure Member States into Consensus

On the *constructive* side of the Commission's powers, the Commission's de facto veto grants it power beyond its exclusive right to initiate legislation. It also heavily weighs in on the final outcome. The reason is the interplay between Article 293(1) and Article 293(2) TFEU, which we can see clearly from the following hypothetical scenario.

Imagine the Commission submits a proposal that aims to reduce the emission of harmful substances into the air. In the Council, Germany wants three amendments to make its industry happy, France wants three amendments to make its agricultural sector happy, and Denmark and Greece each want three amendments flatly contradicting each other. The Council will have to agree on these amendments unanimously as per Article 293(1) TFEU – an impossible task. The Commission, however, can now enter into negotiations with each of the Member States, and agree to take one amendment on board in its new proposal (Article 293(2) TFEU) if the Member State is willing to drop its other amendments. When iterated for each Member State, the outcome is almost invariably consensus among all 27 Member States in the Council for the revised Commission proposal. At first glance this is highly surprising: Why should they concede? A closer look reveals that the Commission is issuing a veiled threat. Whereas Member States need to build a coalition of unanimity within the Council, all the Commission needs to do is build a Council coalition of a qualified majority.

[38] Case C-409/13 *Council v Commission*, EU:C:2015:217.

If a Member State is uncompromising, the Commission will stop negotiating with it and build a coalition without it: it only needs the votes of 15 Member States representing 65 per cent of the EU population. In essence, the Commission enters negotiations with Member States with a dynamic akin to the 'prisoner's dilemma'. Member States know that if they compromise, they will get at least part of their amendments enacted; they also know that if they do not compromise, they will get nothing because the Commission will proceed without them. This, of course, is highly empowering for the Commission, which can manoeuvre to at least partly determine the outcome of legislative negotiations without having to cast a single vote.

The Commission, then, is in a position where it can force Member States into compromise and consensus. This is the reason why so many legislative proceedings that the Treaties allow to be passed with qualified majority voting end with little Member State opposition. Legislative negotiations take place in the shadow of the vote, which distributes the power to build a coalition unequally: Member States in the Council need unanimity, whereas the Commission needs only a qualified majority. The Council believes this amounts to granting the Commission 'an unjustified means of exerting pressure on the conduct of legislative work'.[39] Whether justified or not, it certainly is a powerful tool which strengthens the supranational character of the most important legislative process in the Union considerably.

c) Trilogues Deformalise the Legislative Process

The Treaties structure the ordinary legislative procedure in a way that the three institutions involved (Commission, Parliament, and Council) have an incentive to learn, as fast as possible, the respective positions of the other institutions and reach an agreement as soon as possible. The incentive is so strong that the practical operation of the ordinary legislative procedure has been modified to a degree that is not mirrored in or even prescribed by the law. The most important shift is that not all stages of the ordinary legislative procedure will be used. During recent years, more and more legislative dossiers have been adopted earlier in the process. Almost nine out of ten dossiers are now agreed upon at the first reading, and the rest are adopted at the early second reading. Only one out of 100 dossiers goes beyond that stage, and none reaches the third reading.

[39] Ibid, para 36.

The reason is the so-called 'trilogues'. Trilogues first emerged in the mid-1990s as preparation for the Conciliation Committee. Since then, they have spread to every stage of the ordinary legislative procedure. Normally, no more than 10 representatives altogether from the three institutions are in the room during trilogues. In high-visibility dossiers that number may rise to 10 people from each of the institutions. Trilogues began as a forum where each side could explain its position and where, if possible, agreement could be reached. They are now used to broker compromise as early as at the first reading. The meetings – negotiations over a Commission proposal – are conducted in an informal framework in a closed room. If there is agreement, it will be ratified by the Council and by Parliament. It is that simple. Trilogue numbers are staggering. Thousands of trilogues are conducted each year.

Trilogues are not mentioned in the Treaties. However, they are now reflected in Parliament's Rules of Procedure and mentioned in Joint Declarations of Union institutions. Without any legal basis in primary EU law, they have become standard procedure for legislation and have turned the OLP into a de facto single-reading legislative procedure. Their obvious advantage is efficiency. While the first reading now takes longer (because all contentious issues which might otherwise be dealt with in the second and third readings are now subject to discussion in the first-reading trilogues), the overall legislative process is considerably shorter. That, however, is also the problem. Efficiency is important, but so are representativeness, plurality, and transparency. Trilogues privilege the former over the latter. They sideline checks and balances and lack formality and transparency. Democratic processes are not *l'art pour l'art* ('art for art's sake') but serve highly significant goals. They secure representation and accountability, democratic equality and public justification, inclusion and deliberation. Democratic form makes sure everyone can be heard, and everything can be carefully considered. There are no shortcuts in democracies: procedure without form is what authoritarian regimes do, not democratic ones.

Trilogues are secluded and highly opaque. They deformalise the ordinary legislative procedure. The formal procedures that remain in place do no more than rubberstamp already settled informal agreements. Trilogues involve a restricted number of participants who are selected according to criteria that are not always transparent. This undercuts the representative and inclusive functions of Parliament. Deliberation suffers as well because the negotiating process is truncated. The small number of participants puts the process in danger of being captured by well-informed special interests. Finally, the trilogue procedure has ended up depoliticising Council decision-making further because ministers involve themselves less in negotiations leading up to the trilogue, which weakens ministerial accountability.[40] The EP, for its part, turns into a negotiating parliament, with work primarily done in the committees which precede the trilogue, and by the MEPs who negotiate with the Council. Some call this a 'bureaucratisation of the legislative process'.[41] Even with the European Court of Justice now smoothing some of the rough edges by shedding some democratic light on an otherwise opaque process,[42] trilogue practice will not lead to a 'thickening' of democratic culture.

d) Inter-institutional Agreements Rearrange the Constitutional Settlement

Cooperation and some transparency between the Commission, the Council, and the EP are prerequisites for an efficient policy-making process. Trilogues are one example of cooperation and transparency developing in practice. They are part of tacit understandings about how things should be done. Alongside these understandings, written agreements exist. These are 'inter-institutional' agreements between Union institutions which resolve high-level issues or provide guiding principles. They are a pragmatic means to reduce tensions among the Council, Commission, and Parliament, and have been part of the Union for a long time. They come in many varieties, forms, and names. Such agreements have been concluded in relation to the budget, better rule-making, comitology, subsidiarity, transparency, and the ordinary legislative procedure. Some believe them to be the 'constitutional glue' between these institutions, or at least an important means of informal constitution-building in the EU.[43] The Treaties now acknowledge them and grant they can be binding.[44]

[40] On this latter point see FM Häge and D Naurin, 'The Effect of Codecision on Council Decision-making: Informalization, Politicization and Power', (2013) 20 *Journal of European Public Policy* 953. See also C Roederer-Rynning and J Greenwood, 'The Culture of Trilogues', (2015) 22 *Journal of European Public Policy* 1148; A Rasmussen and C Reh, 'The consequences of concluding codecision early: trilogues and intrainstitutional bargaining success', (2013) 20 *Journal of European Public Policy* 1006.

[41] D Chalmers, G Davies and G Monti, *European Union Law*, Cambridge, Cambridge University Press, 4th edn 2019, 126.

[42] The Court has forced, for instance, access to trilogue documents for citizens and journalists, Case T-540/15 *De Capitani v European Parliament*, EU:T:2018:167.

[43] M Westlake, *The Commission and the Parliament: Partners and Rivals in the European Policy-Making Process*, London, Butterworths 1994, 101; P Slominski, 'The Fabric of Governance: Interinstitutional Agreements in the EU', (2007) 13 *European Law Journal* 2.

[44] Art 17(1) TEU, Art 295 TFEU.

Many inter-institutional agreements detail procedural rules or formalise processes and institutional duties. The Commission finds its policy processes formalised in terms of an elaborate strategic cycle of planning, programming, and reporting. These include five-year strategic objectives adopted by the Commission upon entering office, an annual policy strategy, a Commission work programme building on that strategy, road maps, strategic initiatives, priority initiatives, and lists to be updated monthly, among other specifications. The 2016 Interinstitutional Agreement on Better Law-Making structured a detailed annual policy cycle, which proceeds as follows. First, the President of the Commission gives her 'State of the Union' address in the EP in mid-September and presents a Letter of Intent for the following year to the EP President and the Council presidency. In late October, the Commission presents its annual Work Programme in the EP. Then, the Commission, the Council, and the EP agree on a Joint Declaration of legislative priorities for the following year. Although agenda-setting and policy formulation seem to rest exclusively in the hands of the Commission, the Interinstitutional Agreement turns them into a cooperative undertaking.

There are a number of problems with inter-institutional agreements, which mainly result from the fact that they are not included as part of the Treaties. First, they – not unlike trilogues or the unscripted bargaining power of the Commission – change the character of EU constitutionalism by shifting the balance between institutions. Treaty rules no longer reflect the actual procedures, the real rights and duties of institutions, or the true balance of power. Second, they increase the complexity and decrease the transparency of Union rules. Consulting the Treaties is no longer sufficient, or even helpful, for understanding the institutional processes of the major Union institutions. Treaty law is either too fuzzy (because the agreements have detailed many open-ended processes) or simply misleading (because the agreements have installed formalised procedures or duties where the Treaties have not). Third, this creates a problem of political will. It is the Member States who are the 'masters of the Treaties'. By writing and ratifying the Treaties, they have distributed institutional power and decided on institutional balance. Inter-institutional agreements, however, separate Member State-made law from institution-made practice. Independently from the Member States, they find different answers to the questions of when, and how, and with what relative power, institutions should interact with each other. Even though the Court of Justice of the EU accepts such a practice, it changes the constitutional settlement and thereby threatens its basis of legitimacy.

C. Ambiguities of Union Law-Making

The legislative procedures exemplify one of our major themes: that the institutional and theoretical paradigms of state governance do not fit Union governance. Union processes cannot carry the same authority and legitimacy as state processes. Indeed, they should not, since the Union is not, and is not supposed to be, a superstate. Yet, much of Union law that results from this process supersedes national law, so the process needs to resonate with citizens as a democratic one to retain its legitimacy. There is much ambiguity here.[45] On the one hand, the Union legislator is more pluralistic, equipped with a more panoramic vista than national decision-makers. On the other hand, our analysis of Union legislative practice has revealed many democratic deficiencies. Above all, Union law-making has become dominated by informal practices which curtail deliberation and concentrate decision-making in the hands of a limited number of actors in the name of efficiency. This might suggest a legislative orientation that emphasises plurality.

While pluralising decision-making may persuade citizens that Union legislation is a means of European self-government in the deep sense of a political community, it may also lead to a democratic 'overload'. Such democratic 'unloading' has indeed happened already. Pluralisation leads to a lengthy and crowded decision-making process which loses its utility for many of its protagonists, particularly market players. In response, substitutes for democratic processes have proliferated (such as law-making through regulatory agencies and standardisation organisations) with a 'thinner democratic vernacular of accountability', while EU law-making has shrunk, both in size and content.[46] Perhaps the true virtue of democratic ambiguity is to try and find a way between democratic overload and democratic unloading.

III. HOW THE UNION IS EFFECTIVE IN WHAT IT DOES: DIRECT EFFECT AND PRIMACY

Constitutionalism is, of course, not merely about how law is made, but also about how it is heeded. While the Union legislative process does not

[45] Explored in detail by D Chalmers, 'The Democratic Ambiguity of EU Law Making and Its Enemies', in A Arnull and D Chalmers (eds), *The Oxford Handbook of European Union Law*, Oxford, Oxford University Press 2015, 303.

[46] D Chalmers and M Chaves, 'EU Law-Making and the State of European Democratic Agency', in O Cramme and SB Hobolt (eds), *Democratic Politics in a European Union Under Stress*, Oxford, Oxford University Press 2015, 155.

fit the state template of constitutionalism, the results of that process are surprisingly familiar from the point of view of state constitutionalism. Like states, the Union makes law which Member States do not violate. This is far from normal for an international organisation existing within the 'crowded space' between sovereign states. Ordinary international law may impose obligations on states, but states violate them often and with impunity. EU law, in contrast, comes with a number of assumptions about its own nature. The following paragraphs will lay out these assumptions, explain their emergence, and analyse their consequences.

A. Two Key Questions: Effect and Hierarchy

The first key question is how effective law enforcement is. The answer hinges on two factors, one procedural and one institutional. Procedurally, who can bring a case before the courts? If it is only states, like in garden-variety international law, the result will be way too few cases to build a rule of law. If, on the other hand, it is individuals, like in all national constitutional orders that protect individual rights, the result will be a domestic-like rule of law. Institutionally, who decides the case? If it is a transnational court, with no real enforcement mechanisms at its disposal, the result will be compliance only if nothing is at stake. If, on the other hand, it is (also) national courts, whose decisions have teeth, the result is more likely to be compliance all around.

The second key question is what happens when EU law and national law collide. What, in other words, should happen when there are two different norms covering one set of facts, and they give different responses to the problem at hand? If national law trumps transnational law, as it usually does with orthodox international law, EU law will have little impact because Member States can simply pick and choose which Union commitments they honour. If, on the other hand, the default collision rule works the other way round, and transnational law supersedes national law, Union law – and the legal order it sustains – will be extremely effective.

The first set of questions defines what lawyers call the 'direct effect' of law. Is Union law part of the 'law of the land' within Member States? Does it empower individuals to bring cases, both before the Court of Justice of the EU and before national courts? The answers will profoundly impact the shape of Union constitutionalism. First, they will determine the place of the individual in European integration. Empowering individuals to enforce Union rules in local courts would take the decision over whether or not to comply with those rules out of the hands of governments and place it in the hands of courts seized by ordinary people. Some argue that Union constitutionalism would become a democratic achievement, while others argue that Union constitutionalism would become a depoliticised, self-effecting legal order.[47] Second, answering questions around direct effect will determine whether EU law can be effectively enforced, and thus decide the 'hardness' of Europe's rule of law. Without direct effect, individual enforcement would be absent, leaving the judicial enforcement of Union law to the diverse whims of governments and Union institutions.

The second set of questions relates to what lawyers call 'primacy' or 'supremacy' of Union law. Which norms of Union law trump which norms of national law? Again, the answer will tell us what EU constitutionalism really looks like. There are two important factors to consider here. First, since Union and Member State constitutional orders are interlocked, this poses difficult institutional problems: who does what with what effect, and who is *not* allowed to do what any longer? For example, can national courts still use national fundamental rights to block the application of Union law? Primacy, or supremacy, then, is not merely about what provision overrides what other provision, but also about the distribution of institutional power between the Union and its Member States. Second, and perhaps most importantly, constitutions deploy law to assert the values of a particular political community. Constitutional conflict about primacy is therefore, at its deepest level, a conflict of collective values.

B. The Silence of the Treaties

Oddly, the Treaties have next to nothing to say about the relationship between these orders. They are silent about whether national courts should apply rules sourced at the Union level, and if so, how. Neither do they say which legal order, in the event of conflict, shall prevail. Before European integration, and even in its first decade, it was generally accepted that the status of international legal provisions – including European Union law provisions – would be determined by the constitutional order of every single country. Member State constitutions

[47] See on the one hand F Mancini and D Keeling, 'Democracy and the European Court of Justice', (1994) 57 *Modern Law Review* 175, 183, and M Dawson and F de Witte, *EU Law and Governance*, Cambridge, Cambridge University Press 2022, 102–4, on the other.

dealt with international law in different ways, but few granted international law direct effect within their legal order, and even fewer granted them primacy over national law (the notable exception was the Netherlands).[48]

As a consequence, the Union, at its inception, looked much like an orthodox international organisation. Its legal architecture was not constitutional, but intergovernmental. Few cases reached the European Court of Justice, among them even fewer of political significance. Many large infractions could occur without legal repercussions; most conflicts were resolved out of court.

This changed with interventions from the European Court of Justice: the Union's transformation from a weak international system to what became known as a strong 'supranational' system, and what today is a constitutional order, was orchestrated by the ECJ through bold legal interpretations. Its rulings in the cases *Van Gend & Loos* in 1963 and *Costa v ENEL* in 1964 have not merely shaped, but constituted Europe's legal and political order.[49] These cases mark the moment when a constitutional European order emerged, and since they are a window into the Court's thinking, the following section will detail these iconic cases and their aftermath.

C. Direct Effect: *Van Gend & Loos* 1963

The principle of direct effect allows citizens to invoke EU law provisions in their local courts, even against their own governments; national courts are obliged to disapply national law that conflicts with EU law. The principle was brought about by the *Van Gend & Loos* case in 1963. The facts of the case are quite mundane and revolve around Dutch customs duties. When the Benelux countries modernised their tariff system in 1960, the changes in classification led to occasional increases in tariff rates for a small number of products. Such increases were contrary to Article 12 of the EEC Treaty which, as a standstill clause, prohibited Member

[48] France, from the adoption of the Constitution of the Fourth Republic in 1946, had a constitutional provision as well which seemed to recognise the primacy of international treaty law over subsequent national legislation, but the French courts refused to 'question the popular will as expressed by the representative assembly', see G Berman, 'French Treaties and French Courts: Two Problems in Supremacy', (1979) 28 *International Comparative Law Quarterly* 458, at 461.

[49] *Van Gend & Loos* (n 14); *Costa v ENEL* (n 14).

States from increasing tariffs (this was meant as a first step to dismantling internal tariffs between Member States and establishing the single market). A Dutch road haulier named Van Gend & Loos launched legal actions against the Dutch government because it had to pay a higher duty on certain chemicals imported from Germany. In doing so, it invoked Article 12 EEC in legal proceedings before a Dutch tax court. The Dutch court sent a preliminary reference to the ECJ, asking whether Article 12 EEC could have direct effect: Could a party rely on Treaty provisions in proceedings before a national court?

That question clarifies the effect of EU Treaty law within the Dutch legal order. International law and constitutional law all over the world agreed, at the time, on the answer: the internal effect of international treaty law within a national legal order is decided by national constitutions, not the international treaty. Accordingly, none of the Member States implicated in the case (three out of then six: the Netherlands was a party, Belgium and Germany intervened) argued in favour of direct effect of Article 12 EEC. On the contrary, they claimed the Dutch preliminary reference was inadmissible because it was not about Community law, but about Dutch constitutional law, and therefore a matter for Dutch courts, not the ECJ. The Member States, in other words, remained firmly within settled international law doctrine.

The Commission, on the other hand, presented a highly ambitious brief, arguing that Community law was unlike other international law. While the latter was based on mutual contracts between states, Community law constituted a genuine *droit communautaire*. As a consequence, it was not national constitutional law that decided the effect of European norms within the Member States, but the ECJ's interpretation of Community law. This was a daring position, and it was not well received by the governments of the Member States.

The Court came out against the Member States and followed the Commission's lead, at least to some extent. It stated that

> [t]he objective of the EEC Treaty, which is to establish a Common Market, the functioning of which is of direct concern to interested parties in the Community, implies that this Treaty is *more than an agreement which merely creates mutual obligations between the contracting states*. … The conclusion to be drawn from this is that the *Community constitutes a new legal order of international law for the benefit of which the states have limited their sovereign rights, albeit within limited fields, and the subjects of which comprise not only Member States but also their nationals*. Independently of the legislation of Member States, Community law therefore not only imposes obligations on individuals but is also intended to confer upon them rights

> which become part of their legal heritage. These rights arise not only where they are expressly granted by the Treaty, but also by reason of obligations which the Treaty imposes in a clearly defined way upon individuals as well as upon the Member States and upon the institutions of the Community (emphasis added).[50]

This was an intrepid leap. There was simply nothing in the wording of Article 12 EEC that suggested it might have direct effect. It was directed at the Member States only, did not mention citizens, and did not seem to contain any individual rights. The Court, however, reversed traditional legal methodology and started not with the wording but with goal-oriented interpretation (what lawyers call 'teleological'), which leaves much more room for the Court to manoeuvre. Clearly, the European Court wanted to rule out the possibility that Member States, once they had signed the Treaties, would decide, through subsequent legislation, not to follow the commitments in those Treaties.

Undeterred by the absence of any explicit treatment of direct effect in the Treaty, the Court distanced EC law from orthodox international treaty law. The ECJ did not explain what exact form it envisioned EC law to take, but the ambition to paint it as a constitution is palpable. Imitating the language of national constitutions, the Court held that the Treaty has created a legal order that limits the power of national constitutional law. This was a legal power move: the ECJ claimed that national legal systems no longer formed the exclusive building block for legal authority in Europe. Rather, legal authority flowed from the Treaty, and national orders would have to adapt. The Court reversed the relationship between national and European Treaty law.

In its ruling, the Court made a novel claim about the nature of political community within Europe. While traditional international law only governs mutual obligations between sovereign states, EC law recognises other subjects, namely individuals and corporations. The Community legal order confers rights and obligations on them which set up legal relations that are independent from their relationship to national law. This was the birth of a new legal community, with all that comes with it: mutual commitments, a political community, the constitution of values on the European plane, loyalty and responsibility, peoples and eventually people coming together. In this sense, the Court was setting in motion a founding myth of the European Union as a 'settlement between the peoples of Europe that binds their governments, and not

[50] *Van Gend & Loos* (n 14), at 12.

simply as an agreement between the governments of Europe that binds their peoples'.[51] It is this founding myth that acts as a justification for the legal power claim.

Constitutionally, this was a far-reaching and revolutionary breakthrough. Legally, not that much had happened. All the Court had done was to proclaim one article of the Treaty, Article 12 EEC, to be directly effective. A flurry of subsequent litigation tested what other provisions might have direct effect. In each subsequent case, the Court held Treaty articles were directly effective.

The Court later extended direct effect to secondary Union law, that is to the huge body of legislation coming out of Brussels. Direct effect of regulations and decisions was unsurprising. Their architecture is hierarchical and structured in terms of commands and obedience. The problems for direct effect in this context came from the nature of directives. Their legislative process is less centralising since national parliaments, in a two-step process and with some leeway, need to transform them into national law. Obligations from directives become directly effective only once they have been transposed into domestic law.

In spite of this, the Court strengthened the possibility to enforce directives when Member States did not transpose them or did so in ways deemed incorrect. It held that individuals may rely directly on an un-transposed or mis-transposed directive's provision in order to enforce their rights against a Member State in court (ie, in 'vertical' relations between individual and Member State). While the Court's legal argument was doubtful, its policy argument was quite compelling. First, many important, sensitive, and potentially explosive areas of Union policy (such as banking, insurance, environmental and consumer protection law) rely on Member States properly implementing Union directives for their practical realisation. If Member States fail or refuse to implement them, these policies will be seriously undermined. Second, since these policies are far from uncontested between Member States, the negotiation of such directives is arduous and contentious – Member States' gloves come off in the process. Once a compromise is found, it needs to be protected. Direct effect and the resulting litigation before national courts is the most effective protection mechanism. Third, the more sensitive the policy area is, the more incentives Member States have to break the law simply because the stakes are higher. Close judicial

[51] Chalmers, Davies and Monti (n 20), 17.

monitoring and effective enforcement are essential. From the point of view of integration politics, the Court's constitutional vision is entirely appropriate. From the point of view of legal methodology, however, it was a daredevil move that was met with some resistance from Member State courts because it blurred the distinction between directives and regulations.

The upshot is that much of Treaty law and EU legislation has direct effect, which forms part of a very effective enforcement machinery of European law. To be sure, there are EU provisions that are not directly effective (because they are not sufficiently clear, precise, or do not offer an unconditional individual right), which does leave gaps in enforcement; but here national courts are under an obligation to read all national law in such a way that the outcome still conforms with the demands of EU legislation (lawyers call this doctrine 'indirect effect'). Whether through direct or indirect effect, the making and the enforcement of law are no longer in the hands of the Member States.

D. Primacy: *Costa v ENEL* 1964

The principle of direct effect is undergirded by the principle of primacy (or supremacy) which states that, in cases of conflict, EU law trumps national law, even national constitutional law. It is the twin sibling of direct effect. The European Court established it not long after the 1963 *Van Gend & Loos* case in the 1964 case of *Costa v ENEL*. Italy had nationalised its electricity industry in December 1962 (a hugely important political issue at the time since it pointed to a 'new economic model' beyond capitalism) and created the national electricity corporation, ENEL. Liberals were opposed to this, among them Mr Costa, a Milanese criminal lawyer, who set up a test case to challenge the Italian Nationalisation Act. He refused to pay his 1,925 Lire electricity bill to ENEL (which was less than US $2), arguing that the Nationalisation Act of 1962 was both unconstitutional and in violation of EU law. One *Pretore* – a low-level Milanese judge – referred questions about constitutionality to the Italian Corte Costituzionale; another *Pretore* made a preliminary reference to the ECJ. The Constitutional Court was faster and held that the Italian Constitution allowed for limitations of sovereignty in favour of international organisations such as the EEC, but that this did not affect the domestic status of European law. Existing orthodox international law rules should be applied, so that as a result, the EEC Treaty could not prevail over the later Nationalisation Act.[52] Other courts followed, particularly in France, and law professors were not at all convinced that the ECJ was right in reading the Treaties as a constitution.[53] Convinced of impending victory, the Italian government intervened in the *Costa v ENEL* preliminary reference procedure in Luxembourg and submitted that the case was 'absolutely inadmissible'. Under Italian law, it argued, the *Pretore* had no power to set the Nationalisation Act aside, and therefore its questions could not serve any valid purpose. This meant open political resistance to everything the European Court had held in *Van Gend & Loos*.

In the face of such adversity, the Court stuck to its *Van Gend* rationale and issued another forceful judgment. Resolutely siding with the constitutionalists, it now asserted the primacy of EC law:

> By contrast with ordinary international treaties, the EEC Treaty has created its own legal system which, on the entry into force of the Treaty, became an integral part of the legal systems of the Member States and which their courts are bound to apply.
>
> By creating a Community of unlimited duration, having its own institutions, its own personality, its own legal capacity of representation on the international plane and, more particularly, real powers stemming from a limitation of sovereignty or a transfer of powers from the States to the Community, the Member States have limited their sovereign rights, albeit within limited fields, and have thus created a body of law which binds both their nationals and themselves.
>
> The integration into the laws of each Member State of provisions which derive from the Community, and more generally the terms and the spirit of the Treaty, make it impossible for the States, as a corollary, to accord precedence to a unilateral and subsequent measure over a legal system accepted by them on a basis of reciprocity. Such a measure cannot therefore be inconsistent with that legal system. The executive force of Community law cannot vary from one State to another in deference to subsequent domestic laws, without jeopardizing the attainment of the objectives of the Treaty ....
>
> It follows from all these observations that the law stemming from the Treaty, an independent source of law, could not, because of its special and original nature, be overridden by domestic legal provisions, however framed, without being deprived of its character as Community law and without the legal basis of the Community itself being called into question.[54]

[52] Corte Costituzionale, 7 March 1964, No. 14, Foro Italiano 1964-I, 465.

[53] B Davies, *Resisting the European Court of Justice*, Cambridge, Cambridge University Press 2012, 46 et seq.

[54] *Costa v ENEL* (n 14), 593–94.

Some elements in this judgment – like the emphatic distancing from orthodox international law and the limiting of sovereign rights – are restatements from *Van Gend & Loos*. Others are new. The Court in *Costa v ENEL* claims an unreserved primacy of EC law, which is absolute in two dimensions, hierarchy and time. Hierarchy here means *all* EC law prevails over *all* national law. 'All Union law' means both primary Union law (Treaties, Charter of Fundamental Rights) and secondary Union law (directives, regulations, decisions etc). 'All national law' means not just national statutes but also national constitutional law. In other words, in the Court's view, a Commission decision prevails over core constitutional provisions of any Member State. As to time, the Court sets aside the legal maxim that a later law repeals an earlier law. Union law will trump national law regardless of when either was enacted. The basis for these sweeping claims is the 'special and original nature' of EU law. The Treaties have set up an 'independent source of law' (which the Court later developed into the 'autonomy of the EU legal order'). It is a system of rights and obligations arising from the Treaty which entails a permanent limitation of sovereign rights, against which subsequent unilateral national action cannot prevail.

E. Implications

The first, immediate consequence of direct effect and primacy was the emergence of a transnational rule of law in Europe. While the Commission was able to take Member States to court if they violated EC law, those proceedings could be sporadic, slow, and politically skewed. Direct effect meant that individuals could police Community law in their national courts. Enforcement could now be decentralised and ubiquitous, making it much more effective. Procedurally, the Community had installed a 'dual vigilance' model of judicial remedies: the Commission as one eye, watching and suing Member States with EC interests in mind, and, as the other eye, individuals and corporations suing Member States and one another, with their own rights in mind. Legally, direct effect construed international treaty provisions as individual subjective rights which national courts had to protect, and harnessed the economic, political, and social interests of individuals in vindicating those rights. Institutionally, the European Court was catapulted to the apex of the judicial system, whereas national courts, above all national courts of last resort, were disempowered. Politically, national legislatures were relegated to playing second fiddle in all matters covered by Community law. Direct effect meant, after all, that Community law could be applied without any political involvement from domestic parliaments. National parliaments could no longer infuse democratic legitimacy into obligations resulting from EC law (which now were self-executing), and the Brussels legislative process alone appeared unready to shoulder the democratic legitimacy necessary to justify European output of rules and policy. Unsurprisingly, not everyone was happy about the heightened political role of the European Court; many were troubled by a democratically unaccountable international legal body's ability to overturn laws passed by their democratically elected representatives.

Another consequence was that the European rule of law suffused into national societies. It not only changed the nature of the political process, but also expanded the number of actors involved in the political process. Litigation provided avenues for political and institutional change, and the Court empowered private actors to challenge national policies that arguably conflicted with Union law. Often, these were individuals disadvantaged by their national systems who sought to gain new rights at the Union level. There were also influential interest groups or huge companies which hijacked the legal process as an alternative arena to the political process. Civil society, in any case, was mobilised and, to a certain extent, Europeanised.[55]

A prominent example is the Court's heavy involvement in combatting sex discrimination. In the founding Treaty, there was no general commitment to equal treatment for women and men, but Article 157 TFEU provided for equal pay. This was firmly grounded in an economic rationale: without the provision, Member States could gain a competitive advantage through cheap labour provided by women. A Belgian lawyer in the 1970s tested the compliance of Belgian law with Article 157 by taking up a complaint from an air hostess who had been awarded a pension inferior to that of her male colleagues. The European Court held that Article 157 had direct effect, although this practically contradicted its settled doctrine about clear and unconditional wording.[56] This meant that individuals in all Member States were suddenly positioned to challenge Member State gender discrimination by using Union law. Indeed, the Court's jurisprudence led to an unprecedented increase in litigation testing the compatibility of national laws with Union law, emanating,

[55] R Cichowski, *The European Court and Civil Society: Litigation, Mobilization and Governance*, Cambridge, Cambridge University Press 2007.

[56] Case 43/75 *Defrenne v Société anonyme belge de navigation aérienne – Sabena*, EU:C:1976:56.

in particular, from Ireland and the UK. The Court became a key engine for gender non-discrimination law, fleshing out concepts such as indirect discrimination, shifting the burden of proof from the complainant to the respondent, excluding any prior fixing of an upper limit on compensation, and pushing the boundaries of the material scope of Article 157. Much of subsequent Member State gender equality law was the direct consequence of these rulings. Moreover, the Court began the process of recasting gender equality as a question of fundamental human rights rather than a mere economic expedient, and thus placed it at the centre of the Union's constitutional construct. None of this would have been possible without concerted efforts by lawyers and activists who in turn were empowered by direct effect and primacy.[57]

Finally, Union law was now focused on individuals, their rights, and policing them against Member State encroachments. Mobilising civil society for law enforcement is a bottom-up approach to European integration otherwise underdeveloped. Asserting their European rights, individuals became immediate stakeholders in the fate of the EU. Decades before Union citizenship, direct effect combined with primacy of Union law constituted the individual as a European subject, with some European political identity attaching to his or her national political identity.[58] It is doubtful, however, how deep that identity reaches. If it is self-interest alone that drives the European market-citizen in his or her dealings with Europe, there is little hope for anything close to national allegiance and loyalty (see Chapter seven).

In the light of this, it is all the more problematic that the CJEU continues to demonstrate steadfast bias in favour of centralisation every time it addresses the balance between national and supranational authority. As a result, many people worry that in privileging integration over safeguarding national competences, the Court's jurisprudence may threaten a politically acceptable balance between European and national competences. Recent years have seen the expansion of EU law's reach into ever more politically sensitive areas. While the allocation of competences has always been a contentious issue in the Union, now it has become outright divisive, and the permissive consensus concerning European integration and its Court has faded. Controversial cases see an unprecedented level

[57] See, eg, D Hoskyns, *Integrating Gender – Women, Law and Politics in the EU*, London, Verso 1996.

[58] JHH Weiler, 'Van Gend en Loos: The Individual as Subject and Object and the Dilemma of European Legitimacy', (2014) 12 *I-Con* 94.

of political criticism. Right-wing parties in all Member States build their election platforms on criticism of the Union, and of the Court especially. What does it matter, one might ask, if the European legal system is weaponised with direct effect and primacy so that no government and no parliament can overturn it? The answer is twofold. First, there is a profound unease about a political system that relies on self-executing law and depoliticises politics. The picture that emerges is that of a top-down process controlled by a single court, with little democratic accountability, non-existent feedback from the public, and next to no cultural connection to a society. Second, legal pushback is also on the rise, threatening the principle of primacy. National courts have begun to challenge the EU legal order in a number of areas, such as the alleged breach of national norms central to the constitutional identity of Member States (most of all national fundamental rights), and EU institutions acting beyond the scope of their competences.

It is not surprising that the CJEU and national courts keep clashing over issues of primacy. Neither its theoretical foundations nor its practical implications are uncontested. In fact, there is a deeply rooted irreconcilability at the bottom of these juridical disputes. The disagreement revolves around the question of where the ultimate source of legal authority lies – in national constitutional law or in European Union law. The CJEU claims the 'special and original nature' of the Treaties themselves as the source of authority,[59] whereas Member State courts claim their constitutions as the ultimate source. As for the latter perspective, the thought that Union law can claim primacy within national law on the basis of its self-asserted authority is as 'implausible as Baron von Munchhausen's claim that he had lifted himself from the quicksand by pulling on his bootstraps'.[60]

Who cares what the ultimate source of Union legal authority is? Isn't that like asking how many angels can dance on the head of a pin? It is not, because different answers to the question change its influence and power. National courts who believe that Union law's ultimate authority derives from the authority of national constitutions are much more likely to afford their national constitutions primacy over EU law if those norms are in conflict. Indeed, this is precisely the rationale many national constitutional courts have followed. They thus protect

[59] *Costa v ENEL* (n 14).

[60] B de Witte, 'Direct Effect, Primacy, and the Nature of the Union Legal Order', in P Craig and G de Búrca (eds), *The Evolution of EU Law*, Oxford, Oxford University Press, 3rd edn 2021, 187, at 216.

important provisions of their national constitutions at the expense of Union law. While this seems legitimate from a national point of view, it also threatens the uniform application of Union law across all Member States. This conflict persists today and is heating up.

One example is the German Federal Constitutional Court's judgment on the European Central Bank's (ECB) Public Sector Purchase Programme (PSPP), a quantitative easing programme designed to reduce interest rates, increase the supply of money, and drive more lending to consumers and businesses. The ECB's monetary policy had not been in sync with the general economic environment: the ECB maintained its extremely expansive monetary policy even though the economy in the entire euro area developed significantly above potential over several quarters (until the COVID-19 pandemic hit). Increasingly, it left the impression that it was pursuing goals it would not name. Suspicions arose that an ulterior motive – lowering the refinancing costs for euro area Member States – had become the main objective of its monetary policy. The German Court declared that the ECB had exceeded its competences, and since the CJEU was unwilling to stop it, the CJEU had also acted outside the ambit of its competences. The German Court played hardball, calling the European Court's decision on the matter 'simply not comprehensible' and 'arbitrary from an objective perspective'. It openly disregarded the substantive primacy of Union law and the procedural monopoly of the CJEU to declare Union legal acts illegal, and held that the Court's decision was not binding in Germany.[61] The decision was on newspaper front pages for weeks. Union institutions issued press releases, national parliaments and governments tried to defuse the situation, and the Commission opened, and later dropped, infringement proceedings against Germany because of the German Court's decision.

Direct effect and primacy, then, are doctrines that highlight one of the major themes of this book. On the one hand, political consensus between 27 wildly diverse Member States is complicated and makes legislative decision-making difficult. Law, in contrast, is a pragmatic and efficient way to integrate Europe. On the other hand, advancing European integration by obviating the legislative process, 'integration through stealth', opens European integration up to the attack that it is both depoliticised and devoid of deeper meaning beyond its own

[61] BVerfG, 5 May 2020, 154 BVerfGE 17 – *Public Sector Purchase Programme* (PSPP) (translation at https://bit.ly/3KRpk8d).

efficiency. It is here, in the European Court's greatest success story, that the deepest doubts about the Union's stability reside. The issues of primacy and direct effect place the divide between law and politics, between market and values, and, in the end, between function and democracy centre stage. This leads us seamlessly to the final section of this chapter, which asks how democratic the Union is.

IV. HOW DEMOCRATIC IS THE EUROPEAN UNION?

A. The Unsettled Law/Democracy Divide

Article 10 TEU stipulates that 'the functioning of the Union shall be founded on representative democracy'. But can there be a democracy without a *demos*? There is no European *demos*, and there are no signs of such a *demos* emerging. The citizens of EU Member States *do* know much more about their neighbours than 20 years ago, but knowledge of European Union affairs is still virtually non-existent. European political identity is thin. The political home for most citizens is still the nation-state. Absent pan-European political parties and media coverage, this is unlikely to change. Can the EU be a democracy that deserves the name, or will it always be a construct driven by law rather than political belonging?

The relationship between law and democracy in the EU is troubling. As we have seen, Union law enjoys primacy, which means that the higher (EU) level defeats the lower (Member State) level. This is problematic for its democratic bona fides in two ways. First, it shines an unflattering spotlight on the Union's law-making process. While the *Van Gend & Loos* and *Costa v ENEL* judgments are hailed as the true founding moments of the European Union as we know it, they also created a governance problem so immense that the Union is still trying to get out from under it. The continental shift of direct effect and primacy combined put enormous pressure on the Union legislature. Raising the status and potency of the law commensurately raises the status of the law-maker. Just as Union law trumps national law, the Union legislature became more important than the national legislature; not only was national law driven from its top position, but the national law-maker too. However, the European law-maker in 1963 was no adequate substitute since it was a far cry from what we would accept as a democratic legislature. What the European Court did, in truth, was a serious dilution of democracy and its meaning. Second, Union law's primacy creates a tension at the centre of what many call 'integration through law'. To be sure, primacy of EU law has been widely accepted by national courts, at least with respect to national statutory law. However, the true source of normative authority, and of real power, comes from the lower (Member State) level, not the higher (EU) level. The result may be 'perennial instability'.[62] Indeed, practically all national constitutional courts reserve some form of legal review for themselves which they feel competent to perform in order to protect important constitutional provisions, such as fundamental rights, democracy, or the rule of law, from encroachments by European integration.

This instability has spawned both a palpable popular discontent about the state of the Union and waves of countermeasures (serious institutional reform and less serious public relations campaigns) by the authorities. To many people, the Union is an impersonal and opaque bureaucracy that affects their lives with hardly any opportunities for feedback or input. The response is often that the Union cannot, and should not, be democratic like a state is democratic, since it does not replace states but merely manages their interdependence.[63] This is true insofar as institutional state templates of democracy do not fit the Union. For instance, it is inconceivable that European citizens would accept a European Parliament with a monopoly on legislation and elected by universal suffrage with all votes weighted equally (see Chapter one). However, to argue that the Union should be judged only by its own standard of democracy is close to being fully apologetic (and perhaps analytically lazy), as it is equally obvious that this standard is simply not democracy as we know it.[64]

B. The Standard Version of the Democratic Deficit

The democratic critique of the Union has a 'standard' version going back to the 1990s, which still captures the salient points well.[65] Its first element is the 'inverted regionalism' of European integration. Although

[62] JHH Weiler, 'Federalism Without Constitutionalism: Europe's Sonderweg', in K Nicolaidis and R Howse (eds), *The Federal Vision: Legitimacy and Levels of Governance in the United States and the European Union*, Oxford, Oxford University Press 2001, 57.

[63] Weatherill (n 29), 404. Weatherill's own position is more nuanced.

[64] Chalmers (n 45), 304.

[65] I am relying here on the summary that we drew up in the 1990s: JHH Weiler, U Haltern and F Mayer, 'European Democracy and Its Critique', (1995) 18/3 *West European Politics* 4.

the formal boundaries of the Member States have remained intact, their functional boundaries have been redrawn through the transfer of competences to the Union. Simply due to the enlarged membership of the Union, the specific weight and control of each individual citizen has diminished. EU government is more distant from its subjects, and all the virtues of regionalism (such as local justice) are inverted. The growing alienation that citizens feel towards European authorities is exacerbated by a number of factors. One factor is the Union reaching into areas which were thought to be reserved for the state. The feeling is 'they' (the Union) should not be telling 'us' (the Member State people) how to handle things. Another factor is the Union reaching into areas which were thought to be reserved to individual choices, where 'they' (public authorities) should not be telling 'us' (individuals) how to handle things. Finally, there seems to be no stopping Member State competences from drifting to Brussels, which exacerbates the perception of distance and inverted regionalism.

The second element to the standard account of the Union's democratic deficit is its unresponsiveness to citizen involvement. In states, every government is subject to parliamentary control and can be thrown out in the next elections if the people are unhappy with its performance. In the Union this is impossible. The Commission is not subject to electoral approval, and the Council, the major legislator and decider, is a body that represents national governments. The only body that is directly elected is the European Parliament, but its role is diminished from that of national parliaments. Even if it were further empowered, elections are second-order elections, wholly determined by national political agendas and feature low voter turnout (see Chapter three). Things temporarily improved a bit with the 2014 *Spitzenkandidatensystem* because voters had a say in the decision over who would become Commission President. Still, this is a far cry from nation-state government responsiveness.

The third element is the way the Union institutional arrangements distort the balance of powers in Member States. Most importantly, the *executive* branch is much empowered at the expense of the legislative branch. Member State ministers – members of the national executive power – perform important legislative functions at the Union level over ever-wider and increasingly important policy areas. In contrast, the national *legislature* is disempowered. National parliaments lose their grip on those areas that have migrated to the Union and, in the face of the sheer volume and speed of most Union decision-making, lose control of their ministers in Brussels. The European Parliament cannot compensate for parliamentary disempowerment, as its powers are still limited, its functions are quite different, and its legitimacy is shaky. Both its 'public forum' function and its 'power' function are compromised. Moreover, the national *judicial* branch is weakened. Union law is the law of the land, so national courts lose the ability to control much of the outcome of the legislative process and of its implementation. Since national governments are responsible for the execution of Union law, they escape both parliamentary and judicial oversight of many of their executive functions. Finally, national preferences are distorted in a *substantive* sense. Each of the Member States sends only one of 27 ministers into the Council. Even if the Member State electorate voted for a social democrat government, it is entirely conceivable that it gets a conservative government running the Council if that is where the Europe-wide majority is.

The fourth and final element is the overall lack of transparency of Union governance. Both the institutional and the procedural sides are notoriously prolix and confusing. This extends to the law as well. The fact that there are two Treaties with a host of protocols, declarations and annexes is just the beginning; legislative procedures, trilogues, comitology control, divergent processes, selective inclusion, and hundreds of thousands of pages full of secondary and tertiary legislation leave even the best minds befuddled at times.

C. The Political Deficit

A huge part of the democracy deficit concerns a deeper 'political deficit'. We may describe it as a gap between formal decision-making power and substantive decision-making procedures. It is therefore a gap between law and democracy. While the law robustly moves the *locus* of decision-making to Brussels, the democratic credibility of that process is doubtful. More than 85 per cent of all decisions in the Council are taken at lower levels by preparatory bodies such as COREPER or working parties, where procedures are hidden from public view and accountability mechanisms are largely absent. European elections are determined by domestic rather than EU-level considerations as it appears there is too little at stake in EP elections. What does it say about a polity if much of an election campaign focuses on going to vote rather than who to vote for, and still only half of people cast a vote? There is also a fissure between the opinions of citizens and of domestic political elites regarding European integration. Citizens tend to be more sceptical of the EU than political elites, but it is the latter who make decisions on integration. Political protest is much less common at Union level than at domestic level, and even if protests are mounted against Union policies, they are directed at national governments rather than at Union institutions. Union institutions and office-holders are less vulnerable to public opinion, which is just another way of saying that citizens play a smaller role in EU politics. Political parties at the EU level do not perform the same functions as domestic political parties in that they fail to provide the same types of links between citizens and their political system.

Taken together, Vivien Schmidt's quip about the Union as 'policy without politics' as opposed to Member States as 'politics without policy' on the whole still holds.[66] The law, as an agent of integration and guardian of the integration *acquis*, has divorced the formal power of decision-making from the substantive site of politics and of democratic self-determination, thus immunising the inner, supranational workings of the Union against political reappraisal by Member States or citizens. It is only recently that political debate within Member States has gained a broader European-wide horizon, mostly thanks to the financial and refugee crises and the political developments in Poland and Hungary. This has led to a slight shift in attitude, one in which political elites need to take public opinion more into account when making choices about further integration.

While politics in the Union is 'thinner' than in nation-states, it has not disappeared; European integration as such is not unpolitical. Politics in the Union unfolds in different spaces than those we are used to within the state template of constitutionalism. We have come to expect interests, preferences, and ideology to be bargained over at the place where political decisions are made. However, in the Union, the decision-making process is heavily de-politicised through independent actors and law, and for good reason: how else could the Union get anything 'done' across the diversity of 27 Member States? Still, politics in the Union cannot be suppressed. It migrates to the point where political decisions are contested, most of all by Member State courts. While in state constitutionalism, the space where power is constrained rather than exercised is one of rationality and knowledge, in the Union, it becomes increasingly politicised. National constitutional courts emerge more and more

[66] VA Schmidt, *Democracy in Europe: The EU and National Polities*, Oxford, Oxford University Press 2006.

as political actors. We may speak of 'inverted constitutionalism' which damages the legitimacy of both spaces (see the Conclusion to this book).

D. Democracy Beyond State and International Organisation?

It is important to compare the Union not to some abstract ideal of democracy (which leads to easy judgements out of proper context) but to what we know about other political systems. To some, the appropriate comparison to make is to the nation-state, where, by and large, all the elements of democratic decision-making (like media, political parties, and a *demos*) are present. The argument then would be that anything that obstructs national choices through supranational decision-making – such as the Commission's quasi-exclusive right to legislative initiative, minister decision-making in the Council, qualified majority voting etc – is per se undemocratic. That critique would be a vast overstatement. First, it presupposes the idea of a *demos* with a shared identity that problematically implies some sort of pre-political homogeneity.[67] Second, states are not always able to realise what they want through national politics in national parliaments, either because some harms or risks require cooperative rule-making, or because transnational decision-making infuses national processes with a degree of otherwise missing pluralism. Third, national processes may turn out to be subject to not much closer monitoring by citizens than European ones. It is unclear, for instance, whether French citizens are better informed about the content of their myriad laws or about what goes on in the Elysée than they are about EU politics. Yet, the critique is right in maintaining that the Union cannot be built on crude majoritarianism. The state template does not fit, just as the basic unanimity template of international organisations does not fit. Rather, the Union is based on multiple *demoi* (which has given rise to the notion of 'demoicracy',[68] a concept that has gained traction beyond European integration). In essence, it is one of several ways to understand European integration as a 'third way' between the

[67] Chalmers, Davies and Monti call this idea 'dangerous, even fascistic' (n 20), 151. The strongest rebuttal to the no demos thesis comes from JHH Weiler, 'Does Europe Need a Constitution? Demos, Telos and the German Maastricht Decision', (1995) 1 *European Law Journal* 219.

[68] K Nicolaidis, 'The Idea of European Demoicracy', in J Dickson and P Eleftheriadis (eds), *Philosophical Foundations of European Union Law*, Oxford, Oxford University Press 2012, 247; K Nicolaidis, 'European Demoicracy and its Crisis', (2013) 51 *Journal of Common Market Studies* 351.

concepts and structures of the nation-state on the one hand, and international organisations on the other.

The direction of such a third way remains unclear, however. The manifestations of the Union's continued democratic deficit are persistent. Some of the most fundamental norms of democracy, such as accountability, representation, and transparency, remain compromised. It is the dilemma of Europhiles that, in the face of growing populism, Euroscepticism, and exit options, they strive for a stronger Europe without being able to show how such strength can be established and tamed democratically. Mostly, they propose little more than either a further strengthening of the European Parliament (which may turn out to be exactly the wrong thing to do, since European parliamentarianism on the basis of majoritarianism is precisely what the political context in Europe does *not* sustain) or a narrowing of the Union's ambit of activity. Neither proposal attempts to map any substantive content for an enriched landscape of democracy beyond the state.

E. Thin Constitutionalism

The political deficit at the centre of the Union's highly differentiated system of governance – and consequently at the centre of its audacious transnational constitutionalism – highlights the distinction between 'thin' and 'thick' constitutionalism (see Chapter one). It pinpoints how the law, and the European Court of Justice, are implicated in the democracy and legitimacy crisis that is at the root of the current discontent. It was the Court, after all, which triggered the constitutional transformation away from classic international organisational law in *Van Gend & Loos*. Legally, direct effect constructed European individual subjective rights which national courts had to protect, and shoved individuals to centre-stage in European integration – a truly constitutional move. Institutionally, the European Court catapulted itself to the apex of the system of judicial remedies, forging a fully-fledged system of judicial review and pushing national courts aside. The Court is still acclaimed for these manoeuvres. The trade-off, however, is democracy. Politically, the rulings disempowered national legislatures in all matters covered by Union law, while the Brussels legislative process moved into the spotlight. That spotlight was utterly unflattering. In the 1960s, at the time of *Van Gend & Loos*, the Union legislative process was a long way from being democratic and was certainly unable to bear the weight of EU governance through directly effective law. The Court, writes Joseph Weiler, gave 'its normative imprimatur to a caricature of democracy, not to the thing itself'.[69] It was at that moment that law displaced politics as the primary agent of European integration, with all that came with it: legal texts rather than media; courts rather than parliaments; legal hermeneutics in the courtroom rather than arguments via public debate; lawyers rather than citizens; the narrow expertise of legalese rather than the broad democratic negotiation of values; and individual rights vindicating private interests rather than the public good. Europe created an ambitious, even unprecedented, and in its own way revolutionary legal construct, but it settled, at the same time, for a thin constitutionalism that sailed under the democratic radar. No wonder that people decided to stick to the political thickness and democratic depth of the nation-state rather than reinventing themselves as European citizens.

It may have been possible, in the Union's early years, to rely on the law as the linchpin of the integration process. Pascal Lamy, a member of the Commission, Jacques Delors's lieutenant and later Secretary-General of the WTO, once said that

> Europe was built in a St. Simonian [i.e., technocratic] way from the beginning, this was Monnet's approach: The people weren't ready to agree to integration, so you had to get on without telling them too much about what was happening.[70]

It may have been possible to 'integrate by stealth' in the formative years of European integration.[71] Law certainly played a powerful role in that strategy. It has acted as a constitutional constraint on national action, limiting Member State choices and depoliticising whole fields of activity because they are authoritatively governed by EU law. Regardless of its efficacy, this now strikes us as profoundly undemocratic. The Union and its Member States have done much to supplant legal legitimacy with political and democratic legitimacy, but it has been a cumbersome process with many adversaries, public opinion not the least among them. Union constitutionalism rests on foundations that are contractual and textual rather than spiritual: 'They are not premised on a system of governance

[69] JHH Weiler, 'Deciphering the Political and Legal DNA of European Integration – An Exploratory Essay', in J Dickson and P Eleftheriadis (eds), *Philosophical Foundations of European Union Law*, Oxford, Oxford University Press 2012, 137, at 154.

[70] Quoted in G Majone, *Rethinking the Union of Europe Post-Crisis: Has Integration Gone Too Far?*, Cambridge, Cambridge University Press 2014, at 49 and 217–18.

[71] G Majone, *Dilemmas of European Integration: The Ambiguities and Pitfalls of Integration by Stealth*, Oxford, Oxford University Press 2005.

by, for, and of the people. The system is its only authority'.[72] The Union's thin constitutionalism still rests on the formal rule of law. But that rule often serves to augment the alienation that is palpable across the Union. With Hungary (and, for a while, Poland) in the process of democratic backsliding, it is also under heavy strain. Even so, for the moment, a Europe united with an excess of strict laws, lawyers, and litigation is surely better than a Europe divided without them.[73]

FURTHER READING

Bulmer S, Parker O, Bache I, George S and Burns C, *Politics in the European Union*, Oxford, Oxford University Press, 5th edn 2020.

Chalmers D, 'The Democratic Ambiguity of EU Law Making and Its Enemies', in Arnull A and Chalmers D (eds), *The Oxford Handbook of European Union Law*, Oxford, Oxford University Press 2015, 303.

Cini M and Pérez-Solórzano Borragán N (eds), *European Union Politics*, Oxford, Oxford University Press, 7th edn 2022.

Wallace H, Pollack M, Roederer-Rynning C and Young AR, *Policy-Making in the European Union*, Oxford, Oxford University Press, 8th edn 2020.

Weiler JHH, '*Van Gend en Loos*: The Individual as Subject and Object and the Dilemma of European Legitimacy', (2014) 12 *I-Con* 94.

[72] A Williams, *The Ethos of Europe: Values, Law and Justice in the EU*, Cambridge, Cambridge University Press 2010, 188.

[73] RD Kelemen, *Eurolegalism: The Transformation of Law and Regulation in the European Union*, Cambridge MA, Harvard University Press 2011, 252.

5

Courts and the Rule of Law

I. THE PLACE OF LAW AND THE COURT(S) IN EUROPEAN INTEGRATION

FROM THE START, law has played an extraordinary role in the process of European integration. Walter Hallstein, who served as the first president of the European Commission from 1958 to 1967, famously said that '[i]t is neither force nor subjugation that is the means of [European] integration, but rather an intellectual, a cultural force: the law. The majesty of the law will succeed where, over ages, blood and iron have failed'.[1] Being a law professor, Hallstein had considerable faith in the power of the law; he believed that the rule of law would also replace political pressure and eventually substitute for power as such.[2] The latter clearly has not happened, but violence has indeed been exorcised from Europe. Still today, we call the Union foremost a 'Union of law', or '*Rechtsgemeinschaft*'. The Court reiterates this whenever the opportunity presents itself, which is often.

The 'Union of law' narrative revolves around the constitutional nature of Union law and its application. Substantively, it is foremost about the primacy and direct effect of European Union law (see Chapter four). Institutionally, it revolves around the Union's court, the Court of Justice of the European Union (CJEU), which is both the author and the jealous guardian of the constitutional narrative. The CJEU is at the centre of this chapter, which will explain what it means to govern with judges.

Of course, other international organisations have courts too. But there is a world of difference in how effective those courts are compared to the CJEU. Take the 'World Court', the United Nation's International Court of Justice (ICJ), in The Hague. It decides a handful of cases every

[1] W Hallstein, *Die Europäische Gemeinschaft*, Düsseldorf/Wien, Econ Verlag 1973, 53 (my translation).

[2] W Hallstein, 'Die EWG – eine Rechtsgemeinschaft', in T Oppermann (ed), *Europäische Reden*, Stuttgart, Deutsche Verlags-Anstalt 1979, 341, at 348.

year and appears happy with that. When, a few years ago, it handed down no more than four judgments and 13 orders, it wrote in its report to the UN's General Assembly:

> Over the last 20 years, the Court's workload has grown considerably ... In order to ensure the sound administration of justice, the Court sets itself a very demanding schedule of hearings and deliberations, enabling it to consider several cases simultaneously ... The Court plays a crucial role in maintaining and promoting the rule of law throughout the world.[3]

In contrast, the CJEU decided 1,594 cases within the same period, a staggering yet consistent figure. In terms of numbers alone, no international court can match the CJEU.

Numbers alone, however, do not automatically translate into the rule of law. Court decisions only matter if they are followed. In international law, low quantity in one court is matched by weak and inconsistent compliance with the rulings of another. Sovereign nation-states subject international law, and decisions of transnational tribunals, to a political logic of national interest. National sovereignty and international law seem to be pointing in different directions, and the willingness of nation-states to comply with international law depends on the extent to which it benefits them in any given case. Since there are no effective enforcement mechanisms, violations of international law often remain unsanctioned. While legal academics are highly interested in international courts and tribunals, and make much of their decisions, sovereign states are less impressed, least of all in cases that matter to them, and definitely not in most high-profile cases.[4]

By contrast, the CJEU's decisions are immune to horse-trading and bargaining. While many UN Member States routinely ignore the ICJ, all Member States of the EU see the CJEU as a true court, and almost invariably comply with what the Court says is 'the law'.[5] In many regards,

[3] Report of the International Court of Justice, 1 August 2017–31 July 2018, New York 2018, https://www.icj-cij.org/en/annual-reports. It appears such remarks have become standard in The Hague. The Court's recent report (2022–23) opens with 'During the period under review, the International Court of Justice experienced an extremely high level of activity, including the handing down of four judgments'.

[4] The result is that academia and state practice are out of sync, exposing academics of international law to the charge of idealism and utopianism. For such a critical view, see eg EA Posner, *The Perils of Global Legalism*, Chicago IL, The University of Chicago Press 2009.

[5] But see a more sceptical account outlining recent Member State strategies to 'work around' CJEU case law: A Hofmann, 'Resistance Against the Court of Justice of the European Union', (2018) 14 *International Journal of Law in Context* 258.

the CJEU is the odd-man-out in the field of transnational courts. It is by far the largest, busiest, and most complex and developed of all transnational judicial bodies. The extent of its powers, budget, caseload and staff is unrivalled.

This success story reaches much deeper than institutional design; it touches upon the political imagination of what 'the law' is, and ultimately of who 'we' are. Since law is a tool of self-government, the rule of law, and therefore compliance with the courts, depends on whether the law is perceived as 'our' law.[6] When – and only when – we see courts apply the law that legitimately governs *our* political community, are we willing to listen and follow. For national courts, this is so self-evidently the case that we do not give the dynamic much thought. International courts, by contrast, may have the best legal minds on the bench who engage in legal methodology beyond reproach, and yet we might respond that these are 'foreign judges' who should have no say as to how we should live.[7] The miracle at the heart of the European Union, then, is that its law is accepted as 'our law' – something to be followed, not to be ignored or to be bargained over. In this, EU law is like national, not international law.

Much of this has to do with the architecture of the Union's system of judicial remedies. Crucially, it is not the CJEU alone which has transformed the EU legal order, but the CJEU in cooperation with the courts of the Member States. The construction of the Union's constitution is a tale in which national courts have played as important a role as the CJEU. Constitutionalisation in the EU is, in a sense, a conversation between national courts, with its own language and syntax. The conversation takes place through decisions that 'talk' to each other, whereby judges either follow or ignore the opinions of their judicial brethren, and through involving or not involving the CJEU. Everyone watches everyone else, adjusts accordingly, and sometimes speaks when the right case comes up. That conversation is ongoing, and shifts between differing levels of intensity, varying outcomes, and changing numbers of interlocutors and observers. It is a conversation on law and doctrine; but, as with all conversations, it takes place in particular yet ever-changing environments which are broader than narrow legal rules. The nature and outcome of

[6] The best work on this is by PW Kahn, see eg his *Making the Case*, New Haven CT, Yale University Press 2016.

[7] On 'outsider' constitutional interpreters see R Dixon and VC Jackson, 'Constitutions Inside Out: Outsider Interventions in Domestic Constitutional Contests', (2013) 48 *Wake Forest Law Review* 149, and A Dziedzic and SNM Young (eds), *The Cambridge Handbook of Foreign Judges on Domestic Courts*, Cambridge, Cambridge University Press 2023.

this discourse between the courts depends on their judicial sensibilities (eg, is teleological interpretation the way to go, or should it be the wording that determines a case? German courts may feel differently about this than Polish courts) as well as on the subject-matter (criminal law may warrant a different approach than the law on free movement of services). It also matters who the CJEU 'talks' to and squares up to. A small and possibly marginal first instance court will have a different conversation than a powerful constitutional court. Political and economic factors (such as the financial crisis or the refugee crises) may influence and alter the conversation.

This chapter will explain the tandem system of justice by first outlining what the CJEU, as an institution, looks like and how it works. It will then turn to the normative framework of judicial procedures and highlight the centrepiece of the European judicial system, the so-called preliminary reference procedure. We will see that the CJEU and its many national counterparts are locked into a complex and, at times, fragile tandem system of justice which creates compliance and, more often than not, uniform application of Union law across the Member States. Finally, this chapter will touch upon the complicated relationship between the Court of Justice and the political, which goes well beyond the phenomenon of judicialisation of politics. If law is the means to achieve integration, the integration process is depoliticised.

II. THE CJEU AS AN INSTITUTION: STRUCTURE, COMPOSITION, CASELOAD, ROLE

A. The Judicial Structure

Most constitutional systems have a judicial system that looks like a pyramid, with the first instance courts forming the base, appellate courts forming the narrower middle level, and the supreme jurisdiction forming the top. All levels fulfil different roles and complement each other. The CJEU is nothing like this. It has a more or less unitary judicial structure which is located in Luxembourg. It is divided into the Court of Justice (ECJ) and the General Court (GC). The ECJ hears actions brought by Member States or Union institutions, and preliminary references brought by Member States' courts (which will be explained below). It is the ECJ that has rendered almost every important decision referred to in this book. The GC was created in 1988 to relieve the workload on the ECJ. It hears actions from individuals and some complaints from Member

States not reserved to the ECJ. There is a right to appeal its rulings to the ECJ. While lower on the hierarchy than the ECJ, it hears the bulk of cases and is, in some fields like competition law, the more important actor. A reform is under way which will transfer some preliminary reference cases in selected, highly technical fields (such as VAT, excise duties, and customs) to the GC. There was also a specialised court, the Civil Service Tribunal (CST), which was established in 2004 to ease the ECJ's and GC's workload and adjudicate in staff cases, but its jurisdiction was transferred to the GC and it ceased to operate in 2016. No decentralised or regional EU courts were ever created.

The reason for the CJEU's centralised judicial structure is historical circumstance. It did not follow the logic of gradually building a fully-fledged federal judiciary. Rather, the CJEU started out as a court, or even an arbitration tribunal, much in the vein of courts or tribunals in classical international organisations.[8] Member States attached the GC (and, for a while, the CST) to it because they saw it necessary to unburden the ECJ when, by 1988, the average length of proceedings had reached between 18 and 24 months.

B. The Internal Structure: Chambers, Judges and Advocates General

The ECJ has 27 judges, one from every Member State; the GC has 54 judges, two from every Member State. The Court of Justice started out with seven judges in 1952 and met in a cosy Luxembourg villa; now it has a staff of well over 2,000 people spread across a number of big and symbolic buildings, with a budget of almost €500 million. Having moved from 'a bit of a family' to 'a bit of a factory',[9] the Court's expansion had considerable impact on its working methods. In 1995, when EU membership stood at 15 (and, therefore, the Court had 15 judges), the Court announced that further enlargement would mean crossing the boundary from a collegial court to a deliberative assembly. This happened in 2004 at the latest, when the number of Member States and judges rose from 15 to 25. Since then, the plenary court sits very rarely, and the vast majority of cases are decided by smaller groupings, most of them chambers of

[8] A Cohen, '"Ten Majestic Figures in Long Amaranth Robes": The Formation of the Court of Justice of the European Communities', in A Vauchez and B de Witte (eds), *Lawyering Europe*, Oxford/Portland OR, Hart Publishing 2013, 21.

[9] Interview with Judge S Prechal of the ECJ, Part I: Working at the CJEU, 18 December 2013, http://bit.ly/3ULJRQ3.

three or five judges. The body entrusted with the coherence of the case law is the Grand Chamber, composed of 15 judges. It is the most important body within the CJEU. With its 15 judges, the Grand Chamber is precisely what the Court in its pre-2004 enlargement phase looked like, even though it is now embedded within a larger structure.[10]

The ECJ's decision-making is assisted by 11 Advocates General (AGs). The GC has only ad hoc AGs but will have one or more permanent AGs after the imminent court reform. They are not judges but are impartial and count as full members of the Court. Their office is modelled after the traditional French *commissaire du gouvernement*, whose function is to present arguments to the court that are not in the interest of either party, but to ensure the coherence of the law and its development.[11] It is their task to produce written opinions for the Court which articulate the allocated AG's view of the law and recommend how a case should be decided. Although their opinions are not binding on the Court, they are influential, and the Court follows them more often than not.

The drafting style of the AGs is very different from that of the judges. The Court's offerings in the 1960s and 70s were firmly rooted in the unfortunate French tradition of extremely succinct and syllogistic structure, dry tone, and abstract style – something that has been called the 'grammatical strait-jacket of a single sentence'.[12] Since the 1980s, the Court has moved a bit towards the common law style, but its reasoning is still abstract, concise, and deductive. Part of this is owed to the constrained process of judgment writing. In the words of one of the *référendaires* (who are charged with writing the first drafts, see below),

> you are so bound to what has been said before that you can hardly even use a new verb or express the same thing in a slightly different way ... maybe once in five or six years a case will come along that might have one single paragraph saying something completely new or different.[13]

[10] M Bobek, 'The Court of Justice of the European Union', in A Arnull and D Chalmers (eds), *The Oxford Handbook of European Union Law*, Oxford, Oxford University Press 2015, 153.

[11] For an in-depth account M Bobek, 'A Fourth in the Court: Why are there Advocates General in the Court of Justice?', (2022) 24 *Cambridge Yearbook of European Law Studies* 529.

[12] LN Brown and T Kennedy, *The ECJ of the European Union*, London, Sweet & Maxwell, 5th edn 2000, 55.

[13] K McAuliffe, 'Language and Law in the European Union: The Multilingual Jurisprudence of the ECJ', in LM Solan and PM Tiersma (eds), *The Oxford Handbook of Language and Law*, Oxford, Oxford University Press 2012, 200, at 206.

Due to the absence of any formal separate opinions, dissenting views are often embedded in the judgment itself, couched in unclear language that often 'announces' a solution rather than discusses it.

The AGs are not nearly so constrained. They are much more outspoken and discursive and explain their reasoning at length. Unlike the anonymous collegial Court, with the individuality of the judges actively suppressed, the AGs always write in the first person and with a personalised, sometimes idiosyncratic style. Often their opinions are more enlightening than the actual Court judgments. To understand what a case is about, and what animates the Court, it is important to read both the Court decision and the AG opinion, which taken together, like two transparencies on an old-fashioned projector, create the whole picture. AGs are often 'promoted' to become Judges. However, since AGs have significantly more freedom to emerge as individuals than Judges, some prefer to stay AGs.

Finally, all the judges have a handful of clerks working for them. They are called legal secretaries, or *référendaires*. On average, they are older than law clerks in the US (the average age is almost 40), and they stay significantly longer. They exert no small influence (half of them are French or Belgian, and thus help the non-French-speaking judges draft their opinions in French, the working language of the Court) and many of them become judges later. It is therefore not without problems that many *référendaires* come to the Court from a career path within the Commission,[14] as this suggests a certain bias, or at least an insularity between the Court and the Commission.

C. Selecting Judges

Judges are appointed for six years and can be reappointed. Of course, both these features (the potential for reappointment and a relatively short time in office) have raised questions about the judges' independence. Reform, however, is not in sight. It might be that the Member States enjoy possessing an informal pressure point and so have little incentive to change this structure.

Considering the Court's huge influence on the ever-growing body of Union law, the process of selecting judges is as important as it is political. Traditionally, it was for the respective government to select and nominate

[14] AH Zhang, 'The Faceless Court', (2016) 38 *University of Pennsylvania Journal of International Law* 71.

a candidate, who was then appointed by common accord of all Member State governments. That accord was merely a formality, as governments mutually confirmed the candidates without questioning them. In that iteration, the entire process was as politicised as it was opaque, resting the power exclusively in the hands of the Member States' governments. That changed with the 2009 Treaty of Lisbon, which established a new body specifically charged with giving an opinion on the candidate's suitability to perform the duties of judge or AG. This '255 Panel', named after Article 255 TFEU, aimed to improve the quality of appointments – a good idea given the expansion of the Court and its powers after the 2004 Eastern enlargement.[15] The 255 Panel was staffed with seven judges who were either high-ranking in the CJEU or members of highest national courts; the Council wrote the Rules of Procedure.

There are a number of problems with this. One is the democratic legitimacy of the 92 European judges and AGs (27 ECJ judges, 54 GC judges, and 11 AGs). While it is a good idea to make sure that candidates live up to certain quality standards, and thus to formalise and depoliticise the selection process to a certain extent, some believe it is a different matter to leave the process of selection of an undemocratic institution to a panel of experts that enjoys technocratic rather than democratic legitimacy.[16] The 255 Panel, in other words, is a window into a Union bias towards the technocratic at the expense of the democratic. We saw many examples of the thorny relationship between the Union and democracy in Chapter four, and the selection process for CJEU judges is another one.

Another problem is that neither Article 255 TFEU nor the Council's Rules of Procedure establish any meaningful criteria for the selection. It is the Panel itself that sets substantial requirements (such as legal expertise, professional experience, ability to perform the duties of a judge, language skills, aptitude to work as part of a team in an international environment, impartiality, and independence) and declares them to be objective and unpolitical. None of them are. Take the 'ability to perform the duties of a judge': the Panel writes that it particularly looks at the candidate's position with regard to 'the nature, role and scope of the office of Judge'.[17] What, precisely, does that mean? Is, for instance,

[15] Incidentally, the same idea led to a similar panel for judges of the European Court of Human Rights in Strasbourg at exactly the same time.

[16] For detailed assessments see M Bobek (ed), *Selecting Europe's Judges*, Oxford, Oxford University Press 2015.

[17] First Activity Report of the Panel Provided for by Article 255 TFEU, 17 February 2011, 6509/11.

judicial activism a good or a bad thing in a judge? There can be no objective or technocratic answer, as this is an eminently political question.[18] As is often the case in the Union, politics poses as expertise (for further examples see Chapters three, four, and six). It is not without reason that the Union mode of governance has been called 'policy without politics';[19] progress by stealth, which favours technocratic output over democratic input, is still deeply ingrained in the Union's decision-making mode.

The result of this selection process is that the 255 Panel delivered 243 opinions between 2010 and 2022, 27 of them unfavourable (11 per cent).[20] No unfavourable opinions have been delivered on candidates for renewal of a term of office, which means that about one-fifth of first-time candidates were found unsuitable. None of those candidates were confirmed, meaning the Panel report had the impact of a veto. This, in turn, has led to a formalisation of *national* selection procedures. Keen to avoid embarrassment by the 255 Panel, Member State governments engage in more open selection procedures before they nominate their candidates.

D. The Caseload: Volume

The Court's success has ironically caused serious problems for itself. Its docket is full, and its unitary judicial structure has created a bottleneck ill-suited to deal with the workload. The result was a long backlog in the 1980s and 1990s. It took between two and three years to obtain a ruling, which was a considerable strain on the rule of law. Procedural reforms helped to bring that duration down to 14 months. One was to create the GC. To little surprise, the backlog problem resurfaced in the GC which, at the end of 2012, had more than 1,200 cases pending and an average duration of proceedings between 20 and 48 months. Both the CJEU and the European Court of Human Rights have overturned decisions on the grounds that they violated the applicant's fundamental right to have a case heard within a reasonable period of time. The reaction in 2015 was

[18] Empirical analysis confirms that nation-state governments put judges on international courts according to what their respective position towards judicial activism is. See E Voeten, 'The Politics of International Judicial Appointments', (2007) 61 *International Organisations* 669.

[19] VA Schmidt, *Democracy in Europe*, Oxford, Oxford University Press 2006, 22.

[20] Seventh Activity Report of the Panel Provided for by Article 255 TFEU, adopted on 25 February 2022, 9.

to double the number of judges on the GC (and at the same time to dissolve the CST). This was one of the most radical transformations of the EU judicial architecture since the establishment of the GC in 1988. It was probably not a good reform. The appointment of 27 additional judges (rather than, say, 14) was clearly too many. The choice of 27 arose from the fact that Member States were unable to agree on any reform other than one that would guarantee each of them another judge. That, of course, was costly; the CST was dissolved even though it was working perfectly well.[21]

The Court's workload creates further problems. One is that the quality of CJEU decisions has declined. Given the deluge of cases, there simply is not sufficient time to think them through, especially for those judges who are not the judge-rapporteur. The chamber system has panels of no more than three judges deciding important constitutional issues, which increases the likelihood of mistakes. In addition, cases are complex and involve specialised fields of knowledge, not all of which are legal. A typical week includes cases on competition law (where judges need to be versed in industrial economics), on environmental and patent law (where they will need knowledge of natural science), and anti-dumping law (where knowledge of accountancy is necessary). Being the first and last step in the EU's judicial hierarchy, the Court should have time to carefully ponder and deliberate each and every case, but that is precisely the one thing it does not have.[22]

Another problem is that no one has time to read all the judgments released. Courts are not merely watchdogs of legality; they also oversee and direct the legal evolution in a political community. They can only fulfil that role if their decisions are read, interpreted, digested, debated, and ultimately internalised by all legal actors within the interpretative community. The CJEU's audience is not just the parties to the case, but lawyers, judges, professors and students of law, civil servants in Member State ministries and the European Commission. The Court does not reach that audience any more, and it has not for some time. As early as 2003, the ECJ's official collection of yearly judgments, the European Court Reports, surpassed a total page count of 15,000, plus another 6,000 pages from the GC. The Court subsequently decided to publish

[21] A Alemanno and L Pech, 'Thinking Justice Outside the Docket: A Critical Assessment of the Reform of the EU's Court System', (2017) 54 *CML Rev* 129.

[22] JHH Weiler, 'Epilogue: The Judicial Après-Nice', in G de Búrca and JHH Weiler (eds), *The European Court of Justice*, Oxford, Oxford University Press 2001, 215.

selected judgments only, but even then, the official collection again reached more than 11,000 pages shortly after. Meanwhile there is no printed collection anymore, it has been replaced by a web-based database. Of course, for the modern lawyer this is faster and cheaper, but it also makes partial reception, debate, and internalisation worse.

E. The Caseload: Substance

The Court remains an essentially economic court. It devotes its attention to the usual suspects within a single market: taxation, intellectual property, competition, state aid, free movement of goods and services, agriculture, public procurement, and customs. It is not by accident that the landmark cases of the Court's jurisprudence are economic decisions (see Chapter six); much of the constitutional narrative was born from single market law.[23] The single market is still the cornerstone of European integration, humming away like a well-oiled machine. To be sure, the Union has become much more than a single market, with its powers extending to immigration, environment, security, defence policy, penal law and fiscal policy. The bulk of the Court's substantive jurisprudence is still, however, single market law and, therefore, a mirror of the Union's essentially economic nature.

Still, case law in areas outside the single market is on the rise. The Court is particularly active in the fields of judicial cooperation in civil, administrative and criminal matters, fleshing out complex regimes of mutual recognition (an area particularly contentious with respect to the European arrest warrant, see Chapters five and seven); environmental and consumer protection law; social policy and non-discrimination. Another development is the influence of the EU Charter of Fundamental Rights that became legally binding in 2009 (see Chapter seven). Like human rights charters before – in Germany after World War II, in Eastern European countries after 1989 and in the United Kingdom after the 1998 Human Rights Act – the EU Charter has moved the Court's discourse from 'mere' legality towards constitutionality. The subject matter has remained the same, as has the outcome, but cases are now often framed as a fundamental rights issue. This is not without

[23] It is no coincidence that one of the best Advocates General credits the Court with constructing a 'European Economic Constitution': MP Maduro, *We the Court*, Oxford, Hart Publishing 1998.

problems. While in national law, market policy needs to be exercised in a proportionate manner vis-à-vis fundamental rights, the Court has at times turned the relationship between market policy and rights on its head. For instance, it recognised Finnish workers' right to strike to protect their working conditions, but only if that right is exercised in a proportionate manner vis-à-vis the freedom of establishment of the company that employed them and that sought to relocate to a different EU Member State.[24]

Increasingly, the Court engages in value-based jurisprudence. It strikes down EU legislation where it violates fundamental rights (see Chapter seven), but its more dramatic move is to target national laws not only when they disadvantage minorities and individuals (such as bans on headscarves or differential treatment of Roma, Sinti, or LGBTQ+ persons) but also when they are part of general democratic or rule-of-law backsliding. The aim here is not (merely) individual justice but (also) institutional change. Many of these decisions are directed against Hungary and Poland (see Chapter two), but the Court's doctrinal toolbox can just as well be applied to other countries, and already has been. Of course, this is a highly salient and contested line of jurisprudence, lending more and more urgency to questions about the Union's constitutional architecture and legitimacy. Should it really be possible for the Union's 'thin' constitutionalism to control, and correct, the Member States' 'thick' constitutionalism via an independent institution like the Court no less? While most Member States welcome the Court's interventions into anti-liberal authoritarianism, they feel uneasy about the prospect of being told by Luxembourg how to organise their courts, their media, and their system of governance in general. The Court is becoming the focal point of many of the discussions about the themes that animate this book: what is the best, or acceptable, division of responsibilities between the Union and its Member States? What is the legitimate balance between decisions taken by institutions that are democratically accountable, and those that are not? What is the appropriate place for law, as opposed to political decision-making? Should an organisation with mainly power over markets and no underlying political identity steamroll differences between its constituent members? Many worry that the Court, by entrenching this line of value-based jurisprudence and pushing for more law, more Union, and more hierarchy, is biting off more than it can chew.

[24] Case C-438/05 *International Transport Workers' Federation and Finnish Seamen's Union v Viking Line ABP and OÜ Viking Line Eesti (Viking Lines)*, EU:C:2007:772.

III. THE CJEU AND NATIONAL COURTS OF THE MEMBER STATES

In the introduction to this chapter, we saw that the European Union is a 'Union of law' that is characterised by routine Member State compliance with Union law and judgments by the Union's Court of Justice. Compliance is not something to be taken for granted in international organisations. Their member states have much incentive to breach their international legal obligations, which often limit states' regulatory autonomy and impose costly duties, and international law rarely has the tools to force their compliance. It is here where the European Union legal order is most successful. Member States do not disregard the obligations they dislike. This has very little to do with shared values or common goals – the Newtonian 'big objects at low speed' universe of intergovernmental political relations – and everything to do with the Union's judicial system – the Einsteinian 'small objects at super-high speed' universe of legal doctrine passing between the CJEU and its national counterparts. To understand the macro result (rule of law and compliance) we have to understand the microenvironment – the doctrinal system of judicial remedies in the Treaties.

The Court reviews both the measures of Union institutions and those of the Member States for conformity with Union law. I will concentrate on the latter, for reasons of quantity and quality. In terms of quantity, Member States disregard Union law much more often than the Union institutions do. They are constrained by the Treaties they sometimes dislike, and therefore have an incentive to violate them. In contrast, Union institutions owe their existence to those Treaties and are empowered by them; they have significantly less incentive to violate them, and rather a pronounced interest in keeping the rules, and rule of law, intact. In terms of quality, Member State violations are much more interesting when trying to understand the Union legal system's compliance pull. Since the Member States – sovereign and powerful nation-states – subject judgments by international courts to a test of political utility, they will not habitually obey. Hence, the judicial review of Member State acts (not of Union acts) is the litmus test of compliance.

Judicial review of Member State actions works as a tandem system, with two limbs operating on separate levels. One limb is located at the Union level (the 'infringement procedure'), the other at the Member State level (the 'preliminary reference procedure'). Both limbs individually have considerable weaknesses, but together they create a European rule of law that stands tall enough that the Member States can hardly resist. The decisive factor is the cooptation of Member State courts for the benefit of the Union legal system.

A. Judicial Review at the Union Level

Judicial review of Member State acts at the Union level starts, according to Article 258 TFEU, when the Commission brings an action against a Member State for failure to fulfil its obligations under the Treaty. This procedure is called the 'infringement procedure'. It is a centralised enforcement mechanism with the Commission providing supervision and guardianship over Union law.[25] Much of this process initially looks like classical international law, but the procedure has two remarkable strengths. The first is the existence of a mandatory and exclusive form of adjudication through the CJEU, which sets the infringement procedure apart from many international organisations. The second is the role of the Commission. In international law, enforcement of treaty obligations is in the hands of other contracting parties. Here it is in the hands of the organisation itself, which is much more effective. Moreover, it is not in the hands of the Council (representing Member States' governments) but of the Commission, an independent Union body.

At the same time, both the centralisation and the intergovernmental nature of the procedure produce enforcement weaknesses, which translate into weaknesses in the rule of law. First, there is a monitoring problem. The Commission, seated in Brussels and unable to have its eyes everywhere, cannot always know when and how Member States are breaching Union law. Second, if the Commission knows of a possible breach, it will probably be a violation by a Member State legislator (which is easy to monitor), which can lead to neglect of executive branch violations (which are harder to monitor). Third, the Commission has limited human resources (on the numbers see Chapter three). Even if it knows of an infringement, it may not be able to adequately process it. Fourth, the discretionary nature of the procedure makes it inherently political. The Commission, according to Article 258 TFEU, '*may* bring the matter before the Court of Justice' (emphasis added), or it may not: the instigation and cessation of proceedings is entirely a matter of Commission discretion. The Commission may have non-legal reasons to not initiate the procedure. For example, there may be important negotiations on the horizon with the Member State in question, a known difficult customer; in that case the Commission may determine that it should not alienate that Member State by prosecuting it under

[25] There is a parallel infringement procedure that can be started by other Member States under Art 259 TFEU. It is almost entirely irrelevant.

Article 258. Considering the Commission's many responsibilities (see Chapter three), such behaviour is perfectly legitimate. However, to intentionally *not* prosecute a known violation of the law is a significant problem for what we understand as the rule of law. Fifth, no reliable enforcement mechanism exists. Infringement proceedings lack teeth as they conclude with a merely declaratory judgment of the Court (has a breach occurred or not?). Of course, should a Member State not comply, the Commission may go back to the Court and ask for a lump sum and/or a periodic penalty payment to be imposed on the Member State. But were a Member State to choose open non-compliance there is not much the Commission or the Court could do. Poland is a case in point. It did not repeal measures that undermined the independence of its courts even though the European Court had ordered it to do so; the Court then imposed a daily penalty payment of €1 million on Poland.[26] Still, Polish compliance remained extremely patchy until Poland's access to the EU budget was suspended (see Chapter two). The reason is, of course, that enforcing EU values through infringement proceedings requires the willing cooperation of domestic institutions.

B. Judicial Review at the Member State Level

To a large extent, these weaknesses of the infringement procedure are remedied by the second tier of judicial review, the 'preliminary reference procedure'. It operates at the Member State level and is a court-to-court procedure with national courts acting as gatekeepers to the European Court. Article 267 TFEU provides, inter alia, that when a question concerning the interpretation of the Treaty is raised before a national court, that court may suspend the national proceedings and request a preliminary ruling from the CJEU on the correct interpretation of the Treaty. If the national court is a court of last resort, then it *must* request a preliminary ruling from Luxembourg. Once the ruling is made, it is sent back to the national court which, based upon the preliminary ruling, gives its opinion on the case before it.

The preliminary reference procedure is the crown jewel among the judicial remedies procedures in the Treaties.[27] It structures the

[26] Order of the Vice-President of the Court of 27 October 2021 in Case C-204/21 R, *Commission v Poland*, EU:C:2021:878.

[27] The Court itself calls it the 'keystone' of the judicial system, Opinion 2/13 *Accession to the ECHR II*, EU:C:2014:2454, para 176.

relationship between the CJEU and national courts as one that is reference-based rather than appeal-based: there is no appeal to the CJEU (individuals have no right to a reference, which is entirely within the judge's discretion). Therefore, as we will see later, their relationship is based on voluntary cooperation of national courts, which become functionally, if not institutionally, European Union courts.

The main purpose of the reference system is to ensure uniform interpretation and application of Union law throughout the Member States. The CJEU can clarify ambiguous terms so that domestic courts and administrations from northern Sweden to southern Greece use them in the exact same fashion (which is important for the functioning of the single market). Considering the diversity of economy, culture, and tradition between the Member States, this system is very successful, even if it affords relative sameness rather than complete uniformity.[28]

The true impact of the preliminary reference procedure, however, lies not in quasi-uniform interpretations of Union law. The system has developed into something else entirely: it has become 'the principal vehicle for imposition of judicially driven Community discipline'.[29] Individuals assert before their national courts that a Member State has broken a Union rule which (thanks to direct effect and supremacy) they can enforce via their national courts, and, if the appeal is successful, void the national measure's applicability. In other words, the preliminary reference procedure becomes a decentralised judicial system whereby individuals can test the Member State's measures for conformity with all Union law, both Treaty law and secondary legislation. It has become the most important procedure for the enforcement of Union law and for the effective protection of rights conferred upon individuals by Union law.[30]

One reason is that the preliminary reference procedure hands the CJEU the tools to control and define the *substance* of the law in a given case: it is for the Luxembourg Court to say what the contents of EU law are, and (more often than not) whether Member State law conforms with it.

[28] S Weatherill, *Law and Values in the European Union*, Oxford, Oxford University Press 2016, 155.

[29] JHH Weiler, 'Journey to an Unknown Destination: A Retrospective and Prospective of the European Court of Justice in the Arena of Political Integration', (1993) 31 *Journal of Common Market Studies* 417, at 421.

[30] R Barents, 'EU Procedural Law and Effective Legal Protection', (2014) 51 *CML Rev* 1437, at 1455.

The other reason for its efficacy is that the *form* of the preliminary reference procedure remedies every single weakness of the centralised limb of judicial review at the Union level. It will be remembered that the infringement procedure suffers from a monitoring problem (the Commission cannot have its eyes everywhere), a work overload problem (the Commission has a relatively small legal staff), a political discretion problem (the Commission may choose not to go to Court), a bias problem (many more legislative branch infringements than executive branch infringements), and an enforcement problem (no reliable enforcement mechanism). The preliminary reference procedure has two features that make all of this go away; both utilise features already present within Member States to work for the European rule of law.

The first feature is the cooptation of Member State courts. It is not the CJEU but the national court which renders the final judgment. The national court's decision comes with all the binding effect and enforcement value we expect from domestic courts. This makes the enforcement problem disappear: EU law (coming from the Luxembourg Court in its preliminary ruling) is now spoken through the mouth of the national judiciary. Consequently, it has the teeth that can be found in such a mouth: institutions which will enforce national judgments.[31] Moreover, the cooptation of national courts for the European rule of law makes it possible to dispense with the question of how the EU Courts will coercively enforce their rulings altogether. The democratic legitimacy of governments depends on observing the rule of law, so much so that they develop (in HLA Hart's words) a 'habit of obedience' vis-à-vis their own law and their own courts. The preliminary reference procedure has national courts pronounce the words that the CJEU puts into their mouths; the habit of obedience therefore attaches to EU law as well. Rather than being perceived as 'foreign', as endangering the national interest, and as working against the 'real' (domestic) rule of law, EU law becomes 'the law' in the surrogate hands of national courts. National judges have gradually assumed their new function as agents of the Union legal order, judging and enforcing Union law in their own right. Democratic governments do not disobey their own courts, even if those courts adjudicate on EU law.

The second feature of the preliminary reference procedure is the cooptation of citizens. Rather than one centralised but limited and overworked institution – the Commission – it is a myriad of individual

[31] JHH Weiler, 'A Quiet Revolution: The European Court of Justice and Its Interlocutors', (1994) 26 *Comparative Political Studies* 510, at 519.

litigants that initiates judicial review. This has many advantages. The preliminary reference procedure is not political in nature because it bypasses political actors. Most individual litigants are not politically motivated in bringing their actions. The monitoring problem is solved too because it is now private individuals, who happen to have suffered harm, acting as some sort of private attorney general. Since these individuals challenge executive measures before their domestic courts (they usually lack standing against legislative measures) the bias that favours legislative violations of EU law in infringement proceedings is negated as well. Hence, although acting out of self-interest, individual litigants pursuing their Union rights in their national courts are at the same time acting as public-interest enforcers of the European Union rule of law.

To sum up, centralised and decentralised judicial review complement each other in fortuitous ways, and enforcement of the rule of law is shifted to a mixed market model of public and private resources. Part of it is top-down with public interest in mind (the infringement procedure); another part is bottom-up, emanating from the most immediate stakeholders (the preliminary reference procedure). Since both limbs of this system are enshrined in the Treaties, the European rule of law seems secure.

C. National Court Cooperation: Motives and Dynamic

Success, however, depends on one crucial element – the voluntary cooperation of national courts. The CJEU does not possess mechanisms to coerce or directly control national judges. While it is true that the Luxembourg Court is at the apex of the judicial system and mostly a single instance court, that does not mean it can decide whatever it wants. On the contrary, 'the ECJ can say whatever it wants, the real question is why anyone should heed it'.[32] If national courts do not heed it, the European Court is powerless; it cannot force its national counterparts to heed anything. Again, the Hungarian and Polish courts are a case in point, even though the European Court has recently increased pressure by declaring Member States to be in violation of EU law by their courts.[33] Without the national courts' willingness to play their role in

[32] KJ Alter, 'The European Court's Political Power', (1996) 19 *West European Politics* 458, at 459.

[33] Case C-516/22 *Commission v United Kingdom*, EU:C:2024:231.

this system, and to ask the CJEU for preliminary rulings, the whole thing would fall apart. Without references from national courts, the European Court would be unable to hand down preliminary rulings in response to decentralised oversight. Rather, it would be stuck with centralised judicial review with all its glaring weaknesses. Without national courts accepting the findings of the CJEU, Member States' habit of obedience would break down, and the European judicial system would devolve into an intergovernmental tribunal system with compliance difficulties. Everything, then, hinges upon national courts playing ball.

National courts do in fact play ball. Even as litigation rates skyrocket, Member States' courts still ally themselves with the CJEU (although, as we will see shortly, there is substantial variation in their willingness to send references to Luxembourg, depending on how high up they are within the national court hierarchy). Generally, the preliminary reference procedure has been a great success. About two-thirds of all the judgments the European Court hands down are preliminary rulings. Member States' governments and the Commission are no longer proprietors of Union rules; rather, national judges, individual litigants, and the CJEU have all been given a greater role in rule-making and rule-enforcing.

One example of the preliminary reference procedure's power is the *Francovich* case. From 1980, a Union directive was in place which guaranteed paying out unpaid wages for employees in the event of their employer's insolvency, but Italy did not implement it even though it should have done so by 1983. In 1989, the Commission sued and won under the infringement procedure, but Italy still refused to implement the directive. Therefore, Italian employees who were owed back-pay but did not receive it because their employers were insolvent went without legal protection. Mr Francovich was one of them, being owed roughly €3,000 by an insolvent electronics company. He sued Italy for damages because Italy was in breach of its EU obligation to transpose the directive into domestic law, and convinced the Italian court to ask the CJEU for a preliminary ruling. Many Member States, Italy among them, did not provide a system of governmental liability for breaches of national or Union law. The CJEU, in 1991, held that

> the full effectiveness of Community rules would be impaired and the protection of the rights which they grant would be weakened if individuals were unable to obtain redress when their rights are infringed by a breach of Community law for which a Member State can be held responsible.[34]

[34] Joined Cases C-6/90 and C-9/90 *Francovich and Bonifaci v Italy*, EU:C:1991:428, para 33.

This was a seminal judgment: legislative harmonisation of systems of remedies had failed, with Member States displaying political objections to harmonising or even coordinating legal procedures. The European Court, responding to Mr Francovich's request for a preliminary ruling, intervened by ruling that the principle of state liability is inherent in the EU Treaties and that an action for compensation must be made available by Member States. This was an important move to enhance the effectiveness of unimplemented directives through an alternative remedy – something that both the Commission and the Member States had failed to achieve. Mr Francovich, the referring Italian court and the CJEU succeeded in replacing legislative inaction with court-ordered reform and, at the same time, in strengthening rule enforcement in the Union.

The pressing question is why national courts would willingly go along with this. It is surely not because the CJEU has acted as a faithful agent of Member States' interests. One explanation is that judicial behaviour is based on legal logic and legal reasoning. National judges may look to the CJEU and be convinced by its legal argument; they may also look to their brethren in other Member States and realise there is a transnational trend toward referring cases to Luxembourg. All this takes place in 'legalese', the lawyers' universal term for formalism, which exerts its own pull.[35] Another explanation focuses on power and prestige. The preliminary reference procedure gives national actors a direct stake in continued legal integration. Importantly, lower courts and their judges are given the power of judicial review even in jurisdictions where such power is either weak or reserved to the highest court in the land. This is judicial empowerment, plain and simple, and it is not hard to see why national courts would jump at such an opportunity.[36]

Focusing on power helps to understand the differing attitudes that higher and lower national courts have towards preliminary references. Despite what the Treaty suggests – lower courts *may* make a reference

[35] JHH Weiler, 'Journey to an Unknown Destination', (1993) 31 *Journal of Common Market Studies* 417, at 423–24; Weiler (n 31), 521–23.

[36] To be sure, no single narrative fully explains EU judicial politics. Adjudication and reference rates vary significantly between legal sectors and are strongly affected by external factors. Analysis has to take into account, amongst others, the legal norm (did the EU law-maker enlist the judiciary's help to secure certain policies by enacting this norm?), and the decision by the parties to litigate and to involve the CJEU. See the programmatic D Chalmers and M Chaves, 'The Reference Points of EU Judicial Politics', (2012) 19 *Journal of European Public Policy* 25.

while courts of last instance *must* make a reference[37] – the highest Member State courts have acted diffidently, and sometimes even with outright hostility, whereas lower instance courts have been enthusiastic in their use of references. In terms of power, there are competing interests for lower and higher courts. Lower courts and their judges – in continental Europe mostly career judges entering the judiciary straight from law school in their late twenties or early thirties – gain the power of judicial review over executive and legislative branches by using Union law. In some countries (such as France) such power of judicial review was traditionally weak; in others (such as Germany and Italy) it was reserved within the domestic judicial system to powerful constitutional courts. The constitutionalisation of the Union legal order – its substance being direct effect and primacy of Union law, its form being the preliminary reference procedure – now allowed lower courts to engage in judicial review on a constitutional scale, reversing traditional judicial hierarchies within the country. If a court of first instance is unhappy with its highest court's jurisprudence on a given subject, all it has to do is find a European Union law argument, submit a reference to the European Court, and try to get its stamp of approval. If it succeeds, it may change the direction of jurisprudence regarding that question, even against its own highest court, which may reverse the lower court but which will usually not hold out against the CJEU for longer than a few years. Little wonder that lower court judges, hitherto the underdogs in inter-court competition, have been deluging Luxembourg with references.

In contrast, judges at the highest courts already have that kind of power. They are at the peak of their careers, and the domestic judicial architecture sets their courts up as the most powerful courts in the country. They have a relatively consistent interest in thwarting the expansion and penetration of Union law into the national legal order. Anything that shakes up their national judicial architecture must seem a bit threatening, and anyone using power previously reserved to them must appear as an intruder. It did not take highest and constitutional courts long to realise that ultimately, their power was being eroded through European integration and its new judicial architecture. They decided to fight back on two battlefields. One is national court hierarchy and procedure, where their opponents are their own lower national courts trying to second-guess them. Higher courts frequently try to revoke or amend a lower instance court's request for a preliminary ruling. The CJEU usually thwarts those attempts by insisting that the

[37] Art 267(2) resp. (3) TFEU.

right to request a preliminary reference is a right conferred on the lower courts by the Treaty itself; therefore, appeals courts generally cannot revoke or amend the request. The other battlefield is European Union court relations and procedure, where the opponent is the CJEU. Most of the defiant highest and constitutional courts simply would not make references;[38] others were very vocal on contradicting CJEU rulings in substance. Until 2008 not a single powerful constitutional court had made a reference to the CJEU.

Today, the dust of highest and constitutional court resistance has started to settle. Highest court reference rates are on the rise, as are constitutional courts' references, which is a sign of the maturation of the legal order and of changing sensibilities. The Italian Corte Costituzionale was first in 2008 to request a preliminary ruling from the CJEU, followed by the Spanish Tribunal Constitucional in 2011, the French Conseil constitutionnel in 2013, and even the recalcitrant German Bundesverfassungsgericht requested references in 2014 and 2017. They are now all part of the institutionalised constitutional dialogue within the preliminary reference procedure. Such is the 'intensification' of the Union legal order (as one Advocate General has it[39]), and the growing trust in it.

Despite this trend, national court cooperation is still not a given. The interaction between the European Court and its national interlocutors is dialectical, full of circumspection and deference, occasionally tense, and based on a somewhat unstable judicial bargain.[40] The German Constitutional Court's 2020 *PSPP* decision is a case in point. It held the European Central Bank's Public Sector Asset Purchase Programme (PSPP) which made the central banks of the Member States of the euro area purchase government bonds to be unconstitutional, and set aside a CJEU decision that had found that programme to be well within the ambit of the ECB's powers.[41] It was the first time ever that the German

[38] On the data: KJ Alter, *The European Court's Political Power*, Oxford, Oxford University Press 2009; J Tallberg, *European Governance and Supranational Institutions: Making States Comply*, London, Routledge 2003; A Ward, *Judicial Review and the Rights of Private Parties in EU Law*, Oxford, Oxford University Press, 2nd edn 2007; A Stone Sweet, *Governing With Judges*, Oxford, Oxford University Press 2004.

[39] Advocate General Cruz Villalón, para 40 of his Opinion in Case C-62/14 *Gauweiler and Others v Deutscher Bundestag*, EU:C:2015:7.

[40] T Tridimas, 'The ECJ and the National Courts: Dialogue, Cooperation and Instability', in A Arnull and D Chalmers (eds), *The Oxford Handbook of European Union Law*, Oxford, Oxford University Press 2015, 403.

[41] BVerfG, 5 May 2020, 154 BVerfGE 17 – *Public Sector Asset Purchase Programme (PSPP)* (translation at https://bit.ly/3KRpk8d). The CJEU's ruling was Case C-493/17 *Proceedings brought by Weiss and Others*, EU:C:2018:1000.

Court pronounced a CJEU ruling to be ultra vires (beyond the Court's legal authority), and declared Germany not to be bound by it. In doing so, the German Court endangered the supremacy and uniform application of Union law, jeopardised the preliminary reference procedure, and imperiled the EU's constitutional architecture, sending shockwaves through Europe. Clearly, the German Court was dissatisfied with the erosion of the principle of conferral, and no longer found the balance between Member State powers and Union powers (and the CJEU's role in it) acceptable. The judicial bargain between the courts, then, is not set in stone. Rather, it is just as unstable as the political bargain over the constitutional control either the Member States or the Union institutions exercise over the integration process.

We also know that court cooperation cannot be enforced effectively, neither with respect to lower courts, which do not have a duty to make a reference, nor with respect to highest courts, which do have such a duty but there is no functioning enforcement mechanism.[42] Here, too, the German *PSPP* ruling is instructive. Reacting to it, the Commission started infringement proceedings against Germany, but then decided to close them without involving the CJEU. There is no doubt the CJEU would have ruled the German Constitutional Court decision to be a violation of Union law. However, enforcing such a ruling is all but impossible; it only would have further fanned the flames of discontent. Regardless, the CJEU has since insisted that infringement proceedings are the right way to respond to 'rogue' national courts.[43]

Because the European Court cannot coerce national courts to cooperate, it tries to convince them. Much of what the CJEU does is watch, persuade, coopt, and cajole Member State courts into making references. One way is to write its judgments and opinions in a way that openly woos them, appeals to their sense of responsibility, and advertises the advantages of a cooperative relationship.[44]

Another way for the CJEU to secure national court cooperation is to be alert as to what court, in what circumstances, and under what kind of pressure, has made the reference, and to make sure its decisions are sensitive to the legal, and methodological, sensibilities of that court, and

[42] There are mechanisms outside of Union law, both under domestic law and under the law of the ECHR (on the latter, see ECtHR *Ullens de Schooten and Rezabek v Belgium*, 20 September 2011, Application Nos 3989/07 and 38353/07). However, a Union-wide solution by a Union institution is unavailable.

[43] *Commission v United Kingdom* (n 33).

[44] See, for instance, Opinion of Advocate General Léger delivered in Case C-224/01 *Köbler v Republik Österreich*, EU:C:2003:207, para 53.

of other important courts who might be watching. A preliminary ruling responding to a reference from the German Federal Constitutional Court therefore looks different from a ruling in response to an Italian small claims court; a judgment responding to a Bulgarian tax court would probably look different if the same question had come up in a French criminal court. French and German courts, for instance, especially value an interpretation that takes the wording of a legal provision very seriously. The CJEU, prone to teleological reasoning, will therefore jump through the hoops of a carefully worded exegesis if the referred question is of interest to French or German courts. This may go so far as to create differences in the substance of the judgment.

A recent example is the European Arrest Warrant saga. The European Arrest Warrant (EAW) is a judicial decision issued by a Member State requesting the extradition of individuals from another Member State for the purposes of criminal prosecution or to execute a prison sentence or a detention order. It is controversial because at its heart lies the idea that a Member State must surrender any person, even its own citizens, when that person has been charged with or convicted of a crime that may not be punishable in the citizen's own state. The EAW includes a range of exceptions that permit non-execution; the European Court has held that this list of exceptions is exhaustive. The Spanish Constitutional Court, however, saw some 'wiggle room', as the Spanish Constitution, due to its high level of fundamental rights protection in this area, has a shorter list of conditions for surrendering persons, and believed that that meant there was room for another exception. It asked the CJEU for a preliminary ruling in a case of an Italian citizen sentenced to prison in absentia. The European Court, in a sharp and almost derisive decision,[45] told the Spanish Constitutional Court off, reiterating that the list of exceptions was exhaustive, and the Spanish Constitution would be trumped by the EAW law given its primacy over national law. The Spanish Court was unhappy but swallowed this. The German Constitutional Court, however, was outraged. When a similar case – also an Italian EAW relating to a person tried in absentia – came up in Germany, it repeated the Spanish argument and added that the principle of proven individual guilt is part of the inviolability of human dignity and therefore one of the core provisions of the German Constitution. Should the EAW law breach the German human dignity provision, European Union law would be null and void

[45] Case C-399/11 *Melloni v Ministerio Fiscal*, EU:C:2013:107.

in Germany.[46] This, of course, was a major threat to the EU's constitutional authority because it would destroy the principle of uniform application throughout the Union. The European Court responded within a few weeks, basically repeating what the German Court had said:[47] Yes, proven individual guilt is part of human dignity which is also protected by the European Union Charter of Fundamental Rights; the EAW will not encroach on that fundamental right, and therefore the list of exceptions is not quite as exhaustive as the Court had said before. In other words, we have here a European Court judgment (responding to the powerful German Constitutional Court) plainly contradicting an earlier European Court judgment (responding to the not so powerful Spanish Constitutional Court), all within a matter of months. Clearly, it matters who sends the request for a preliminary judgment.

For readers of European Court decisions, this is very important methodologically because it means that such decisions need to be approached with a mindset different than the one we use to read national court decisions. National courts do not have to coopt or cajole; they are part of a strict judicial hierarchy and a legal culture with strong coercive force and compliance pull. Established legal methodology does not have to consider the power dynamics involved in a judicial dialogue and, therefore, cannot explain what the CJEU actually does. To read a Luxembourg judgment as a decision concerning two litigants according to settled legal methodology would in all likelihood mean missing the most important context. Judgments by the CJEU are always messages to its interlocutors as part of an ongoing conversation about legal methodology and substance, with undertones of woos, threats, and appeals to trust.

While the European Court has been more or less successful, there have been instances when national courts lost trust in the CJEU and reacted by ceasing to make references. One such instance was when the European Court, in the 1974 *Van Duyn* case,[48] declared directives to be directly effective (see Chapter four). Since losing trust and references is the worst-case-scenario for the European Court, it will always respond swiftly and decisively, often by implicitly overruling its earlier decision

[46] BVerfG, 15 December 2015, 140 BVerfGE 317 – *European Arrest Warrant II* (translation at https://bit.ly/3zaCzyt).

[47] Joined Cases C-404/15 and C-659/15 PPU *Aranyosi and Căldăraru v Generalstaatsanwaltschaft Bremen*, EU:C:2016:198.

[48] Case 41/74 *Van Duyn v Home Office*, ECLI:EU:C:1974:133.

to appease angry reactions. None of this is illegitimate or a betrayal of justice. The Court cannot fulfil its mission to ensure that the law is protected if the decentralised review procedure breaks down.

IV. THE COURT'S POLITICAL IMPACT

The Treaty on the EU provides that the Court 'shall ensure that in the interpretation and application of the Treaties the law is observed'.[49] While this sounds either nondescript or self-evident, the Court has applied this provision extensively and in surprising ways. It extended review to cover bodies which were not explicitly subject to it, and to measures that were not listed in the Treaty. It developed principles of a constitutional nature as part of EU law, which bind the Union institutions and Member States when they act within the sphere of Union law. As interpreter of the Treaties, the Court adjudicates the limits of Union competence against the Member States. Moreover, the Court fashioned seminal principles of the Union legal order, such as direct effect, supremacy, state liability in damages, and the protection of fundamental rights without a written catalogue. These principles define the very nature of the Union: they constitutionalise it and distinguish it from classical international treaties. They are also the toolbox the Court has used to assert the autonomy of the Union legal order in the strongest terms. Taken together, these doctrines helped the Court articulate a juridical universe in which the Union legal order was treated as independent of those of the Member States and as taking priority over national law in areas of overlap. As guardian of the supranational legal order, the Court understood itself to have competence over the limits of its own, and of the Union's, jurisdiction. This too has reinforced a sense of its autonomy, especially as the Court has conceived of its jurisdictional frontiers in highly open-ended terms, curtailed neither by express restrictions in the Treaties nor by recognising the superior normative authority of any other legal site. It then protected its claim of autonomy against encroachments of state constitutional law by declaring that respect for fundamental rights is an integral part of Union law (this was decades before the Charter) and by cultivating and stewarding the Union's constitutional identity (see Chapter seven). The cumulative result of these manoeuvres is a constitutional law that subjects all Union

[49] Art 19(1) TEU.

institutions to internal supervision, fends off competing transnational courts or tribunals, and forces Member State governments to respect their European legal obligations.

The consequences are enormous. Governments can be held to their transnational legal obligations in court: a transnational rule of law has emerged in Europe. That transnational rule of law has spilled out into national legal and political orders. Member State political processes have changed. What had once been national governance with control over international commitments has transformed into a hybrid of national and supranational governance. The balance of powers between national political institutions has changed (with national executives at the winning end, and national parliaments at the losing end), and the making and implementation of policy has turned into a hybrid, compound process. The number of actors involved in political processes has expanded. Judicial control of laws and their application has become a matter of judicial cooperation between national courts and the CJEU. EU law litigation has mobilised civil society and brought both institutional and political change. Much of that change is clearly progress, such as the furthering of gender equality. It does, however, build on processes which often lack democratic credentials (see Chapter four).

In addition, the Court fashioned itself into a policy-maker when political channels were blocked. Its interventions into the political process at times of political sclerosis are too numerous to fully recount. One famous instance of this which we have already seen is the way it came up with its doctrines of supremacy and direct effect, creating a rule of law precisely at a time when the retention of the veto in the Council and the Luxembourg Accord paralysed political decision-making (see Chapter two). Another famous example we have yet to discuss is the Court's case law on mutual recognition as a reaction to harmonisation legislation falling through again and again, thus helping the Union's single market to materialise (see Chapter six).

While integration did benefit from the Court's interventions, there are misgivings about legal processes replacing political ones, and courts substituting for actors with a political mandate. If integration does not depend on political consent, it becomes self-executing. Lawyers celebrate this as progress, and it is in substance, because Union objectives are achieved in a reliable and efficient manner. However, integration through law lacks the robust legitimacy that comes with the approval by elected actors. Indeed, citizens' sense of democratic self-government attenuates, and with it the deeper aspects of constitutionalism come into question.

European constitutionalism contends with legal questions of enforcement and compliance, but these questions exclude deeper questions of political identity, political imaginations, belonging, loyalty and responsibility. All of them are beyond the reach of the law.

FURTHER READING

Alter K, *The European Court's Political Power: Selected Essays*, Oxford, Oxford University Press 2009.

Conant L, *Justice Contained: Law and Politics in the European Union*, Ithaca NY, Cornell University Press 2002.

Kelemen RD, *Eurolegalism: The Transformation of Law and Regulation in the European Union*, Cambridge MA, Harvard University Press 2011.

Stone Sweet A, *Governing with Judges: Constitutional Politics in Europe*, Oxford, Oxford University Press 2000.

Weiler JHH, 'The Transformation of Europe', (1991) 100 *Yale Law Journal* 2403.

6

Regulation and Single Market Constitutionalism

I. EU CONSTITUTIONALISM AND MARKET REGULATION

THE STATE TEMPLATE of constitutionalism provides for no more than a marginal role for market regulation. This is entirely different in EU constitutionalism, for several reasons. The first is historical and relates to the centrality of market regulation within the political community's raison d'être. While economic integration is a regulatory afterthought to state constitutionalism, in the Union it was meant to expedite the post-WWII peace project. Foreign and defence policy might initially seem better suited for achieving that goal. However, European states chose to defend each other within a transatlantic rather than a European organisation, with the US and Canada being part of NATO. Defence and foreign policy were therefore never central to European integration and have only recently gained more saliency. By contrast, economic integration laid the groundwork for future political cooperation. Economic policy, including regulation, thus had a privileged, high-profile role for the EU from the beginning. The single market – or common market, or internal market, as it was formerly called – was the 'concrete achievement' mentioned in the Schuman Declaration (see Chapter two), adding the prospect of prosperity to peace and political cooperation.

Second, due to its privileged place within European integration, the single market is the place where economic objectives and political objectives intersect. While states create social cohesion through a rich tapestry of history, political identity and loyalty, the market is what first and foremost binds European societies together into the Union. Flourishing economic integration is therefore crucial to the advance of Europe as an 'ever closer Union'. Its success depends on two things. First, the integration of markets needs rules to achieve a level of uniformity acceptable to all members. This requires a functioning decision-making system which allows Member States to make rules collectively and shape them accordingly. Second, these rules need to be enforced so that members cannot backtrack on their commitments. This requires an enforcement system sturdy enough to pressure sovereign states and market players into compliance. Both decision-making and enforcement go to the heart of European constitutionalism. It is no accident that the Union's legislative apparatus was devised to meet the needs of market regulation, and that almost all of the European Court's constitutionalising judgments were delivered in the context of the single market.

Third, and arguably most importantly, the single market is not only where European constitutionalism was designed through institution-building and legal doctrine, but it is also where it 'happens', where it plays out, evolves and accentuates the intricate balancing acts and pay-offs that make the EU unique. Much of this has to do with the European Court's role in shaping the interaction between decision-making and enforcement. As was discussed earlier, Union decision-making is a tightrope act where Member State powers and Union powers are weighed within a complex and delicate institutional and procedural architecture (see Chapters three and four). Union enforcement, while hybrid in the sense that it binds the CJEU and its national counterparts together, is different. Its overarching feature is less the sharing of power (which lies overwhelmingly with the CJEU) than the consensual cooptation of power (which national courts supply in order to accomplish domestic compliance with CJEU rulings). In contrast to its decision-making apparatus, the Union's enforcement apparatus – with the Court's monopoly on interpreting the meaning of EU law, and its doctrines of direct effect and primacy – is monolithic and centralising. Indeed, the Court insists on its position at the apex of the enforcement system and fights fragmentation tooth and nail (see Chapter five). In short, EU law-making looks utterly unfamiliar from the perspective of state constitutionalism, whereas enforcement is not altogether different from what we see in nation-states. However, these two different architectures interact in ways that are, again, peculiar to EU constitutionalism. The European Court goes well beyond simply enforcing the rules made by the EU legislator. More often than not, the Court (rather than the legislator) defines the reach of Union powers, and sometimes the CJEU even fashions itself into a genuine policy-maker. The legal process, then, replaces the political process. The field where this happens is the Union's single market – the most important and most successful policy area of European integration which fuels all the rest.

As a consequence, market regulation throws into sharp relief those features of EU constitutionalism that make the Union such a unique constitutional creature, while, at the same time, it raises serious questions about the themes that animate this book. Is the balance between democratic and technocratic decision-making acceptable, or is the Union sacrificing too much accountability for gains in efficiency and effectiveness? Is the balance between Member State and Union powers acceptable, or should Member States worry about the ever-expanding reach of EU law? Is the balance between the Union legislator and the European Court acceptable, or are we dealing with a self-executing legal machinery that displaces politics? Finally, what values are involved here? Is European constitutionalism ultimately nothing more than pompous garb worn, and used, by the market and its economic interests?

This chapter turns to each of these questions because they relate to how EU constitutionalism actually works. It will not go into the intricate details of how the single market functions. But since EU constitutionalism unfolds within the single market, I will need to touch on a few of the basic single market principles first.

II. ECONOMIC INTEGRATION AND ITS INSTRUMENTS

Within the broad range of market integration regimes, Europe chose a customs union and, more importantly, a single market. (Other terms are common market or internal market. There are subtle differences,[1] but I will use them more or less interchangeably and prefer, as the Union does now, the term single market.) Semantics aside, the core idea is that of an 'area without internal frontiers in which the free movement of goods, persons, services, and capital is ensured'.[2] Economically, the territories of the 27 Member States are to be a single space. The cross-border sale of goods and services, the establishment of companies, or employment agreements should be no more complicated within other single market countries than domestic transactions. Economic actors in one Member State do not enjoy any protection against competitors from other Member States.

[1] J Shaw, J Hunt and C Wallace, *Economic and Social Law of the European Union*, Basingstoke, Palgrave Macmillan 2007, 13.

[2] Art 26(2) TFEU.

There are two principal techniques to attain a single market, 'negative' and 'positive' integration. Negative forms of integration are deregulatory in nature, seeking to eliminate barriers to trade by prohibiting national rules that hinder cross-border trade. As the name suggests, this form of integration stipulates what governments *cannot* do, for example, prohibitions are placed on using customs tariffs or levies at the border between Member States, discriminating on the grounds of nationality, implementing quotas, or adopting a law or a policy that benefits domestic producers to the detriment of producers from other states. Since negative integration is about declaring Member State practices illegal if they hinder unencumbered trade, it is a tool that is essential to market-building. Institutionally, it is mostly a matter for the courts because it does not require political agreement between Member States' governments, but instead relies on breaking down national barriers to trade.

Negative integration does have several drawbacks. First, it is cumbersome. Market actors (or their states) have to go to court if they feel that a law or a policy of another state imposes a barrier to trade. This is costly and takes time; and all the while products, services, firms or individuals are not allowed into the market of that state and suffer great damages.

Second, it is impossible to simply prohibit all laws that impact cross-border trade. Some laws hinder trade but nonetheless serve a legitimate purpose and may therefore be allowed. Such purposes include protecting the environment, consumers, public safety, public morals, or public health. A state may, for example, impose an import ban on drilling machines it deems unsafe for users. There are good policy reasons to leave barriers to trade in place if they serve a superseding public purpose and are the least restrictive means to achieve it. However noble the purpose, they are still barriers to trade, making it hard to achieve a single market.

Third, competition and its virtues depend on fairness. It is not possible, however, to establish a level playing-field through negative integration alone. A producer in one Member State may be disadvantaged by the regulatory environment its government sets. Due to minimum wage legislation, labour may be costlier than elsewhere; due to restrictive monetary policy, capital may be more expensive; due to high consumer taxes, services may be pricier; and environmental or health and safety at work policies may push production costs through the roof. Negative integration does not level out these imbalances. What helps, in contrast, is adopting common standards.

Fourth, some barriers to trade result from diversity between states' rules. In some product lines there are genuine differences in regulatory regimes. Imagine, for example, that the ground (or earth) wire of plug-in electrical devices in Ireland has to be green; in Italy it has to be red, while in Germany it has to be striped. The only way to achieve a single market for such devices without the danger of users electrocuting themselves is to harmonise the regulatory regimes across all states. Here, legislation is needed in order to create one standard for the entire Union, as has in fact occurred.

The adoption of common standards requires legislation that overcomes the diversity of state regulatory regimes through harmonisation. Accomplishing this requires crafting legislation the courts lack authority to do. This approach is called 'positive integration'. It does not merely try to maximise inter-state trade by capitalising on difference (which is the basis of classical economic theory: states do not do everything equally well; therefore trade is beneficial to everyone). Rather, it aims to reduce difference in order to establish a level playing-field.

The European Union has adopted both negative and positive integration strategies. (It has also added legal strategies to control subsidies and trade barriers resulting from the behaviour of private actors, such as cartels or monopolies.)

Its regime on negative integration is comprehensive and involves a prohibition of customs duties and of discriminatory taxation. Its centrepiece, however, is its body of law relating to the 'Four Freedoms' – the free movement of goods, services, capital, and labour. The free movement provisions in the Treaty are structurally symmetrical. They each have a ground rule that requires Member States to refrain from adopting any measures that restrict free movement. They also have a justificatory rule that allows Member States to adopt such measures if they are truly necessary for essential public interests. Written in 1957, these provisions have hardly been amended despite many Treaty revisions. The main reason is that the European Court has amply elaborated on their nature, scope, and rationale in thousands of cases, and adapted them to their changing economic and political circumstances.

The Union's regime on positive integration features several Treaty provisions that provide a legal basis for harmonising legislation relevant to the single market. Of these provisions, Article 114 of the TFEU is unquestionably the most important (we encountered this provision in Chapter four: this article is one of the reasons for competence creep). It accords the Union the competence to adopt harmonised rules in order to replace Member State rules which fragment the Union's market along national lines. It allows the Union legislator to choose between regulations (which lay down a single set of standards for the entire EU) and directives (which need to be transposed into national law by the Member State legislatures, leaving room for variation among Member States). Harmonisation is, in other words, not a binary choice but exists on a spectrum. Harmonisation has the discretion to lift a whole policy area from Member State regulation to Union regulation, or it may choose to subject only a specific part of a policy area to common European norms. Harmonisation can also choose the extent to which it reforms divergent standards. It may seek to replace Member State standards with equivalent European ones, with detailed technical legislation for each product, or it may choose a more minimalist approach with general demands at a high level of abstraction. In contrast to negative integration, positive integration requires political agreement because it relies on the Union legislature to impose common standards rather than on courts to enforce prohibitions.

The decisive conceptual contrast between negative and positive integration lies in their differing answers to the question of how much diversity between Member State markets is tolerable. This is, of course, a distinction of the highest constitutional significance: the degree to which the Union interferes with domestic legal orders impacts far more than just the market. Negative integration leaves Member States some autonomy to regulate their internal markets because all it requires is breaking down barriers between them. Diversity in domestic market regulation is, from this viewpoint, not a problem as such. Positive integration, in contrast, must impose uniform regulations on Member States in order to equalise their internal markets. It is therefore much less tolerant of diversity.

We should not overstate this conceptual distinction. In practice, each of these two strategies is pulled into the direction of the other. Positive integration provides the legislator with choices on how expansive and intrusive they want harmonisation, often still leaving room for considerable diversity between Member States, since finding political agreement for harmonising measures is easier said than done. There are many reasons why a Member State would be opposed to harmonisation. One is that its regulatory regime may afford it some competitive advantage over other Member States, which in turn attracts investments. If, for instance, a Member State has merely rudimentary rules on environmental protection or on social security, companies located there save a lot of money in producing cheap goods there. Another reason for a Member State to oppose harmonisation is that its national standard is culturally dear to it. It is hard to imagine the UK, for example, assenting to a European regulation replacing its pint with the continental litre as the measuring unit for beer, because the pint is an established feature of British identity. Expressions of cultural values often supersede economically prudent harmonisation. The upshot is that positive integration often results in careful, measured harmonising provisions in situations where Member States find common ground.

Negative integration, on the other hand, tends to limit national regulatory autonomy more than its focus on market access (rather than market regulation) suggests. Imagine that Germany does not restrict market access of enterprises offering gambling, but it does ban online gambling. Such a rule is uniformly (lawyers prefer 'indistinctly') applicable to German and non-German enterprises alike, but it would surely affect foreign gambling providers more than German providers, who have stores on the ground. Once indistinctly applicable rules are rejected by a negative integration provision (like the 'Four Freedoms'), Member States have fewer and fewer choices in how to regulate their markets.

Both the positive and negative integration of market rules can create regulatory tension for the Union. On the one hand, the Union needs to establish some measure of uniformity in order to free up trade, and to furnish conditions for fair competition between market actors. Without serious enforcement of such rules, the single market would flounder and the Union would not be the global economic powerhouse that it is. On the other hand, the more the Union interferes with national regulatory autonomy, the more it will hollow out national competences and override the heterogeneity of national preferences, interests, and traditions. This is all the more important since market rules, while operating on economic premises, affect much more than just the market. They redistribute resources among market actors and Member States, allocate values, affect the way life feels, and are an expression of how a political community gives itself a particular shape that distinguishes it from other communities. What, then, is the appropriate balance between diversity and uniformity? It is here where the single market and European constitutionalism intersect.

III. CONSTITUTIONALISM WITHIN THE SINGLE MARKET

The intersection of the single market and European constitutionalism raises several questions of constitutional import that must be answered. All of them have been asked repeatedly throughout this book. First, who decides on the balance between diversity and uniformity, the Union or the Member States? Since the market pulls into two directions, there is a sound argument to be made that it should be a hybrid decision-maker, with an eye to the efficiency of the Union's single market but still sensitive to Member States' powers and sensibilities. We will see, however, that both negative and positive integration shift the decision away from the Member States and give much power to the Union. The theme here is the vertical distribution of power. Second, if the decision on balancing uniformity and diversity lies predominantly with the EU, who within the Union should make it? Again, there is a sound argument to be made that a decision of this magnitude should be backed by robust democratic accountability. We will see, however, that independent actors with little connection to voters are the primary decision-makers. Here, the issue of horizontal distribution of power, the divide between law and politics, and the divide between efficiency and accountability reappears. Finally, if market choices are value-laden, what are the values that underpin European constitutionalism in the area of the single market? The theme here is the balancing of economic interests and public goods.

A. The Vertical Dimension of Single Market Constitutionalism

Where do the powers of the Member States end and those of the Union begin? We will have to examine what kind of power is at stake before we can find the hotly contested boundary between the Union and its Member States. Power appears in single market law in two forms. One form of power lies in determining the reach of the Treaty's rules on negative integration. The greater the remit of those Treaty articles, the greater the reach of Union control, and the smaller the Member States' ambit of regulatory autonomy. Since the interpretation of those provisions lies in the hands of the CJEU, it is the European Court that defines the domain of Union competences in the single market. A second kind of power involves setting the permissible scope of positive integration. The Union legislator may harmonise national laws when it relates to the functioning of the single market,[3] but it is not clear what that precisely means. The single market does not demand complete regulatory homogeneity, so some Member State diversity is allowed. How far,

[3] Arts 114(1) and 115(1) TFEU.

then, is the Union legislator authorised to go under the Treaty's harmonisation rules? The precise extent of permissible harmonisation is a matter of definition, and that too lies in the hands of the CJEU.

(i) Regulatory Power vs Spending Power

The question of how power in the single market is distributed between the Union and its Member States needs to start with the observation that the power being distributed is mostly regulatory power. The political architecture of the Union's single market oversight is different from classical state markets in this regard. States organise markets through regulation (that is, by setting rules that influence the behaviour of market actors) *and* through spending power (that is, by collecting money from market actors through taxes, and by spending that money through social and welfare policy). The Union, in contrast, largely lacks the power to do the latter. Taxation, labour law, and social and welfare policy are areas that Member States have retained for themselves. As elements in the 'power of the purse', these powers are conceived of as being part of the core of state sovereignty, which Member States are reluctant to cede to the Union. With the growing drift of competences to the Union and the many crises in need of resolution, this separation of regulation and spending is coming under increasing pressure and starting to break down. But as of now, the Union overwhelmingly wields its power by making rules rather than by collecting and spending money.

Still, regulatory power is real power. Regulatory choices are choices on important moral, political, and cultural questions. How much risk is a political community willing to take with regard to genetically modified food? Should the producers of unhealthy sugary drinks be allowed to target their commercials at small children? How does one strike a balance between desires for supply chains that protect human rights and the global competitiveness of European companies? Answering these questions involves hard choices which have a huge impact on everyday life, and thus it matters a great deal where and how they are made.

(ii) The Reach of Negative Integration

States feel entitled, and competent, to make such choices through legislation. However, what the Member States can and cannot do when they regulate their internal markets depends on whether such laws violate

Union rules, notably the 'Four Freedoms' in the Treaty. Such negative integration cases typically come before the European Court which is seized by the Commission according to the infringement procedure, or by a domestic court by way of a preliminary reference (see Chapter five). The European Court then proceeds in three steps. First, it asks whether the national law can be construed, in principle, as violating the Union prohibitions. Second, the offending Member State has the opportunity to justify its law, usually citing exceptions to the Union prohibition contained in the Treaty itself. Examples of such grounds for justification are, for instance, the protection of public morality and security, of public health, or of the environment. Third, the European Court assesses whether the national law is proportionate, in that it checks whether the law really aims at such a legitimate purpose, whether it is the least burdensome means of achieving its policy objective, and whether the national policy objective outweighs the Union policy of establishing and maintaining a single market.

For our present purpose of determining the distribution of powers between the Union and the Member States, we need to focus on the first stage of the Court's methodology. What precisely do the Union rules prohibit? Do they only outlaw national rules that discriminate, either directly or indirectly, against foreign goods, services, or companies? Or do the rules outlaw all national laws that negatively affect the flow of goods or services, even though they do not discriminate against foreign products? For instance, may Italy impose a charge at the border for statistical purposes, payable by both importers and exporters, Italians and foreigners alike? If the single market is merely about non-discrimination, it can, because the charge is not discriminatory. If the single market is about more, namely the unrestricted flow of trade, it cannot, even though the charge is not discriminatory.[4] The answer, which is far from clear from a reading of the vague Treaty rules alone, decides how far negative integration reaches, and to what extent Member States can still regulate their markets. It is also probably the most hotly debated question in free movement law, and for good reason, since it has significant constitutional implications.

The further the European Court goes in applying the Treaty's free movement provisions, the more it transfers the power to regulate the market from national legislators to courts, mostly to the CJEU itself

[4] Case 24/68 *Commission v Italy*, EU:C:1969:29. Technically speaking, this is a case about customs duties and charges having equivalent effect, Art 28 TFEU, not four freedoms law.

(which then co-opts national courts to drive up national compliance, see Chapter five). The wider the CJEU casts the ambit of the Union's negative integration rules, the further democratic preferences are displaced and the more decision-making is both removed from democratic accountability and depoliticised. Economic integration, however, is a deeply political process, as was discussed above. Should the Union merely pursue a non-discrimination regime, Member States would largely retain control and preserve their socio-economic choices and options, tempered only by a European rule that prohibits discrimination. Should the Court choose a regime of trade liberalisation, Member States would lose much of their regulatory autonomy.

The European Court did not hesitate and committed the Union to a much more extensive regulatory regime than mere non-discrimination. In one of its most famous decisions ever, the 1974 *Dassonville* judgment, it decided that 'all trading rules enacted by Member States which are capable of hindering, directly or indirectly, actually or potentially, intra-[Union] trade' are prohibited.[5] The single market, according to the Court, is about eliminating all unjustified obstacles to trade. The breadth of this formula is striking. In the market for goods alone, it catches (among other things) inspections and controls, obligations to produce certificates, bans on selling goods of a certain description, requirements for the presentation or labelling of products, incentives to purchase domestic products in preference to imports, and restrictions on use, possession and storage. Negative integration rules, therefore, extend to smoking bans in the workplace, age restrictions on sale/purchase of alcohol, and rules limiting Sunday trading; they all are, at least, indirect and potential obstacles to trade.

On the one hand, removing all obstructions to trade is an effective tool to 'cull the dead wood of centuries of accumulated legislation' and set it ablaze in 'a bonfire of red tape on the pyre of [negative integration provisions]'.[6] A regime that removes obstacles to trade liberalises trade and frees up markets. The Court basically kept Member States from regulating market interactions and thus from obstructing the efficient functioning of the single market. On the other hand, the formula feels extreme in that it provides for an exceedingly broad standard when

[5] Case 8/74 *Procureur du Roi v Dassonville*, EU:C:1974:82, para 5.

[6] The first quote is from C Barnard, *The Substantive Law of the EU*, Oxford, Oxford University Press, 6th edn 2019, 72, the second from S Weatherill, 'Pre-emption, harmonization and the distribution of competence', in C Barnard and J Scott (eds), *The Law of the Single European Market: Unpacking the Premises*, Oxford, Hart Publishing 2002, 49.

evaluating national laws banned under the Treaty. If everything is subject to review in the name of the single market, the Union exercises de facto control over all Member State regulations. This is a serious threat to Member State competences since it undermines the principle of conferral (which states that the Union can act only where Member States have expressly transferred powers to it, and which suggests that Member States control the nature and scope of European integration). Simply by construing the possible reach of negative integration as broadly as it did, the Court created a huge constitutional problem.

That problem became salient when the Court decided to extend negative integration provisions to innocuous situations. Imagine, for example, that Spain prohibits sales of goods on Sundays and fines those who breach that prohibition, among them the owner of a hardware store. The Spanish measure affects domestic and foreign producers in precisely the same way. It is, in law, not directly discriminatory as it applies to domestic and imported goods alike. It is also, in fact, not more burdensome on foreign producers: there are no adaptation costs. And yet, it is an obstacle to trade that is, prima facie, prohibited under EU law because it is 'capable of hindering, directly or indirectly, actually or potentially, intra-[Union] trade'. If hardware stores cannot sell on Sundays, fewer hammers and nails are sold including the imported hammers and nails; consequently, fewer hammers and nails are imported into Spain.

For a number of reasons this is a constitutional problem. First, there is little reason to force Member States through the hoops of justification merely because a (hypothetical) reduction in the volume of sales might lead to a (also hypothetical) reduction in the volume of imports.[7] Secondly, the Court is now dragged into intervening in vibrant political fields. Sunday trading rules, for instance, are the product of delicate and ongoing national discussions between churches, employers, unions, and consumer organisations. Subjecting such rules to a legal test along narrow economic parameters designed to create uniformity throughout Europe is probably not a good idea across socially and culturally diverse Member States. Thirdly, these rules are not related to the product itself but to the way the product is marketed. They are 'market circumstance rules': who sells the product, and when, where and how?[8]

[7] This is how one Advocate General put it in a different case, Case C-368/95 *Vereinigte Familiapress Zeitungsverlags- und vertriebs GmbH v Heinrich Bauer Verlag*, EU:C:1997:150, para 10.

[8] K Mortelmans, 'Article 30 of the EEC Treaty and legislation relating to market circumstances: Time to consider a new definition', (1991) 28 *CML Rev* 115, at 116.

As such, they generally do not affect the producer or importer of the product, but only its retailer.

With the negative implications of the endless encroachment of negative integration rules becoming clear, the European Court retreated a bit. It took some market circumstance rules out of the ambit of the Treaty's negative integration provisions[9] and started to check whether others might impede free competition within the internal market too much.[10] Even with course-correction, the fundamental problem is far from gone, and neither are its constitutional implications.

(iii) The Reach of Positive Integration

The power to decide the balance between uniformity and diversity through regulation gets taken away from Member States not just in the judicial arena (through negative integration), but in the legislative arena too (through positive integration). The Treaty has provisions that allow for the harmonisation of national laws, notably Article 114 TFEU. While it is meant as an instrument to counter the de-regulative mechanics of negative integration by way of European re-regulative legislation, harmonisation entails a vertical transfer of power from the Member States to the Union. From a constitutional perspective, it is therefore important that Union harmonising power is clearly set out and limited.

In reality, it is not. On the contrary, even absent an express conferral of legislative power in specific areas, the Union legislator is able to harmonise. There are two main reasons for this. The first is the nature of Article 114 TFEU. It confers on the Union the competence to harmonise national laws that stand in the way of a level playing-field within the single market. That competence is so broad that it may impinge on other competences retained by the Member States. Public health, for instance, is a competence where the Union has little room to act. However, the Union legislator regulated tobacco products by banning menthol cigarettes, by prescribing warnings on the packaging, etc. Its purpose was clearly to prevent and reduce smoking, but it based its directive on Article 114 TFEU. Tobacco producers tried to fight this in court, arguing

[9] Joined Cases C-267/91 and C-268/91 *Criminal proceedings against Keck and Mithouard*, EU:C:1993:905, para 16.

[10] Case C-142/05 *Åklagaren v Mickelsson and Roos*, EU:C:2009:336; Case C-333/14 *Scotch Whisky Association and Others v The Lord Advocate and The Advocate General for Scotland*, EU:C:2015:845.

that such a measure should be left to Member State regulation and that the Union lacked the competence to impose it. The European Court, however, held that the Union is not barred from pursuing other policy objectives under Article 114 so long as it also aims to remove obstacles to trade (the aim, in the tobacco case, was to create a level playing-field for sale of tobacco products). Needless to say, this opens the door to countless regulatory powers drifting from the Member States to the Union. For instance, criminal law is another area where Union competences are severely limited. Still, the CJEU allowed a Union data retention directive (the material objective of which is to contribute to the fight against serious crime) to be based on the Union's competence to harmonise the single market according to Article 114 TFEU.[11]

The other reason for competence creep is the way positive integration interacts with negative integration. The Union legislator's room for manoeuvring is tied to the European Court's methodology of checking Member State laws for compliance with the four freedoms. As has been discussed above, once the Court has determined, as a first step, that the national law violates the Union prohibition on obstacles to trade, it offers the Member State, as a second step, the opportunity to justify its law. It is possible that the Member State will succeed by showing that the law serves a public purpose recognised by EU law and that it is the least restrictive means to fulfil it. In that case the measure may stand. We know it harms the single market (because it is an obstacle to trade, as the Court concluded in its first step), but still it is allowed to remain in place. This is for good reasons, but still the single market cannot be achieved.

The wider the Court casts its net when assessing which obstacles to trade are forbidden (and as we saw, the Court, due to the enormous breadth of its definition of obstacles to trade, casts it very wide), the more pressure it puts on Member States to justify their regulatory action. The number of cases where Member State measures are determined to be in violation of negative integration rules but are still allowed to stand is growing, and these cases cover more and more areas.

Every time that happens (and it happens more and more often), market fragmentation follows. This is precisely where Article 114 TFEU comes in as a check: if there is market fragmentation, the Commission has a legal competence that enables it to propose harmonisation

[11] Case C-301/06 *Ireland v Parliament and Council*, EU:C:2009:68; Joined Cases C-293/12 and C-594/12 *Digital Rights Ireland Ltd v Minister for Communications, Marine and Natural Resources and Others*, EU:C:2014:238.

measures. Imagine, hypothetically, that the Union legislator has no competence to harmonise national Sunday trading rules. If the Court finds that a national Sunday trading law is an obstacle to trade, but that it can be justified, the Union legislator gets to harmonise Sunday trading laws across all Member States in spite of its lack of express legislative competence. The Member State wins in court (its Sunday trading law is allowed to remain in place), but that win proves a Pyrrhic victory because now the national law may be replaced by a harmonising Union rule.

In other words, the European Court controls the Union's space for legislative action (positive integration) through its jurisprudence when determining obstacles to trade (negative integration). The wide reach of its negative integration judgments, which already shifts much power from the Member States to the Union, enables the wide reach of Union harmonisation. The two systems in tandem further shift power from the states to the Union and diminish individual Member State regulatory autonomy. As always, there is the danger that democratic preferences may be distorted because harmonising legislation which passes the Council by qualified majority is removed from voters and their democratic feedback to the point of depoliticisation. All this happens without express conferral of legislative power in the Treaties, which damages the Union's constitutional authority and risks challenges by Member State courts to constitutional doctrines, above all primacy. The economic efficiency of the Union's single market thus comes at a steep constitutional price.

B. The Horizontal Dimension of Single Market Constitutionalism

The loss of democratic accountability is felt acutely given how regulative power, once it has reached the EU plane, is distributed horizontally between Union institutions. The tension here is not so much between the Union and its Member States, but relates to regulatory rationale (expertise vs democratic accountability) and regulatory instruments (law vs politics). In both dimensions, Union decision-making tends strongly towards technocratic, legalistic efficiency.

(i) Expertise vs Democratic Accountability

Regulation may be anchored more in scientific expertise or more in political sensitivity to democratic preferences (another way of describing this tension would be to distinguish between specialisation and pluralisation[12]). The fact that regulatory decisions in positive integration are usually made by Ordinary Legislative Procedure seems to point in the direction of the latter, lending EU regulation some measure of democratic legitimacy and sensitivity to cultural or societal interests. However, such appearances are deceptive. Union regulation is overwhelmingly technocratic and expertise-based. That alone does not make it illegitimate in any meaningful sense; on the contrary, we want health and safety measures to be based on scientific knowledge. But we also want evidence-based assessments embedded within a sense of social and cultural conscience. We know that *Nutella* is bad for us and that the production of *foie gras* tortures ducks and geese.[13] To decide what to do with *Nutella* and *foie gras* is to decide whether we are willing to accept the health and moral risks involved. That, of course, is a political decision that the EU, relying on expertise, cannot hope to make for citizens.

The political aspect of EU regulatory decision-making is thin at best. In positive integration, the EU legislator is informed and supported by a host of independent actors. The Commission, for instance, has the power to adopt delegated and implementing legislation.[14] Since Parliament and the Council cannot regulate thousands and thousands of foodstuffs, in the vast majority of cases they merely set down general principles, which are then expounded into concrete standards adopted by the Commission. The Commission legislates within the framework set by the EU legislator; the theory here is that delegation allows for a division of labour when dealing with problems of complexity and required knowledge. The legislature is further assisted by independent EU agencies. They are tasked with advising the Commission on specific areas of regulation (for instance, the European Food Safety Authority, the European Chemicals Agency, the European Environment Agency, or the European Agency for Safety and Health at Work) and bring unassailable scientific knowledge to the table. The Commission has to consult with them and take their opinions into account.

[12] D Chalmers and M Chaves, 'EU Law-Making and the State of European Democratic Agency', in O Cramme and SB Hobolt (eds), *Democratic Politics in a European Union under Stress*, Oxford, Oxford University Press 2015, 155.

[13] These examples are from M Dawson and F de Witte, *EU Law and Governance*, Cambridge, Cambridge University Press 2022, 73–74.

[14] Arts 290 and 291 TFEU.

On paper, the powers of these independent actors are clearly limited. In reality, they are not nearly so limited. If the EU legislator delegates the adoption of a specific standard to the Commission because it lacks scientific expertise, how would the legislator be in a position to check whether the Commission did its job of providing risk-adequate standards, or whether the Commission did more than it was supposed to do by regulating further aspects? In theory, regulatory Commission legislation is overseen by working groups staffed with national experts who have the power to alert the Council, prevent implementing acts, and revoke delegation.[15] In practice, however, they work to improve Commission measures rather than to veto them. These experts have established a culture of consensus, entrenching the mode of expert and technocratic decision-making. The same dynamic is true for regulatory agencies. Their powers seem limited mostly to informing, and consulting with, the Commission, but in fact their opinions have de facto binding effect. The Commission neither has the same expertise nor can it satisfy the high burden of justification when it wants to go against agency opinions. As a result, regulatory decision-making goes back to independent bodies that are insulated from oversight by the extraordinary complexity of their regulatory task and their own expertise.

The picture that emerges is a regulatory process strongly tilting to science-based, technocratic decision-making that marginalises the political aspects of market integration. Its actors present themselves, more often than not, as bodies engaged in technocratic management with the function of simply executing the broad decisions that Member States have taken in the Treaties, or that the EU legislator has taken in legislative measures. This feigned stance is taken in a variety of regulatory arenas, such as free movement of goods, services, companies and labour. We also find it in EU competition policy (if you consider merger control) and EU state aid policy – policy fields that are politically charged and hotly contested. Here, too, the Commission enjoys great political powers and a large degree of autonomy but presents itself as a mere watchdog of the commitments the Member States have undertaken, or as an impartial arbiter who removes distortions to competition in the single market. However, we know that there is no such thing as 'neutral' political decision-making. Pretending that there

[15] This system of committee oversight and governance has evolved gradually and is called 'comitology'. Its most important legal basis today is Regulation (EU) No 182/2011 of 16 February 2011, OJ L 55/13.

is alters the inner logic of constitutionalism. European integration and its constitutionalism rest on both expertise and democracy. A Union that solves problems very efficiently, but without democratic accountability, runs into legitimacy problems. When democratic logic weakens, so too does the constitutional construct. European constitutionalism then appears, indeed, as 'constitutionalism-lite' or 'as if' constitutionalism (see Chapter one).

(ii) Law vs Politics

While regulation through legislation still needs approval by political actors, the Union employs regulatory tools that circumvent the democratic connection the legislator affords. Among these tools, the most important and efficient one is 'mutual recognition'. Its core idea is that national standards are recognised as being of equivalent value. If, for instance, France adopts safety standards for drilling machines and French-manufactured drilling machines are lawfully produced and marketed in France, there is, according to 'mutual recognition', no reason why these machines should not also be marketable in Germany, regardless of what the German safety standard for manufacturing and selling such machines is (unless Germany is able to show that the French standard is unsafe). Clearly, this is a regulatory strategy that manages the balance between uniformity and diversity by discarding the need for harmonising national rules through EU regulation, as long as the Member States can be trusted to aim for roughly the same outcome.

Mutual recognition is widely used. Usually, the EU legislator sets minimum standards, leaves the rest to national regulators, and deems their certification valid for all other Member States. This technique has spread far beyond the single market. For instance, administrative decisions granting or denying asylum, judicial decisions by family courts, and arrest warrants are all governed by mutual recognition.

The true power of mutual recognition, however, emerges when it is in the hands of the European Court. The CJEU uses it as a legal doctrine in single market law, and the technicalities of that doctrine affect the bigger constitutional architecture in a profound way.

The first case involving mutual recognition, the 1978 *Cassis de Dijon* case,[16] remains one of the Court's most celebrated judgments to this day.

[16] Case 120/78 *Rewe-Zentrale v Bundesmonopolverwaltung für Branntwein (Cassis de Dijon)*, EU:C:1979:42.

Cassis de Dijon is a blackcurrant liqueur which is commonly drunk with white wine. It contains a maximum of 20 per cent alcohol per volume and was lawfully produced and marketed in France. German law, however, banned the sale of liqueurs with an alcohol content of less than 25 per cent,[17] so Cassis de Dijon could not be sold in Germany. The rule was not discriminatory, since it applied to all liqueurs marketed in Germany irrespective of their origin, but its effect was obviously an obstacle to trade. The European market for fruit liqueur was fragmented simply because Germany and France had different legal standards for alcohol content, which resulted from different traditions.

The Court responded to this fragmentation not by trying to figure out if the German rule, while not discriminatory in law, might be discriminatory in fact; nor did it let the German rule stand and hand the management of market fragmentation to the EU legislator for harmonisation. Rather, it articulated the mutual recognition doctrine: Germany must recognise the French standard on alcohol content and allow French liqueurs that conform to that standard to be marketed in Germany, even if they do not conform to the German rule. In other words, if a certain liqueur is produced in France and sold in Germany, it is French law that determines the legality of selling it. German laws on how liqueurs should be made, and what ingredients they should contain, are not applicable (unless Germany can show that the French rules are unsafe in some way, which in the *Cassis de Dijon* case it could not: German doubts over consumer protection should be taken care of by labelling the French liqueur bottles appropriately). Member States have to recognise the adequacy of other Member States' laws if they are functionally equivalent. If products have been lawfully produced and marketed in a Member State, other Member States are prohibited from applying their own national regulations to those goods. Products should only be subject to the regulation of their country of origin, not of the country of sale. While it is possible to derogate from mutual recognition for legitimate and proportionate reasons, those derogations are strictly policed by the Court, and the burden of proof lies with the country of sale.

[17] The reader may wonder why the German authorities would do such a thing. Germany claimed that the rule served to protect consumers: lowering the content of alcohol in beverages (which is by far the most expensive ingredient due to its high tax rate) gives such beverages a competitive advantage in relation to beverages with high alcohol content. German consumers, expecting liqueur to have a high alcohol content and willing to pay a high price for it, might be deceived.

It is hard to overstate the economic impact of the Court's use of mutual recognition. Member States could no longer apply their own national standards to products from other Member States and thereby keep them off the supermarket shelves. Producers were relieved from checking, and adapting to, two different standards, one from their home state and the other from the Member State they wanted to import to. Trade in goods and services was freed up; consumers enjoyed a much broader range of products and services. Competition, both between market actors and between regulatory regimes, was fostered. 'The CJEU, in *Cassis*, did more for the creation of the internal market than the EU legislator has done in sixty years'.[18]

And that, precisely, is the problem if we look at mutual recognition, through a constitutional lens rather than an economic one. First, mutual recognition radically alters the position of the CJEU in the process of European integration. Dramatically turning itself into a market regulator, the European Court is now at the very centre of substantive policy determinations. This is a role distinct from what courts usually do, and it arguably goes a step further than even the Court's revolutionary jurisprudence on direct effect and primacy. The latter can be summed up as 'free bargaining but no free riders', with the Court rigorously enforcing bargains once struck between the Member States and the Union's political institutions. The free movement jurisprudence, in contrast, sees the Court making its own policy determination. Making one's own bargains, however, is a different ballgame from enforcing the bargains of others.[19]

Second, mutual recognition fundamentally alters the constitutional construct by recasting the relationship between legislative and judicial market-building. Before mutual recognition, it was up to the Union legislator to intervene if negative integration proved dysfunctional or insufficient. After *Cassis*, it seems that the Court can complete the single market through adjudication alone. Indeed, the Commission, shortly after the Court introduced mutual recognition, wrote a letter to the Member States, asserting that mutual recognition, as a constitutional principle, obviated the need for harmonisation. That of course was a bit over-enthusiastic, since there are areas where functional equivalence, and thus mutual recognition, do not apply (our earlier example of different

[18] Dawson and de Witte (n 13), 141.

[19] JHH Weiler, 'Epilogue: Towards a Common Law of International Trade', in JHH Weiler (ed), *The EU, the WTO and the NAFTA. Towards a Common Law of International Trade*, Oxford, Oxford University Press 2000, 201, at 217–18.

colours for the ground wires of plug-in electrical devices is such a case). Still, the doctrine of mutual recognition placed 'the relationship between negative and positive integration in the shadow of the law'.[20] The Commission letter indicates the extent to which the Court had reconfigured the relationship of adjudication and legislation, of Court and Union legislator, and of law and politics. One former Advocate General mused that 'what is taking place in the Court is a kind of [Union] legislative process, with the Court trying to harmonise national rules …'.[21] Clearly, the Court was in part responding to the blockage of the legislative harmonisation process in the Council: *Cassis de Dijon* was decided at a time when the Luxembourg Compromise was in place, which forced the Council into unanimous decision-making and paralysed the decision-making apparatus. But this raises the questions whether institutions that are not directly democratically accountable should ever fill the shoes of directly elected rule-makers, and whether policy-making should make way for self-executing law. After all, this is what indeed happened: to this day, single market politics in the Council has to some degree been substituted with single market law in the Court.

The implication is that EU constitutionalism, in its most important field of application, looks different from what we would expect from our analysis of the institutional and procedural set-up. As was discussed in Chapters four and five, and again in the introduction to this chapter, EU rule-making is nominally a hybrid process that navigates Union and Member State interests in a unique tightrope act of balancing, whereas EU rule-enforcement is a much more unitary and centralising process that is reminiscent of states. Single market constitutionalism, however, applies the institutions (Court), the instruments (law), and the characteristics (neutral decision-making) of enforcing rules to making rules. Thus, the whole logic of the Union's enforcement mechanism now attaches to rule-making. The Union process of making choices, which is hybrid and points in many different representational directions, now looks unitary, mono-representational, and state-like. Alas, it is still not really state-like because states use institutions which exhibit robust democratic accountability and supply ample legitimation for unitary decision-making, while the Union cannot muster those features. Without reliable democratic backing, the

[20] A Stone Sweet, *The Judicial Construction of Europe*, Oxford, Oxford University Press 2004, 136.

[21] MP Maduro, *We the Court: The European Court of Justice and the European Economic Constitution*, London, Bloomsbury 1997, 78.

Court entering into the regulatory arena looks like an overreach, like a constitutional claim without the necessary constitutional foundation. As such, *Cassis* creates the same unease detectable in responses to *Van Gend & Loos* and *Costa v ENEL*.

C. The Value Dimension of Single Market Constitutionalism

Finally, European single market constitutionalism links back to our earlier suspicion that EU constitutionalism, compared to the state template of constitutionalism, is located at the thinner end of the constitutionalist scale. That lack of richness is not merely a question of form and process, but also of values. Constitutions are expressive in that they communicate and reinforce values and identity. Single market constitutionalism, in contrast, is clearly dominated by an economic rationale. It is wholly instrumental to creating the single market. All non-economic policies will have to stand the test of legality measured against the single market's economic rationale, with the burden of proof placed on the national regulator. This creates an inbuilt bias in favour of free trade. Since hardly any regulation escapes the free movement rules, everything hinges on the availability of a justification. The ethos is that any obstacle to free trade is in some way improper and needs justification.

Public goods do exist, but they exist at the national level as the result of a process of political contestation and social negotiation. They show what a political community values and how it allocates individual and collective rights. They are the outcome, and in some way the essence, of the national democratic process. Single market law subjects them to close review by the CJEU, a transnational body without direct democratic accountability, every time they collide with trans-border trade. Where exactly the CJEU comes down on collisions will decide the reach of the market and, conversely, determine what rights, values, principles, and democratic processes are worth.

With the Court reviewing so many democratic and political choices, its methodology comes under scrutiny. How precisely does it balance economic interests, non-economic interests, and rights? In view of the Union's leanings towards an ethos of technocracy and expert management, and of its strained relationship with democracy, it comes as no surprise that the Court favours scientific voices and arguments. Its methodology and, above all, its proportionality review, present scientific perspectives as objective, neutral, and more important than moral, social, or democratic preferences. The market, however, is deeply embedded in such preferences. It is a way of life, not just a mechanism of allocating factors of production to the host that most welcomes them. Yet, in its free movement jurisprudence and elsewhere, the Court shows a strong bias towards the material and measurable, and little understanding of how the single market uproots and undermines a way of life. Traditional but somewhat inefficient businesses, for instance, have been replaced by much bigger, cheaper and more alien businesses, causing non-trivial social discomfort despite the fact that this brings variety, higher quality and lower prices. Some of that discomfort is with the primacy of individual choice over the shared experience of common goods.[22] Predictably, single market constitutionalism, both in its undemocratic processes and favouritism for market-driven homogeneity, has been unable to tap into the social resources that animate state constitutionalism, like allegiance, belonging, and identity.

Citizen unease drifts into policy areas that rely on completely different modes of decision-making. For instance, the Economic and Monetary Union (EMU), which is about the common currency, relies on regulatory instruments that are wide-ranging, novel, fluid, extremely complex, and often informal. There is a multiplicity of bodies involved in discharging its functions, partly within and partly outside the Union, some of which are markedly different from those governing the single market. The ECB has assumed the role as lender of last resort; the Commission has a host of competences in fiscal and economic surveillance that are prioritised when responding to problems. The Eurogroup, an informal forum comprising euro area finance ministers, is the lead body for economic policy coordination and decision-making; and the European Council involves itself heavily and directly in day-to-day euro area decision-making, cutting deeper into domestic politics than ever before. While much about these institutions is different from single market constitutionalism, the unease citizens feel toward them is the same. The alienation even finds violent outlets. A case in point is the financial crisis, when emergency support to struggling states had 'austerity' conditions attached that were extremely harsh and caused massive social harms. The fine print of EU support often came from institutions like the Commission and the ECB, which sometimes acted together with the International Monetary Fund under the name of the

[22] The best work on this is by G Davies: 'Internal Market Adjudication and Quality of Life in Europe', (2015) 21 *Columbia Journal of European Law* 289; and 'Democracy and Legitimacy in the Shadow of Purposive Competence', (2015) 21 *European Law Journal* 2.

'Troika'. These harsh austerity measures exacerbated the baseline sense in many Member States that national democracy had been undermined by a transnational bureaucracy, and that economic values had superseded constitutional values, like care and social security. '#ThisIsACoup' was the hashtag in Greece that reacted to the imposition of such conditions, while strikes and demonstrations ensued and young Greeks, faced with a youth unemployment rate of 50 per cent, threw Molotov cocktails. There is an acute tension between national self-government and transnational problem-solving, and one of its deepest sources is the tension between the values that underlie the Union as opposed to Member States.

The tension of constitutional values, however, is not carved in stone. In some respects, European constitutional values have broadened and started to more closely mimic what state constitutional values embody. One example is, ironically, the single market itself. Single market constitutionalism works because the European Court allows individuals to invoke EU law provisions in their local courts and to vindicate their EU-given economic rights against the Member States. The constitutional rationale behind the direct effect doctrine is that it turns national courts into allies in the European Court's quest for a European rule of law. At the same time, direct effect equips citizens with individual rights and catapults them into the centre of legal enforcement. At first, these rights were exclusively economic, which made national citizens European 'market citizens'.[23] Soon after, however, their scope broadened; the Court protected the whole range of fundamental rights familiar from national constitutions. Meanwhile the Union has its own Charter of Fundamental Rights, with no economic bias (see Chapter seven).

An example of this shift is the Treaty's prescription of equal pay for men and women.[24] Originally, this was a market-building instrument as it was inserted to protect countries like France, where the equal pay principle was respected, from unfair competition from countries that did not respect it and had lower labour costs, like Italy. While the CJEU had recognised the market-building function in its earlier jurisprudence,[25] it now says that

[23] M Everson, 'The Legacy of the Market Citizen', in J Shaw and G More (eds), *New Legal Dynamics of European Union*, Oxford, Oxford University Press 1995, 73.

[24] Art 157 TFEU.

[25] Case 43/75 *Defrenne v Société anonyme belge de navigation aérienne Sabena II*, EU:C:1976:56.

> the economic aim pursued by [equal pay] ..., namely the elimination of distortions of competition between undertakings established in different Member States, is secondary to the social aim pursued by the same provision, which constitutes the expression of a fundamental human right.[26]

Another example is environmental policy, which plays an important role in market-building. Rooting out differences in Member State environmental regulations through harmonising legislation is vital for the creation of a level playing-field. This economic rationale is the reason why the EU became active in environmental regulation long before it was on the agenda of the Member States: it affected trade in goods, particularly in automobiles. However, with Member States and the Union increasingly environmentally conscious, focus on the environment was widened into areas that are not market-related, such as the protection of sensitive natural habitats.

If we turn to policy fields other than the market, we see values in flux, too. Most Union policies have grown out of the increasingly sophisticated single market and have, therefore, taken on board a focus on economic values, but that does not mean that market values are always the focus of EU institutions. Take the Area of Freedom, Security and Justice (AFSJ), the Treaty name for policies that involve asylum and immigration policies, the management of the EU's external borders, and police and judicial cooperation in matters of civil and criminal law.[27] It is part of the 'market-cushioning' policies which compensate for the single market's harmful effects on some people, the environment, or security. In this compensatory process, it touches on the social and security dimension of economic integration. The AFSJ responds to the danger that the main beneficiaries of the single market's abolishment of border checks would be organised crime. It borrows directly from the free movement architecture in the single market by applying the principle of mutual recognition to court judgments in civil and criminal matters as well as European arrest warrants. The underlying constitutional value here is not trust in a shared functionality of regulatory standardisation, but trust in decisions from other Member States to similarly value human dignity and personal freedom. Successfully applying mutual recognition to non-market values sows the seeds for growing a shared constitutional culture: Union institutions have

[26] Joined Cases C-270/97 and C-271/97 *Deutsche Post AG v Sievers and Schrage*, EU:C:2000:76, para 57.

[27] Arts 67–89 TFEU.

argued that the AFSJ should lead citizens to feel that a 'proper sense of "European public order" has taken shape and is actually visible in their daily lives'.[28] These are not values of the market, nor even of rights, but of collective identity.

FURTHER READING

Barnard C, *The Substantive Law of the European Union*, Oxford, Oxford University Press, 7th edn 2022.

Davies G, *European Union Internal Market Law*, London, Routledge, 2nd edn 2003.

Egan M, *Single Markets: Economic Integration in Europe and the United States*, Oxford, Oxford University Press 2015.

Snell J, 'The internal market and the philosophies of market integration', in Barnard C and Peers S (eds), *European Union Law*, Oxford, Oxford University Press, 4th edn 2023, 336.

Weatherill S, *The Internal Market as a Legal Concept*, Oxford, Oxford University Press 2017.

[28] European Convention, *Final Report of Working Group X 'Freedom, Security and Justice'*, CONV 426/02, 2.

7

Rights and the Individual in EU Constitutionalism

FUNDAMENTAL RIGHTS (OR human rights; I will use these terms interchangeably) are the hallmark of any constitutional template. Essentially, they perform two functions. The first is to express the identity of a political community. Constitutions do not merely establish abstract rules of government; they also determine the substantive values those rules express within the political community, like equality, liberty, dignity, family, and faith. This 'realm of meaning'[1] is how a political community understands itself. Their second function is to subject all exercise of public power – including even by the legislature – to a higher law, in order to protect individuals from the threat of a government abusing its power. The rights are understood as 'fundamental' because they are deemed so important for individual liberty that they should be beyond the reach of the political process.

This chapter examines the protection of rights in European Union constitutional law. It will focus on Article 6 of the Treaty on European Union and on the Charter of Fundamental Rights of the European Union, which is surely the most salient instrument for rights protection. But the European Court adjudicated on fundamental rights long before Article 6 and the Charter, even with no formal basis in written law. It did so because fundamental rights, in Union constitutionalism, perform crucial functions in addition to those we know from state constitutionalism. They stabilise the Union rule of law, are an indispensable corollary to the doctrine of primacy of Union law, clarify the distribution of power and competences between the Union and its Member States, and contribute to the autonomy of the Union constitutional order.

[1] R Cover, 'Foreword: Nomos and Narrative', (1983) 97 *Harvard Law Review* 4, at 28.

The European Court pays attention to all these functions in addition to the core functions articulated at the beginning of this chapter. Unlike courts in states, it balances these functions against one another. On the one hand, pragmatic trade-offs between the functions of fundamental rights help to stabilise the Union order. On the other, trading on functions of purportedly fundamental rights casts doubt on how serious the Court really is about treating individual rights as surpassing more expedient considerations. Can we trust it to protect European citizens when an important Union policy or Union value other than fundamental rights is also at stake? What precisely happens when the Court weighs the importance of multiple factors? In a complex constitutional order like the European Union, we can imagine a number of unintended consequences that could destabilise the constitutional architecture.

Finally, this chapter will zoom in on the citizen protected under EU fundamental rights law. This book began with the observation that one of the features missing from Union constitutionalism is a European political identity felt by its citizens. With so many incommensurable values balanced by rights, some are inevitably sidelined by the Court in favour of other policy objectives. We need to ask whether EU fundamental rights can be the foundation for genuine forms of belonging and attachment.

I. EU FUNDAMENTAL RIGHTS: SOURCES AND USES

The Treaties today are so deeply suffused with human rights commitments that the Court calls them a 'premise' of the Union legal order.[2] Article 2 of the TEU states that the Union 'is founded on the values of respect for human dignity, freedom, democracy, equality, the rule of law and respect for human rights, including the rights of persons belonging to minorities'. The central human rights provision, since the 2009 Lisbon Treaty amendment, is Article 6 of the TEU:

> (1) The Union recognises the rights, freedoms and principles set out in the Charter of Fundamental Rights of the European Union of 7 December 2000, as adapted at Strasbourg, on 12 December 2007, which shall have the same legal value as the Treaties. …

[2] Opinion 2/13 *Accession to the ECHR II*, EU:C:2014:2454, paras 167–8. See also Advocate General Maduro in his Opinion on Case C-380/05 *Centro Europa 7 Srl v Ministero delle Comunicazioni e Autorità per le garanzie nelle comunicazioni*, EU:C:2007:505, para 19 ('the very existence of the European Union is predicated on respect for fundamental rights').

(2) The Union shall accede to the European Convention for the Protection of Human Rights and Fundamental Freedoms. Such accession shall not affect the Union's competences as defined in the Treaties.
(3) Fundamental rights, as guaranteed by the European Convention for the Protection of Human Rights and Fundamental Freedoms and as they result from the constitutional traditions common to the Member States, shall constitute general principles of the Union's law.

This article identifies three legal sources for fundamental rights protection. The first, in paragraph 1, is the 'Charter of Fundamental Rights of the European Union', which was first established in 2000 and made legally binding in 2009. It has become the document that both the European Court and the EU legislator increasingly cite to explain their decisions. The Court uses it as its main point of legal reference in fundamental rights cases, and EU legislation often justifies itself as elaborating the Charter. As to the Charter's substance, some things are noteworthy. First, the Charter covers a wider array of topics than traditional human rights instruments, and includes, for example, the protection of ecological and cultural interests. Clearly, this is meant to be ambitious, but it has the perverse effect of diluting the value of rights: if everything is a right, nothing is a right. Moreover, the choice of what gets mentioned, and what does not, is sometimes mystifying. For instance, the right to (employment) placement services, Article 29 of the Charter, is a good thing, but so would be a right to housing. Second, some rights are 'recognised' only in accordance with the rules laid down in Member State or EU legal orders, which means that national laws get to determine what counts as an EU fundamental right. Third, the Charter distinguishes between rights and principles; the latter 'may be implemented by legislative and executive acts' taken by the Union or Member States implementing Union law; 'they shall be judicially cognisable only in the interpretation of such acts and in the ruling on their legality'.[3] This entails a difference in the scope of judicial protection for Charter provisions, the details of which are still unclear. Finally, it is not clear that courts, rather than political institutions, are well-placed to decide on the conditions for a good life, for a decent society, or for good ecology.

The second source of fundamental rights, in Article 6, paragraph 2, will be the European Convention for the Protection of Human Rights and Fundamental Freedoms of 1950 (ECHR), as soon as the Union accedes. The ECHR is an international convention to protect human

[3] Art 52(5) of the Charter.

rights in Europe and was drafted in 1950 under the auspices of the Council of Europe, an international organisation independent of the European Union. The ECHR has 46 members, every EU Member State among them, and has its own enforcement mechanism, above all the European Court of Human Rights (ECtHR) in Strasbourg. Accession to the Convention has been under discussion for more than 40 years and was made mandatory with the Lisbon Treaty in 2009. However, it still has not happened because the European Court, in 2013, declared a Draft Agreement on Accession to be incompatible with Union law,[4] mostly to protect the autonomy of the Union legal order and its own position from interference by the ECtHR (we will see more details below). Since that time, it has been unclear what the path forward is. The Draft Agreement on Accession is currently being re-negotiated, but accession seems, for the time being, difficult. Since the Union is not a member of the Convention yet, it is currently not directly bound by it.

The third source of EU fundamental rights, in Article 6, paragraph 3, is the 'general principles of the Union's law'. This source reads comparatively obscurely. It refers to the fundamental rights jurisprudence of the European Court. The Court, beginning in the late 1960s, had started to read human rights into the Founding Treaties which, at the time, were silent on the matter. The Court was willing to protect fundamental rights, but because the Treaties did not enumerate any such rights, it had to look elsewhere. It found several bills of rights, both in the Member States' constitutions and in the ECHR, to which all Member States were parties. In an act of judicial activism, the Court announced it would distil Union fundamental rights from these two sources and wrap them up in the Union's 'general principles' in order to make them part of the Union legal order.[5] Paragraph 3 of Article 6 codifies that case law.

The triple, overlapping formal sources for human rights within one legal order have been criticised for creating confusion: what precisely is the content of a Union fundamental right? One might be tempted to interpret the complexity of human rights sources as yet another instance of compound Union constitutionalism bridging multiple legal orders: after all, 'general principles' derive from national constitutions and the ECHR. The Court, however, has made it clear that it is the Charter that serves as the main basis of its interpretation.

[4] *Accession to the ECHR II* (n 2).

[5] Case 29/69 *Stauder v City of Ulm, Sozialamt*, EU:C:1969:57; Case 11/70 *Internationale Handelsgesellschaft v Einfuhr- und Vorratsstelle für Getreide und Futtermittel*, EU:C:1970:114; Case 4/73 *J Nold, Kohlen- und Baustoffgroßhandlung v Commission*, EU:C:1974:51.

While the dominant focus of the Union remains on economic matters, the influence of the Union's fundamental rights on the European Court and on the EU legislator has been huge. It is most visible when the Court uses fundamental rights to strike down EU legislation. While that happens rarely, it is always dramatic. One example was a draconian Union regulation of 2002, implementing the United Nation's 1999 terrorist sanctioning regime. Under these sanctions, individuals could have their assets frozen with almost no reasoning provided and no effective recourse to judicial remedies. The Court annulled the regulation in a string of emphatic judgments.[6] Most of the time, however, the Court upholds EU legislation, which indicates that it has a mixed record with regard to human rights challenges. However, in cases where Union law is left standing, the Court uses the Charter to interpret the law in a way that makes sure it lives up to high human rights standards.

The Union's political institutions, too, have developed instruments to integrate the Charter into their policy-making process. They conduct, for instance, fundamental rights impact assessments. Again, the record is mixed: the Commission conducts these assessments more regularly than the Council, but often its analysis is cursory and a bit self-congratulatory. Parliament has a powerful fundamental rights committee, which pushes for legislative interactions between Parliament, Council, and Commission to more deeply consider human rights. Beyond the central institutions, an independent agency, the Fundamental Rights Agency, was established in 1995 to further raise human rights awareness. Taken together, these mechanisms form a respectable framework to integrate fundamental rights values into the political process.

EU fundamental rights determine what is fundamental for the Union, not for the Member States. This has important ramifications for their scope of application. They apply first and foremost to acts of Union institutions, but can also interfere in Member State decisions under special circumstances. Article 51(1) of the Charter of Fundamental Rights states that 'the provisions of this Charter are addressed to the institutions, bodies, offices and agencies of the Union … and to the Member States only when they are implementing Union law'. National measures are subject to Union fundamental rights review only when Member States act as 'agents' of the EU. In contrast, when they are acting in purely

[6] The most important ones were Joined Cases C-402/05 P and C-415/05 P *Kadi and Al Barakaat International Foundation v Council and Commission (Kadi I)*, EU:C:2008:461, and Joined Cases C-584/10 P, C-593/10 P and C-595/10 P *Commission v Kadi and Others (Kadi II)*, EU:C:2013:518.

internal situations, where Union law does not apply, possible fundamental rights violations must only be assessed against national standards. The upshot is a division of labour in regard to both the applicable standard of review and the competent institution performing the review. It is for the CJEU to apply European fundamental rights, whereas it is for the national courts to apply domestic standards (unless their Member States are acting in the context of EU law). This allows for a diversity of values, but it also creates some confusion, since the dividing line is far from clear, as we will see later.

II. THE ROLE OF FUNDAMENTAL RIGHTS IN EU CONSTITUTIONALISM

The prominent place of human rights in the Treaties, which mimics the prominent place of a Bill of Rights in state constitutional systems, suggests that this is where EU constitutionalism and state constitutionalism are most similar. There are, however, still significant differences. Human rights in the state template of constitutionalism safeguard individual rights by defining the limits of governmental authority in the state's relationship to individuals, and thereby help articulate the political community's common identity. Hence, in state constitutionalism, fundamental rights reflect a constitutional ethos that grounds its deepest values in the individual, who may not have their rights compromised by anyone.

In EU constitutionalism, fundamental rights share that ethos, but they also perform functions unknown to state constitutionalism. Above all, the European Court uses them in order to stabilise the Union's system of governance. In the European Union, fundamental rights perform a role that strengthens European government. At first blush, this may sound counter-intuitive because rights are, by definition, counter-majoritarian, and set firm limits on what governments can legally do. Remember, however, that the Union exists in a 'crowded space' between powerful sovereign nation-states, where it is itself the subject of serious contestation. In response, it uses fundamental rights in order to secure its constitutional authority against outside challenges. These challenges target vital building-blocks of EU constitutionalism and threaten the whole edifice. Fundamental rights are therefore a tool to save the Union from being crushed by nation-states jostling in that crowded space. We can organise these building-blocks into four groups: the rule of law, the primacy of EU law, the safeguarding of competences, and the autonomy of the Union legal order. None of these building-blocks are contested within states, which therefore do not need the stabilising function of fundamental rights that we find in the Union. This dimension of Union human rights ties them into the system of Union governance that has been the subject of this book's previous chapters.

A. Stabilising the Rule of Law

The European Court relies on fundamental rights to stabilise the European rule of law, both generally and in specific areas. Starting with the former, the EU rule of law evolved out of CJEU case law and depends on the Court's continuing heavy involvement. However, the Court cannot act of its own accord, but only when it is presented with a problem or disagreement on which it can adjudicate. The vast majority of its cases arise from the preliminary ruling procedure. For the CJEU to ensure that 'the law is observed', as Article 19 of the TEU states, and to control and define the substance of the law in any given case, it depends on Member State courts asking for a preliminary ruling. The extent and scope of European rule of law, then, hinges on cases that involve EU law and the voluntary cooperation of domestic courts to send these cases up to Luxembourg (see Chapter five).

The rule of law in Europe, then, is in part contingent on the quantity of EU case law. Fundamental rights reviews help ensure a healthy number of cases, strengthening European rule of law. Fundamental rights review has spread across all Member States and all areas of law. Its ubiquity in national courts dramatically widens the circle of cases that are eligible for preliminary rulings by the CJEU. Since the 'applicability of European Union law entails applicability of the fundamental rights guaranteed by the Charter',[7] the Court has made considerable progress in attracting more cases – and more cases of consequence – which it uses to shape the law.

The quantity of cases, however, is only part of what a functioning European rule of law requires. Domestic courts refer cases to the CJEU when they trust the European Court to share their sense of what a just decision involves. The balancing of public goods and individual interests surely is part of that sense of justice. Fundamental rights review in Luxembourg feeds into the perception that both national courts and the

[7] Case C-617/10 *Åklagaren v Åkerberg Fransson*, EU:C:2013:105, para 21.

European Court share a common understanding of what justice demands and what a 'correct' application of the law necessitates. Stabilising the European rule of law in this general way is all the more important since it is declining in some Member States. Especially in Member States where populist or far-right parties are in power (Hungary), or influencing power (such as, at the time of writing, Italy and Sweden), the deterioration of the rule of law, while gradual, risks becoming systemic.[8]

In addition, the European Court sometimes uses fundamental rights to stabilise the EU rule of law in specific areas where it perceives weakness in the rule of law. A case in point is the enforcement of directives. Directives, one will recall, are EU injunctions which need to be transposed into the domestic legal order by Member State parliaments. If the process of implementation goes awry and a Member State fails to transpose an individual right found within the directive, individuals should be able to rely directly on the pre-transposed directive. That, however, is possible only under specific circumstances. In the absence of such circumstances, rights from the directive cannot be enforced and citizens in that Member State go unprotected (see Chapter four), which creates a significant problem for the Union's rule of law. In response, the Court remedied that problem by using fundamental rights.

The prime example is the Court's 2005 *Mangold* decision.[9] German law allowed fixed-term contracts with employees who were 52 years or older, whereas such contracts with employees younger than this required an 'objective justification' and were generally prohibited. Mr Mangold, a 56-year-old lawyer employed by a law firm under an eight-month fixed-term contract, challenged the German law as violating a Union directive that prohibited age-based discrimination. That directive, however, was neither implemented in Germany, nor directly applicable. Since Mr Mangold could not rely on it directly, he should have lost the case. The CJEU decided otherwise. Wanting to help Mr Mangold, but unable to enforce the directive as such, it maintained that the directive's content, the prohibition of age-based discrimination, had actually been an unwritten Union fundamental right all along (this was before the Charter entered into force). Consequently, the Court invalidated the German law. By doing so, it helped to enforce not the directive as a formal law but its substance as an individual right, and thus strengthened the European rule of law.

[8] See, for instance, Civil Liberties Union for Europe, *Liberties Rule of Law Report 2024*, https://bit.ly/4aYkfpt.

[9] Case C-144/04 *Mangold v Helm*, EU:C:2005:709.

B. Stabilising Primacy

European fundamental rights review performs another important constitutional function in that it stabilises the hugely significant doctrine of primacy (which states that when there is a conflict between national law and Union law, the latter should take precedence, so EU law can never be assessed by reference to national law). Again, the relationship between the European Court and its national counterparts is at issue, this time in its substantive rather than its procedural dimension.

As has been discussed, primacy is the cornerstone of the new constitutional environment established by the European Court in its seminal 1963–64 *Van Gend & Loos* and *Costa v ENEL* decisions (see Chapter four).[10] Union law became not only directly effective, but could also reach directly into an individual's legal sphere and, like national laws, violate his or her fundamental rights. Imagine that a Union regulation bars a German vintner from planting new vines on her property because it aims to avoid overproduction of wine in the EU.[11] Had that prohibition come from the German legislature, the vintner could argue it was unlawful because it interfered with her German fundamental right to pursue a trade and her right to property. Had the prohibition come from international law, it would have had to be transposed into German law, and again, the vintner could ask her national courts for protection pursuant to German fundamental rights. Since the prohibition comes from Union law, however, this is not possible: the principle of EU law primacy prevents such appeals. Union law takes precedence over national law, including national fundamental rights. Every Union measure, even a lowly regulation, trumps every Member State law, even a constitutional right. National courts cannot assess the legality of Union law because they would undermine the uniform application of EU law across all Member States. Union law need not defer to a particular national fundamental right. In other words, primacy means that national fundamental rights do not protect individuals against the effects of Union measures.

Of course, Member States would be reluctant to accept primacy if that meant they had to sacrifice fundamental rights protection for their citizens. Surely Member States like Germany and Italy would refuse

[10] Case 26/62 *NV Algemene Transport- en Expeditie Onderneming van Gend & Loos v Netherlands Inland Revenue Administration*, EU:C:1963:1; Case 6/64 *Costa v ENEL (Ente Nationale Energia Elettrica)*, EU:C:1964:66.

[11] Case 44/79 *Hauer v Land Rheinland-Pfalz*, EU:C:1979:290.

primacy because they have made respect for human rights the cornerstone of their constitutional raison d'être, as one of the lessons learned from their fascist pasts.

Indeed, both the German and Italian Constitutional Courts challenged primacy on the basis of their national fundamental rights, at a time when the Treaties had no fundamental rights provisions and the Charter did not yet exist. The German Court held that Article 24 of the German Constitution (dealing with transfers of sovereign rights to interstate institutions) did not cover a transfer of power that compromised its 'inalienable essential features' such as fundamental rights protection. It added that, as long as the European Court did not protect fundamental rights in a way that was 'substantially similar to the protection of fundamental rights required unconditionally by the [German] Constitution', it would not surrender its jurisdiction over national fundamental rights and would instead continue ensuring that those rights took precedence over Union law. The German Court did not beat around the bush about its direct attack on primacy, stating,

> it is not enough simply to speak of the 'precedence' [another term for primacy] of Community law over national constitutional law in order to justify the conclusion that Community law must always prevail over national constitutional law because, otherwise, the Community would be put in question.

Similarly, the Italian Constitutional Court vowed to review the domestic applicability of Union legal obligations in the light of Italian national fundamental rights.[12] It was only when the European Court established its bold doctrine of European fundamental rights review as part of the Union's 'general principles' that Member State courts recognised primacy.[13]

Given Member State resistance, it is fair to say that EU fundamental rights are the de facto precondition for primacy. Primacy is the reason why the European Court, with no legal basis in the Treaties, created fundamental rights review in the first place. 'The "surface language" of the Court', wrote Weiler, '… is the language of human rights. The "deep

[12] BVerfG, 29 May 1974, 37 BVerfGE 271 – *Solange I*; Corte costituzionale, 18 December 1973, No 183/73, Foro italiano 1974-I, 314 – *Frontini v Amministrazione delle finanze dello Stato*.

[13] This is one of the most familiar sagas in European integration. The best work on this is B Davies, *Resisting the European Court of Justice: West Germany's Confrontation with European law, 1949–1979*, Cambridge, Cambridge University Press 2012.

structure" is all about supremacy'.[14] The Court's activist human rights case law is the inevitable sequel to *Van Gend & Loos* and *Costa v ENEL*.

C. Stabilising Competences

The third function that EU fundamental rights perform within the Union's constitutional order is revealed in helping to stabilise the relationship between Member States' governments and the Union legislator via balancing competences between Member States and the EU.

This might come as a surprise, since comparing federalist experiences across constitutional societies repeatedly shows the highly centralising effect of fundamental rights. However, that effect is mostly the result of federal courts applying federal fundamental rights to limit or invalidate State action. A well-known example is the US Supreme Court's use in 1925 of the Fourteenth Amendment's Due Process Clause to apply blanket protections afforded by the Bill of Rights to every State,[15] and its subsequent 'New Deal' expansion of federal power.[16] Article 51(1) of the EU Charter of Fundamental Rights, however, rejects, or appears to reject, the 'incorporation' of EU fundamental rights in that it clearly identifies Union institutions as the primary addressees of the Charter, and in doing so, limits the Charter's application to the Member States to situations when they are 'implementing' Union law. With Union government, and not Member States' governments, bound by EU fundamental rights, its powers are legally limited by fundamental rights, and its authority depends on it observing these limitations. For Member State governments, which are deeply suspicious of competence creep, this is good news. Union fundamental rights are a legal boundary for Commission, Council, and Parliament. Their legislative activity is subject to an additional body of law that controls what they do.

[14] JHH Weiler, 'Eurocracy and Distrust', (1986) 61 *Washington Law Review* 1103, at 1119.

[15] US Supreme Court, *Gitlow v New York*, 268 US 652 (1925).

[16] See, eg, 'Symposium Federalism and Rights: Europe and the United States Compared', (2017) 15 *I-Con* 1066–1173. The Member States were well aware of the federalist tendency towards centralisation, and tried to avoid a similar dynamic. Article 51(2) of the Charter asserts that 'the Charter does not extend the field of application of Union law beyond the powers of the Union or establish any new power or task for the Union, or modify powers and tasks as defined in the Treaties'. Similarly, Article 6(1) of the TEU states that 'the provisions of the Charter shall not extend in any way the competences of the Union as defined in the Treaties'.

There is another layer to understanding the stabilising effect of EU fundamental rights for the distribution of competences between Union and Member States. It hinges on the restricted applicability of Union fundamental rights. The absence of EU fundamental rights 'incorporation' – ie, the fact that Union fundamental rights review is, in principle, limited to Union measures and does not extend to Member State measures unless Member States are 'implementing' EU law – means that, at least as a matter of principle, there are 28 different sets of human rights in the Union: one EU order and 27 different Member State orders, just as there are 28 different court systems that apply them. The limited scope of application of Union fundamental rights, and the resulting division of labour, acknowledges the diverse sensibilities of national political communities within the Union.

This is a point that deeply resonates with one of the major themes of this book. What is the balance that EU constitutionalism strikes on the spectrum of uniformity and diversity? We have seen many different answers to this question since the balance is contingent upon the policy field. In the Area of Freedom, Security and Justice (court and police cooperation in criminal matters, asylum etc), for instance, EU constitutionalism privileges diversity through a greater amount of Member State control, whereas in the single market it privileges uniformity through greater Union control. What about fundamental rights? The substantive and institutional division of labour we have observed suggests that diversity is a good thing.

But is it? Do 'human rights', by definition, not reside within the dignity of all human beings by virtue of their humanity? One would expect, then, that fundamental rights protection throughout Europe rests upon a single standard.

This was, indeed, the opinion of an influential Advocate General before the European Court. The case in question was about a Greek national living in Germany, Χρήστος Κωνσταντινίδης, transliterated in his passport as Christos Konstantinidis, who became engaged in a Kafkaesque dispute with the German authorities over nothing less than his right to his name. He had applied to the German Registry Office to correct a misspelling of his name on the marriage register. Upon examining his application, however, the German authorities determined that his name had, from the outset, been improperly transliterated under German law, and ordered that he must henceforth be known as Hrēstos Kōnstantinidēs (the German typewriters, as the ones at the European Court in Luxembourg, had trouble writing macrons above letters, and used accents instead, which made things even worse). The poor man was horrified. He feared loss of business, believed that the new spelling disguised his ethnic origin (Hrēstos, as the Advocate General observed, does not look or sound like a Greek name and has a vaguely Slavic flavour), and felt offended in his religious sentiments: owing his name to his date of birth on 25 December, the new spelling destroyed the Christian (not 'Hrēstian') character of his name. He sought protection in a German court, which promptly requested a preliminary ruling from the CJEU. The Court's Advocate General argued that Mr Konstantinidis was protected by human rights and suggested that he should be able to invoke European Union human rights against Germany. Wherever a Community national goes to earn his living in the European Community, he claimed, 'he will be treated in accordance with a common code of fundamental values', adding: 'In other words, he is entitled to say "*civis europeus sum*"', I am a European citizen, 'and to invoke that status in order to oppose any violation of his fundamental rights'. Hence, the Advocate General invited the Court to 'incorporate' Union fundamental rights and to apply them to Member State acts across the board.[17]

The European Court did not agree with the Advocate General's argument (it protected Konstantinidis' right to his name using free movement law rather than fundamental human rights), and arguably with good reason. While fundamental rights do have a 'longing for universality'[18] in that they protect people by appealing to what they, as individual human beings, have in common, that is only one part of their nature. The fundamental rights enumerated in a society also protect the particularities of political communities. Rights are expressive of the political culture and identity of democratic societies bargaining about competing public goods and social values. One fundamental value is to empower the individual against governmental authority; another is to empower collective social interests that are represented by government (think of fighting crime, land reform, or nationalisation). Invariably, the result is a compromise, which is informed by the traditions and self-perceptions of a political community. That compromise reflects more than merely the level of individual rights protection. It is about the balance that communities strike between individual interests and public goods, and that balance indicates what a community finds fundamental and how it wants to live.

[17] Opinion of Advocate General Jacobs, Case C-168/91 *Konstantinidis v Stadt Altensteig – Standesamt and Landratsamt Calw – Ordnungsamt*, EU:C:1992:504, para 46.

[18] M Cartabia, 'Europe and Rights: Taking Dialogue Seriously', (2009) 5 *European Constitutional Law Review* 5, at 20–21.

To illustrate, the scope of free speech for neo-Nazis is not, and arguably should not be, the same in political communities that have a fascist past, and those that do not. Germany criminalises those who deny the Holocaust and bans neo-Nazis from marching through the Brandenburg Gate. Other countries, like the US, do not.[19] One might conclude that the US 'better protects' free speech in that more speech is legally protected from state censure. But how meaningful is such a statement? Given the historical and cultural context of a society, different balances between the individual right to speech and the communal right to censure have to be struck in order to preserve the very social order that makes liberal constitutional order possible. Germany, with its fascist past, must clearly be more sensitive towards forms of speech which would facilitate its return. To give another example, Sweden has high taxes, and funds schools, preschools, hospitals, sheltered housing, and a good communications network; citizens enjoy a high level of welfare and are able to live well even when they are ill or unemployed. Other countries have much lower taxes, aim to end dependence on public support and use the market as the template for the welfare state. Again, one might conclude that Sweden does not protect private property rights as thoroughly as other societies. While that may be legally true, it is trivial given the fact that Sweden has struck a different balance between welfare and private property rights, and weakens the latter to more efficaciously advance others.

The division of labour between the Union and its Member States on fundamental rights is reflective of the balance that European constitutionalism strikes between cohesion and efficiency on the one hand, and national values on the other. It acknowledges that fundamental rights jurisprudence is a way of articulating the constitutional ethos that defines, and is expressive of, different polities and their constitutional texts.[20] The Union, just like the Member States, finds its own fundamental balance and thus allows for separate identities with separate values and competences. To come back to our earlier example of US constitutional history, the US Supreme Court, *before* incorporating the Bill of Rights into the Fourteenth Amendment, stated that

> we have in our political system a government of the United States and a government of the several States. Each one of these governments is distinct from the others, and each has citizens of its own who owe it allegiance, and

[19] US Supreme Court, *National Socialist Party of America v Village of Skokie*, 432 US 43 (1977).

[20] The best work on this is JHH Weiler, *The Constitution of Europe*, Cambridge, Cambridge University Press 1999, 102–29.

> whose rights, within its jurisdiction, it must protect. The same person may be at the same time a citizen of the United States and a citizen of a State, but his rights of citizenship under one of these governments will be different from those he has under the other.[21]

The Supreme Court voiced precisely the sensibility reflected in Article 51(1) of the EU Charter of Fundamental Rights, which in turn reflects how Member States imagine themselves within the Union. It is, in short, the idea that there is more than one sovereign.

D. Stabilising Autonomy

The final function that EU fundamental rights perform is reinforcing the autonomy of the Union legal order. By 'autonomy' of the Union legal order, I mean that it is independent from other legal orders and only Union institutions are competent to interpret its rules. This, at least, is how the European Court understands it. EU law, according to the Court, does not depend on national or international law for its validity, and requires that national and international courts do not interfere with the law set out in the Treaties. The Court laid the foundation for this claim in its seminal *Van Gend & Loos* and *Costa v ENEL* decisions (see Chapter four), and later continued that EU law 'stems from an independent source of law'.[22]

Asserting the Union legal order's autonomy is not only the basis of doctrines such as direct effect and primacy, but also informs the Court's own self-perception and position within the institutional architecture. If the Union legal order is self-contained and self-sufficient, the European Court is the supreme and constitutional court of a federal-type Union, even if it stands in a rivalry with Member States' highest courts (see Chapter five). Disputes relating to Union law cannot be settled by institutions other than the CJEU, and no other court can outrank it.

The autonomy of Union law, and with it the Court's position, will come under pressure once the Union accedes to the European Convention on Human rights (ECHR), as Article 6(2) of the TEU prescribes. Accession to the ECHR is meant to align the legal duties

[21] US Supreme Court, *United States v Cruikshank*, 92 US 542 (1875).

[22] *EU Accession to the ECHR II* (n 2), para 166; Case C-621/18 *Andy Wightman and Others v Secretary of State for Exiting the EU*, EU:C:2018:999, para 45.

of Union Member States under the ECHR with those of the Union. Especially when Member States transpose Union law into their own domestic legal orders, alignment helps to ensure they are not exposed to contradictory legal commands they are obliged to follow, eg, one under Union law that obliges them to implement something, and one under ECHR law that prohibits them from implementing it. Alignment is also meant to submit the Union legal order to outside supervision: the Union legal order, including the European Court, is not immune from making mistakes. With the ECtHR judging the legality of Union measures under the ECHR, such cases would be decided without a Union institution having the last say.

It is precisely this rationale that poses a problem for the autonomy of Union law, and, obviously, for the European Court. By acceding, the ECtHR is allowed to rule on matters of EU law, perhaps even before the CJEU has the opportunity to do so. The Union Court might lose its position as the 'highest' court in all matters relating to Union law.

This is not merely a question of judicial power. It also links back to our earlier discussion of values and competences. The precise balance between individual interests and public goods is what makes a polity unique and provides for diversity. Accession to the ECHR would tilt that balance towards uniformity and, while wiping out blind spots in Union justice, would also wipe out much of the delicate balance between Union and Member States as well.

It is, then, perhaps not all that surprising that the European Court pronounced the Draft Agreement on Accession incompatible with EU law and averted accession of the Union to the ECHR, at least for the time being.[23] The reason it was able to do so was the Union's own fundamental rights order, especially the Charter. Without it, it would have been virtually impossible to argue against accession and insist on Union autonomy.

III. REPERCUSSIONS OF THE ROLE OF FUNDAMENTAL RIGHTS IN EU CONSTITUTIONALISM

The role of fundamental rights in EU constitutional issues that are not, or not predominantly, about the protection of individual rights per se has significant unintended consequences. The European Court envisions

[23] *Accession to the ECHR II* (n 2). See D Halberstam, '"It's the Autonomy, Stupid!": A Modest Defense of Opinion 2/13 on EU Accession to the ECHR, and the Way Forward', (2015) 16 *German Law Journal* 105.

rights as stabilising the EU constitutional construct, and often they do. Sometimes, however, the EU's conception of fundamental rights can destabilise EU constitutionalism. One of the main reasons is that they are in the hands of the European Court, which sometimes miscalculates, and that other courts, both Member State courts and international tribunals, challenge the CJEU in the ongoing process of judicial bargaining. This affects all four constitutional building-blocks: the rule of law, the doctrine of primacy, the safeguarding of competences, and autonomy.

A. Destabilising the Rule of Law

The very fact *that* EU constitutionalism has additional roles for fundamental rights beyond the protection of individual interests is a problem, both procedurally and substantively. The problem is one of instrumentalisation. Just as the preliminary reference procedure is in place not just to strengthen rights, but to buttress the Union system of remedies, so too the EU fundamental rights order is in place not just to protect individuals, but to also safeguard primacy and autonomy. Where does that leave our liberal understanding of fundamental rights, which are emphatically not instrumental? Such strategic use of rights to ends different from individual freedom, equality, and agency raises the question of how credible the EU's commitment to protecting rights really is. Is the European Court truly interested in protecting individual rights for their own sake, or is it just a means to an ulterior end?

Usually, fundamental rights protection and protection of the integrity and effectiveness of the Union legal order go hand in hand. However, if rights are instrumental, what happens if a case decouples individual rights from an important Union policy? Will the right be robust enough to be protected by the CJEU, or will it have to give way to the effectiveness of Union law? A right that is discarded any time it conflicts with expediency is not a right in any recognisable sense. The Court's jurisprudence has given rise to misgivings.

One example is the case of an Afghan refugee, Mr NS, who had entered the EU via Greece, was deported to Turkey, and then somehow ended up in the UK where he claimed asylum. Union rules stipulate, however, that it is the state of first entry, in this case Greece, where asylum claims have to be considered. When British authorities sought to deport him there, Mr NS protested on human rights grounds. Since there was widespread evidence that asylum seekers were kept in appalling conditions in Greece, he claimed that deporting him back to Greece would violate two rights within the Charter: the prohibition of inhuman and degrading treatment, and the right to asylum. The Court pitted Mr NS's individual rights against an important integration value, the integrity of the Common European Asylum System (CEAS), which is a key part of the Union's Area of Freedom, Security and Justice. It maintained that the CEAS embodies a policy value that overrides individual rights, and established a presumption that Member States were acting in conformity with human rights (a claim, one might add, that lacked any basis in reality). Consequently, the Court decided to afford protection not against any instance of human rights violation, but only against violations that are part of a 'systemic deficiency'.[24] This is a massive retreat from the idea that fundamental rights are inherent to the individual. Instead, several human rights abuses have to be tallied before the Court may step in (with the triggering threshold quite nebulous). The Court in *NS* privileged an important Union policy, and protected the integrity of CEAS over individual rights.

The Court, in short, balances individual rights with other Union objectives, and sometimes favours those other objectives. The point here is not that balancing these different objectives is, as such, illegitimate. However, it does undermine the Court's credibility in human rights jurisprudence, which hurts the rule of law.[25]

B. Destabilising Primacy

At times, the European Court's instrumentalised use of fundamental rights is so glaring that it creates a huge backlash among Member State governments or courts. The backlash can be severe enough to threaten vital constitutional doctrines such as primacy. One example is, ironically, the *Mangold* case discussed earlier, the very case that was meant to expand the EU rule of law by strengthening the enforcement of directives by appealing to unwritten fundamental rights within them. The European Court's judgment met with fierce criticism of several aspects: the articulation of an unwritten fundamental right in a way that seemed

[24] Joined Cases C-411/10 and C-493/10 *NS v Secretary of State for the Home Department*, EU:C:2011:865, paras 75 et seq.

[25] See, for instance, A Williams, 'Human Rights in the EU', in A Arnull and D Chalmers (eds), *The Oxford Handbook of European Union Law*, Oxford, Oxford University Press 2015, 249, at 250 (concluding that the Court was not 'constructed with the realization of human rights as a constituting principle', and that it therefore may not be a 'credible institution for the fulfilment of human rights').

to contradict the Court's own methodology; the undermining of carefully negotiated detail within the directive; the interference with democratic policy choices; and the creation of a new EU social right. German law review articles appeared under headlines such as 'The end of rational jurisprudence in Luxembourg' and 'Yet another tale from the loony-bin'. Former President of Germany and former President of the German Federal Constitutional Court, Roman Herzog, published a newspaper article calling for both strategies to 'stop the European Court of Justice' and civil disobedience.[26] The Court's reputation was in tatters, its legitimacy seriously questioned. To many it appeared interested only in its own self-aggrandisement.

Perhaps worse, the *Mangold* decision was challenged before the German Federal Constitutional Court. The European Court, the argument went, had exceeded its competences under Union law. Therefore, the judgment, as an act ultra vires, did not have any legal force and should be ignored by German authorities. This argument was a direct attack on primacy. The German Constitutional Court did not agree and allowed the European Court considerable room to manoeuvre.[27] However, it did not conclude that challenges to primacy, and to European Court decisions, were, in themselves, illegitimate. Rather, it insisted on its competence to invalidate European Court judgments, even though it agreed that such invalidations should not be made lightly. Primacy, while generally accepted, remained highly tenuous. Indeed, a few years later the German Court 'toughened' its conception of what constituted an ultra vires measure,[28] and another few years later it did declare certain Union measures, including a European Court decision, to be ultra vires.[29]

C. Destabilising Competences

The stabilising effect of EU fundamental rights on the distribution of powers and the protection of national values depends on maintaining

[26] R Herzog and L Gerken, *Frankfurter Allgemeine Zeitung*, 8 September 2008, 8.

[27] BVerfG, 6 July 2010, 126 BVerfGE 286 – *Ultra-vires Kontrolle Mangold (In re Honeywell)* (translation at https://bit.ly/367BfLa).

[28] BVerfG, 14 January 2014, 134 BVerfGE 366 – *Outright Monetary Transactions (OMT) Referral* (translation at https://bit.ly/2MbK1kA); BVerfG, 21 June 2016, 142 BVerfGE 123 – *Outright Monetary Transactions (OMT) Decision* (translation at https://bit.ly/2MsTX9D).

[29] BVerfG, 5 May 2020, 154 BVerfGE 17 – *Public Sector Purchase Programme (PSPP)* (translation at https://bit.ly/3qMoBcj).

the limited scope of application of EU fundamental rights, and on a functional division of labour between Union fundamental rights (and the CJEU) and national fundamental rights (and national courts). Alas, the legal boundary, Article 51(1) of the Charter, does not hold. The federal experience, with its tendency towards centralisation, manifests itself within the Union too. Just as in federal states, the reason is that the central court (the CJEU) uses central (EU) fundamental rights to more and more frequently intervene in Member States' measures.

We would be mistaken to imagine a clear and unambiguous distinction between the space where EU fundamental rights are applicable, and the space where they are not. What appears to be a boundary is, in fact, a pretty large grey area. While we are able to recognise situations where the answer is obvious one way or the other, plenty of cases reside in the nebulous grey area. The answers within that grey zone are provided by the European Court, which behaves like a federal constitutional court.

What is clear, first, is that situations not covered by EU law, like purely internal situations, are left to *national* fundamental rights. These are situations where there is no doubt that the values expressed through national fundamental rights must be allowed to unfold. If German authorities, for instance, decide to prohibit a rally of German neo-Nazis near the Holocaust Memorial in Berlin, German fundamental rights apply. What is also clear, secondly, is that Union institutions are not bound by national, but by *Union* fundamental rights. When the Union legislator, for example, passes a directive that introduces the European Arrest Warrant (which forces Member State courts to recognise and execute arrest warrants from other Member States), that directive must be measured against EU fundamental rights. Since the Union relies on Member States to execute European law, the same goes for Member State execution of European law when Union law leaves no discretion. Here the Member States' authorities act substantively as the Union's executive branch in addition to their national authority. If, for instance, the Spanish authorities execute a European arrest warrant from Italy, they act under Union law as 'agents' of the Union, and therefore Union fundamental rights apply. To give another example, if the Croatian Parliament transposes the European Arrest Warrant Directive into Croatian law, it is under a European Union legal obligation to do so; therefore it, too, is an agent of the Union. The law that it passes is, formally, a Croatian law, but substantively it is the product of an 'agent' of the European Union. Challenges to the Croatian law must therefore be based on it violating Union fundamental rights. This is what Article 51(1) of the EU Charter of Fundamental Rights means when it states that the Charter applies 'to the Member States only when they are implementing Union law'.

Everything in-between these two clear-cut situations is murky and needs elucidation. That task lies with the European Court, which went about its mission by equating 'implementing Union law' with 'acting within the scope of application of EU law', a much broader formulation.[30] The Court's conflation ties the scope of applying Union fundamental rights to the scope of Union law's general application. As the Court states,

> since the fundamental rights guaranteed by the Charter must ... be complied with where national legislation falls within the scope of European Union law, situations cannot exist which are covered in that way by European Union law without those fundamental rights being applicable. The applicability of European Union law entails applicability of the fundamental rights guaranteed by the Charter.[31]

The Court's jurisprudence expanding the scope of Union fundamental rights feeds directly into the pressing constitutional problems surrounding competence creep (see Chapter four). The broader the scope of Union law becomes, the broader the scope of application of Union fundamental rights becomes. The space where national fundamental rights can express national values and national identity shrinks.

The Court even goes so far as to intervene in policy areas considered core sovereign rights, such as tax law and criminal law, which Member States have retained for themselves. In the 2013 *Åkerberg Fransson* case, the Court was faced with a Swedish citizen, Mr Åkerberg Fransson, who had already been sanctioned for VAT fraud by Swedish administrative courts, and who was now subject to further penalties by Swedish criminal courts. He argued that this violated the principle of *ne bis in idem*, the right not to be tried twice for the same offence, codified in the Charter. The Commission (which has not been known for its timidity in making the most of sparse Union provisions) and several Member States interceded before the CJEU to argue that Union human rights were inapplicable for the simple reason that the Swedish sanctions law did not in any way implement Union law. One would tend to agree. The Swedish law had nothing to do with Union law, and it is hard to imagine

[30] The Court based its interpretation on the Explanations relating to the Charter (OJ 14 December 2007, C 303/17) produced during the Charter's original drafting, which also use the term 'scope' ('binding on the Member States when they act in the scope of Union law') and which were given interpretative effect, Article 6(1) of the TEU and Article 52(7) of the Charter.

[31] *Åklagaren v Åkerberg Fransson* (n 7), para 21.

a case closer to the Member States' sovereign 'power of the purse' and 'power of the sword' than this one. The Court, however, disagreed. It reasoned that because part of Member State VAT revenues is destined for the Union's own resources, and Article 325 of the TFEU declares that Member States have an obligation to counter fraud affecting the financial interests of the Union, there was a sufficient link between the Swedish sanctions law and Union law to satisfy the requirements of Article 51(1) of the Charter and thereby bind Sweden to Union fundamental rights.[32] The case is illustrative of how tight the space for Member States asserting their national fundamental rights under the Court's jurisprudence has become. With the loss of distinct balances of fundamental rights comes a loss of ability to meaningfully express national values through them.

To be sure, the Court allows Member States to apply national fundamental rights, but only insofar as they observe 'the level of protection provided for by the Charter, as interpreted by the Court, and the primacy, unity, and effectiveness of European Union law are not thereby compromised'.[33] In other words, the Charter is decisive, just as primacy, unity and effectiveness of Union law are. This is the case even when a national fundamental right affords a higher level of protection to an individual than the Charter and despite the Charter itself stating that 'nothing in this Charter shall be interpreted as restricting or adversely affecting human rights and fundamental freedoms as recognised, in their respective fields of application, by … the Member States' constitutions'.[34] The Spanish Constitutional Court, in the 2013 *Melloni* case, interpreted this clause as possibly calling into question the doctrine of primacy (this is the European Arrest Warrant saga discussed, from a different perspective, in Chapter five). It was unwilling to execute a European arrest warrant from Italy because the person in question had been sentenced in Italy *in absentia* which, under the right to a fair trial as formulated in the Spanish Constitution, was sufficient reason not to surrender him. Under the EU law regulating the European arrest warrant and under the Charter, it was *not* a reason not to surrender him. The Spanish constitutional right to a fair trial thus afforded a higher level of protection; would that not mean, according to the Charter itself, that the European law should be interpreted in the light of the Spanish right to a fair trial?

[32] *Åklagaren v Åkerberg Fransson* (n 7).
[33] Ibid, para 29.
[34] Art 53 of the Charter.

Constitutionally speaking, here, at last, was a chance to reverse the federalist logic of relentless centralisation, to let national fundamental rights prevail, and to vindicate national sensibilities while the overall level of human rights protection in the Union would go up. The European Court, however, responded with a terse decision denying space for the Spanish fundamental right. Its line of reasoning was basically a restatement of its decades-old primacy doctrine since *Van Gend & Loos* and *Costa v ENEL*. The Spanish Constitutional Court, the highest court of its land, was forced to disapply its own constitutional fundamental right because it conflicted with the European Court's reading of the European Arrest Warrant law and the Charter, even though the Spanish fundamental right afforded better individual protection.[35]

The picture of European constitutionalism that emerges from *Melloni* and *Åkerberg Fransson* is one of centralisation led by the European Court. When deciding between the values of uniformity and diversity, the Court invariably chooses the former by privileging primacy over individual rights. In doing so, it not only steamrolls national values, but also seems to confirm suspicions that its fundamental rights jurisprudence has motives ulterior to protecting individuals from the power of the state.

That, however, is not the whole picture. European constitutionalism's central feature is its compound, hybrid nature. It provides plenty of safety valves if the pressure on either side, Member State or Union, becomes too great. The safety valve in the case of judicial centralisation is judicial dialogue. Member State courts are not subservient recipients and executors of European Court pronouncements, but self-confident and, at times, defiant partners. It is them the European Court needs to convince for the system to function; if that fails, there is little it can do to enforce its authority.

In that vein, neither the *Åkerberg Fransson* nor the *Melloni* saga ended with the European Court's judgment. In both cases the German Federal Constitutional Court applied counter-pressure. Merely two months after *Åkerberg Fransson*, it decided an unrelated case about a German counterterrorism database law that was challenged as being incompatible, inter alia, with EU human rights. The German Court rejected that argument. It maintained that the German law did not 'implement' EU law, and that the link between the German law and Union law was too weak for the challenge to succeed. It then added that

[35] Case C-399/11 *Melloni v Ministerio Fiscal*, EU:C:2013:107.

should the CJEU decide differently by following its *Åkerberg Fransson* logic, such a judgment would be declared ultra vires and ignored within Germany.[36] Similarly, following *Melloni*, the German Court decided that the European Arrest Warrant law would have to be read in the light of the German Constitution's fundamental right to human dignity, which is central to the German Constitution, otherwise it would be invalid under German constitutional law.[37] Both decisions explicitly threatened to violate EU law primacy. In both cases, the European Court partially recanted its prior decision and followed the German court's lead. It agreed that the link between national measures and EU fundamental rights needed to be stronger than what *Åkerberg Fransson* had suggested,[38] and it reinterpreted the Charter and the European Arrest Warrant law in the light of the (Charter) fundamental right to human dignity.[39]

The safety valve of judicial dialogue with mutual threats and retreats, however, is not a fine-tuning instrument for balancing the EU and member interests. Its blunt nature has several drawbacks. One is that pressure needs to build to a breaking point before it is released. National courts only intervene when the degree of centralisation has become blatantly unacceptable. Another problem is that the safety valve for Member States itself raises the stakes considerably. National courts threaten to undermine primacy and the European Court's interpretative monopoly, and thus move outside, and even against, the Union legal order. The European Court is then confronted with serious constitutional dangers since the uniform application of Union law is on the line. Dialogue between the courts turns into a game of chicken. Finally, results are usually unsatisfactory. Even if the European Court yields, typically two things happen. First, the Court retreats only momentarily. In our examples, it overruled neither *Åkerberg Fransson* nor *Melloni*, but kept them as precedents and merely readjusted on the details. Readjustment takes place on a level of generality that allows the Court, in future decisions, to backtrack and continue its original centralising course.

[36] BVerfG, 24 April 2013, 133 BVerfGE 277, paras 88–91 – *Counterterrorism Database* (translation at https://bit.ly/4czCuCR).

[37] BVerfG, 15 December 2015, 140 BVerfGE 317 – *European Arrest Warrant II* (translation at https://bit.ly/3zaCzyt).

[38] Case C-206/13 *Cruciano Siragusa v Regione Sicilia*, EU:C:2014:126; Case C-198/13 *Julian Hernández v Reino de España (Subdelegación del Gobierno de España en Alicante)*, EU:C:2014:2055.

[39] Joined Cases C-404/15 and C-659/15 PPU *Aranyosi and Căldăraru v Generalstaatsanwaltschaft Bremen*, EU:C:2016:198.

Second, a safety valve does not replace the basic logic of competence creep and centralisation. Pressure will rebuild. It is not guaranteed that national courts will be ready and able to intervene again. Questioning the CJEU's primacy comes with political risks. National courts have to spend a good deal of 'social capital' when moving against the Union legal order (the German Constitutional Court, for instance, came under heavy attack from the Union and most of European legal academia when it invalidated a European Court decision in 2020). Utilising the safety valve is something they cannot do every year. This complex logic aside, they may also simply be inattentive.

D. Destabilising Autonomy

Court-led autonomy of the Union's fundamental rights vis-à-vis the ECHR is part of a larger line of jurisprudence that insulates the Union from the influence of the international legal order. The Court is notoriously sceptical of the idea that international law might constrain the Union's freedom to make or adjudicate law. Its rejection of WTO law is a case in point. The CJEU fiercely defends the autonomy of the Union against the direct effect of WTO provisions, and against oversight from the WTO's judicial bodies, thus shielding EU law from challenges based on international treaties.

There are, however, two problems that make protecting autonomy in fundamental rights law, as distinct from autonomy in market law, difficult. One is that autonomy with respect to the ECHR is not working. The other is that the pre-accession status quo may even place the Union Court, and its rights regime, at a disadvantage compared to its position after the Union's ECHR accession.

Autonomy from ECHR influence must fail for two reasons. First, the Member States, as 'masters of the Treaties', have conceived the European fundamental rights regime as an order inextricably intertwining Union and ECHR rights. They have mandated accession, and drawn up the Charter as a legal instrument that orients itself, at least partially, towards the ECHR. Article 52(3) of the Charter states that

> in so far as this Charter contains rights which correspond to rights guaranteed by the Convention for the Protection of Human Rights and Fundamental Freedoms, the meaning and scope of those rights shall be the same as those laid down by the said Convention. This provision shall not prevent Union law providing more extensive protection.

Union rights and ECHR rights are joined from their very foundations. The Court's jurisprudence, in contrast, raises the possibility of a conflict between pronouncements of the CJEU and ECtHR on identical issues, which explicitly contravenes the Treaty and the Charter.

Second, the ECtHR already reviews Union legal acts, albeit indirectly. In 1999, the ECtHR ruled that while the ECHR does not stand in the way of Member States transferring sovereign powers to the Union, the responsibility for violations of the Convention would remain with the Member State even after such a transfer.[40] That put Union Member States, which are also without exception member states of the ECHR, in a bind because now there was a danger of contradictory legal demands from the Convention and the Union: Union law (as read by the CJEU) might demand implementation of a rule, the Convention (as read by the ECtHR) might prohibit it. In 2005, the ECtHR therefore came up with a legal presumption of lawfulness. As long as Union law offered a standard of protection at least equivalent to that offered by the ECHR, Member States implementing EU law would only be found in breach of the Convention if the protection of rights was 'manifestly deficient'.[41] This 'presumption of equivalence' is a lower threshold than what applies to ECHR member states acting outside the scope of EU law. This, however, does not keep the ECtHR from severely criticising Union law and, at times, pronouncing laws as violating Convention obligations. In 2016, for instance, it came very close to declaring part of the Union's instruments in the Area of Freedom, Security and Justice a breach of ECHR law because of their low level of fundamental rights protection.[42]

The second problem with fundamental rights autonomy is that the Union Court may have weaker standing now that it has stopped accession. The Draft Agreement on Accession provided two mechanisms that worked *in favour* of Union law. One was a procedure that facilitated involving the Court of Justice in ECtHR decisions. It stipulated that, when an issue before the ECtHR has not previously been examined by the CJEU, the latter may be called on to decide on its compatibility with EU law. The idea was that the EU has its own normative and interpretative universe, and judgments about its compatibility with the Convention

[40] ECtHR *Matthews v United Kingdom*, 18 February 1999, Application No 24833/94.

[41] ECtHR (Grand Chamber) *Bosphorus v Ireland*, 30 June 2005, Application No 45036/98 (pre-Charter); largely confirmed in ECtHR *Michaud v France*, 6 December 2012, Application No 12323/11 (post-Charter).

[42] ECtHR *Avotiņš v Latvia*, 23 May 2016, Application No 17502/07, concerning the AFSJ's 'principle of mutual trust'.

should not be made solely by judges on the ECtHR bench who are versed only in Convention law and in national law, not in Union law. The other mechanism, the so-called co-respondent mechanism, would allow the Union (and, in addition, one or several Member States) to become party to ECHR proceedings against a Member State, where the compatibility of Union law with the ECHR might be at issue. Here, the idea was the ECtHR would not have to unilaterally examine the division of powers as it would deal jointly with the Union and its Member States.

Both mechanisms would have worked to the benefit not just of Union law but also of the ideas behind the autonomy of Union law. Failing accession, Union law is subject to ECHR review anyway, with the Union Court not necessarily being involved, the competence questions being unilaterally decided by the ECtHR, and the CJEU garnering a bad reputation for failing to take ECHR review seriously.

IV. THE INDIVIDUAL IN EU CONSTITUTIONALISM

The strategic use of fundamental rights by the European Court impacts not only the Union's system of governance but also the standing of Union citizens. 'The Union places the individual at the heart of its activities', claims the Preamble to the Charter. This is a bold claim, considering that for the longest time, international organisations were so far removed from individuals. Rather, it was states who were the subjects of international law, which conditioned the status of their citizens. It is perhaps for this reason that European integration is seen, to this day, as a predominantly institutional phenomenon.

However, the Union has reconfigured institutions, processes, and policies far beyond the usual reach of international organisations. European integration rearranges the institutions of Member State political communities, and with it the relationship between citizens and public authority. Since Union law can directly entitle and disentitle citizens, individuals are no longer 'mediated' subjects of the transnational legal order, but directly implicated like they would be living in a traditional state.

What is different is the fact that in the Union, legal entitlement does not translate into political allegiance. In contrast to states, the Union almost entirely fails at constructing an imaginary fabric that would allow citizens to incorporate the Union into their sense of identity. It lacks the necessary social and cultural tools to do so. Above all, there is no 'We the people' inscribed into the memory of European citizens. In nation-states, imaginations of shared sovereignty furnish citizens with a political identity so strong that they conceive of themselves as part of a communal project. States give their citizens a past stretching from before their birth to a future beyond their death. Individual and collective identities merge in ways which benefit both the individual and the state: individuals find meaning for their lives in the collective project of the society, and states gain historical presence and with it the gravitas needed for authority. We map these socio-cultural elements of political identity onto concepts like citizenship. While the Union does have 'Union citizenship', the associative bond between the Union and its citizens is nowhere near as deep and strong as it is between states and their citizens.[43] In what way, then, does the Union 'place the individual at the heart of its activities'?

Fundamental rights promise a solution. They could offer a way to both protect the individual and at the same time forge a community. To have fundamental rights is, in a democratic community, a marker of belonging and membership. Many hoped that a written Charter of Fundamental Rights would enrich the Union with moral values and ethical grounding. Human rights connect with civic republicanism, opening up legal discourse to discussions about the spiritual foundations of Europe. The promise of conjoining these discourses seemed like an answer to the question of European identity.[44]

It was not to be. Rights are an ambivalent tool for creating political identity. While they can have the virtues I have mentioned, they produce inherent challenges to creating a community. First, they are often uncompromising and individualise the rights-bearer rather than embed her in community. They play individual interests against each other and operate on the basis that the winning right trumps the losing right. The consequence may well be an atomised society, which is the opposite of a closely-knit community. Secondly, rights are counter-majoritarian. They work against constructing a sense of 'we' because they are designed to protect individuals against the power of the many. This accentuates

[43] There is a burgeoning literature on the lack of European political identity. Just to name a few, see N Fligstein, *Euro-Clash*, Oxford, Oxford University Press 2008; JT Checkel and PJ Katzenstein (eds), *European Identity*, Cambridge, Cambridge University Press 2009; C Bottici and B Challand, *Imagining Europe*, Cambridge, Cambridge University Press 2013; KR McNamara, *The Politics of Everyday Europe*, Oxford, Oxford University Press 2015; B Westle and P Segatti (eds), *European Identity in the Context of National Identity*, Oxford, Oxford University Press 2016; V Kaina, I Pawel Karolewski and S Kuhn (eds), *European Identity Revisited*, London, Routledge 2016.

[44] On the symbolic gestures that came with the Charter, see U Haltern, 'Pathos and Patina', (2003) 9 *European Law Journal* 14.

tensions between individuals and collectives. Democratic societies are able to withstand such tensions because rights-based counter-majoritarianism is part of their democratic culture. That culture requires societal maturity and an already settled political community capable of tolerating the Other as a matter of course. Thirdly, rights lead to an impoverished public discourse. Some things – the objects of fundamental rights – are not the object of public discourse any longer. They become somehow unquestioned background assumptions for political disagreements because they are largely inaccessible for public or political revision. Political identity, however, draws on discourse rather different from judicial decision-making. The 'rueful rhetoric of rights'[45] has individual claims, not shared allegiance, at centre stage.

Even beyond the weaknesses inherent in rights, the European Court's strategic functionalism about rights discussed earlier inhibits the creation of a European identity because it shades into a strategic functionalism of the European citizen. Fundamental rights in the Union grew from *Van Gend & Loos* (see Chapter four). The rights granted in that decision, and the legal proceedings that allowed individuals to enforce them, strategically serve the Union and the single market it wants to achieve. In the words of Judge Lecourt, who sat on the bench when the Court handed down *Van Gend & Loos*, 'When an individual appears before the judge to defend the rights he derives from the Treaties, that individual does not only act in his own interest, he immediately becomes an auxiliary agent of the [Union]'.[46] The citizen becomes an agent of the Union and, ultimately, an agent of the market. Creating such rights does not create meaningful citizenship or even allegiance. Rather, it creates market citizenship. The market citizen makes use of these rights when interacting with the European market, 'in the service not of Europe but of self-interest. Being instrumentalized, the market citizen had no choice but to become instrumentalist'.[47] Rotating around the centripetal force of the market and its values, the Union and its citizens have a mutually instrumentalist attitude towards each other. For the Union, this means to reward those who are ready (and able) to make use of the

[45] P Westen, 'The Rueful Rhetoric of "Rights"', (1986) 33 *UCLA Law Review* 977.

[46] R Lecourt, 'L'Europe des juges, Brussels 1967', 260, quoted in L Azoulai, S Barbou des Places and E Pataut, 'Being a Person in the European Union', in L Azoulai, S Barbou des Places and E Pataut (eds), *Constructing the Person in EU Law – Rights, Roles, Identities*, London, Bloomsbury 2016, 3, at 5.

[47] M Everson, 'The Legacy of the Market Citizen', in J Shaw and G More (eds), *New Legal Dynamics of European Union*, Oxford, Oxford University Press 1995, 73, at 88.

market: it 'empowers those who are agile and adaptable'.[48] For individuals, this means to ask, 'what do I get out of it?' It pushes the Union deep into an output-legitimacy mentality, a kind of 'bread and circus' polity[49] which is always precarious.

The deeper worry about the instrumentalism at the heart of market citizenship through rights is their inexorable connection to the market. *Van Gend & Loos* is steeped in market-building. The single market is, to a large degree, about offering individuals more choices – of goods and services, but also of how and where to work, how and where to live, what to believe, etc. There is much emancipatory potential in wider choices. Union law, however, explicitly articulates emancipation through the individual's 'release from communitarian constraints'.[50] Somek writes that those who become part of the market by increased mobility are relieved 'from dependence on received social bonds and hierarchies' and that 'solidarity is treated as a resource to be tapped by individuals'.[51] It is not just a mutually instrumentalising relationship between individuals and Union that is the cause of worry. Rather it is that Union law, in its attempt to construct a market, at the same time constructs, and rewards, a concept of what people should be like which misunderstands and thus undermines solidarity. Critics fear that such a legal order not only trivialises itself, but in turn trivialises its subjects. A myopic focus on market choices thus harms the social conditions that facilitate individual agency. A market values neither individuality (the market does not care who we are when we conclude a contract or spend money) nor history (it does not matter why we have become who we are). Both individuality and history are, however, indispensable for constructing a political community. Markets cannot tell us who we are as individuals, let alone who we are as a political community.

While the Charter loosens the link between rights and the market, it does not sever it, nor does it soften the strategic character of rights. The overwhelming share of fundamental rights litigation still concerns single market matters. The rest deals with policies that grew from the single market, as market-correcting or market-cushioning policies

[48] A Somek, 'Alienation, Despair and Social Freedom', in L Azoulai, S Barbou des Places and E Pataut (n 46), 35, at 52.

[49] JHH Weiler, 'Bread and Circus: The State of the Union', (1998) 4 *Columbia Journal European Law* 223.

[50] F de Witte, 'Emancipation Through Law?', in L Azoulai, S Barbou des Places and E Pataut (n 46), 15, at 16.

[51] Somek (n 48).

(see Chapter six). Those areas exhibit weak Union competences and make it difficult for the European Court to clear the hurdle of Article 51(1) of the Charter, as *Åkerberg Fransson* demonstrated. The Court's continued instrumentalist approach to fundamental rights keeps alive the instrumentalist nature of the European citizen. As has been discussed, fundamental rights sit alongside other Union goals and are sometimes jettisoned by the Court to protect the integrity of other policy objectives. If the Court is not fully guided by the values embedded in rights, there is no reason to expect any deeper sense of attachment from Europe's citizens.

The 'Union citizenship' provisions of the Treaty[52] are not well suited to bringing citizens and Union closer together either. Unlike national citizenship regimes, they do not offer a consistent set of substantive rights for all citizens. Some are applicable only when individuals cross the border into another Member State, others apply regardless of where they live. Even more worrying, rights change depending on one's employment status and place within the market economy. Workers are treated differently from retired persons, students from healthcare patients. This introduces a degree of intentional fragmentation and inequality into the concept of citizenship that is anathema to values codified by the state template of constitutionalism. Citizenship rights, in the Union, do not have an egalitarian core, but instead depend on what citizens do. They distinguish between those who 'deserve', and those who do not 'deserve' them. This connects them, of course, to what we would expect from market rights. Indeed, Union citizenship has come to be criticised as a commodification of values.[53]

FURTHER READING

Azoulai L, Barbou des Places S and Pataut E (eds), *Constructing the Person in EU Law: Rights, Roles, Identities*, Oxford, Hart Publishing 2016.

De Búrca G, 'The Evolution of EU Human Rights Law', in Craig P and de Búrca G (eds), *The Evolution of EU Law*, Oxford, Oxford University Press, 3rd edn 2021, 480.

Dawson M, *The Governance of EU Fundamental Rights*, Cambridge, Cambridge University Press 2017.

[52] Arts 20–25 TFEU.

[53] See, for instance, C O'Brien, 'Civis Capitalist Sum: Class as the New Guiding Principle of EU Free Movement Rights', (2016) 53 *CML Rev* 937.

Weiler JHH, 'Eurocracy and Distrust: Some Questions Concerning the Role of the European Court of Justice in the Protection of Fundamental Human Rights Within the Legal Order of the European Communities', (1986) 61 *Washington Law Review* 1103.

Williams A, *EU Human Rights Policies: A Study in Irony*, Oxford, Oxford University Press 2004.

Conclusion

THIS BOOK BEGAN with the expectation that EU constitutionalism would significantly diverge from the state template of constitutionalism. The Union's constitutional text was constructed from treaties between sovereign Member States; its institutions exist within a 'crowded space' of overlapping boundaries where these states intersect; its obligations, while backed by a court, lack the teeth that domestic enforcement mechanisms have; its policy horizon is restricted to only those areas in which its Member States have expressly conferred powers; its claim to whom it represents is fractured and unclear. EU constitutionalism is in want of sovereign legal power, political *pouvoir constituant*, and cultural allegiance. It is, therefore, a constitutional order that is compound, hybrid, and unsettled.

Having explored the Union's institutional architecture, its decision-making system, and its mechanisms of economic integration and individual rights protection, we can now pull the strands together and examine how our expectations play out against the backdrop of the state's conceptual landscape of constitutionalism. While this Conclusion only outlines an interpretation of an immensely complex and dynamic set of issues, it is safe to say that this book has encountered tensions and dynamics that can be organised into three groups. First is the Union's decision-making apparatus between supranationalism and intergovernmentalism. The second is a momentum that leads from law-making to law-enforcing. The third is a reversal of the relationship between the exercise of power and its constraints. After discussing them each in turn, we will examine some challenges that Union constitutionalism will face in the years to come.

I. DECISION-MAKING: FROM SEPARATING POWERS TO FUSING POWERS

The Union's decision-making apparatus consciously avoids mimicry of state structures; its singular, distinguishing feature is the collaboration of Union and Member States. The Union does not replace its Member States, but rather manages their interdependence by working with them in a host of different political processes. These processes share one trait, which is the interlocking of polities in a composite architecture. Herein lies the deepest reason why constitutional similarities between state institutional structures and Union institutional structures should not be overstated. The Union places a premium on hybridity in that it has no single centre of gravity. Its separation of powers is folded into a compound institutional structure that avoids privileging the authority of either the Union or the Member States.

Within that compound institutional structure, the EU's constitutional framework is informed by a blend of supranational effectiveness (secured by some degree of autonomy from partisan state interests) and intergovernmental control (exercised by the Member States' heavy involvement in the Union's day-to-day operation). It is this balance between the 'supranational' and the 'intergovernmental' that is the Union's basic working system. Institutional functions and powers have been designed to represent and balance diverse interests along that supranational/intergovernmental divide.

In nation-states based upon popular sovereignty, representation of interests is achieved by ensuring citizens' direct influence on the composition of parliament and the head of government. Popular sovereignty, however, is not the leading principle of Union representation. While the Union *does* make sure that its citizens can directly influence the composition of one of its institutions, the European Parliament, it integrates democratic sovereignty into a wider range of interests. Broadly speaking, Member States are represented in the Council and the European Council; the interests of the citizens are represented by the Parliament; and the interests of the Union as its own entity are represented by the Commission. These interests and their distribution among the Union's institutions determine their role in governing the EU. In the legislative process, for example, the Commission enjoys a degree of autonomy that is deemed vital to secure progress by cutting through partisan state interests. It is therefore charged with the responsibility to initiate legislation. Its lack of democratic accountability, however, is the reason why it does not formally make law, which is the preserve of the Council and the European Parliament. Still, the Commission retains a good degree of control over the content of its proposals throughout the legislative process. It is this complex interdependence of its institutions that distinguishes the Union's legislative processes from the ones found in classic international organisations on the one hand, and in nation-states on the other.

The same dynamic exists with respect to decision-making processes beyond law-making. Thus, even as the institutions rarely act unilaterally, they all have a breadth of influence that makes the interdependent structure of EU institutions distinct from the principle of separating powers that is crucial in states. The Council appears chameleonic precisely because it has its fingers in every pie. The Commission enjoys not only an exclusive right to propose legislation, and the influence over the policy and legislative agenda that comes with it, but also the power to colour in the details of the regulatory framework that the Union legislator provides and to regulate some areas directly. Furthermore, the Commission has a judicial role, since it is tasked with ensuring that the terms of the Treaties are observed: the Commission investigates non-compliance and brings infringement proceedings against Member States. Finally, in terms of executive powers, it shares a general responsibility for ensuring that the Member States are implementing in practice what they have agreed to do.

It is difficult to say whether supranational or intergovernmental institutions are driving integration forward. There is open and fierce debate on how power is precisely allocated between them. Proponents of both sides have good arguments to buttress their case. For instance, the fact that more and more issues are decided by qualified majority voting in the Council indicates that supranationalism is on the rise. On the other hand, the fact that the European Council has grabbed more power, especially during the financial crisis, indicates the opposite.

In part, the reason why it is difficult to determine whether the EU fundamentally exemplifies supranationalism or intergovernmentalism lies in the fact that the complex mix of interlocking interests and powers has led the institutions to evolve beyond such labels. The Commission, for instance, is no longer archetypically supranational, with one of its Vice-Presidents – the High Representative of the Union for Foreign Affairs and Security Policy – being also part of the Council system, which may divide his or her loyalty between the College of Commissioners and the Council. Similarly, the Council is no longer quintessentially intergovernmental, with COREPER and its working groups doing much of their work in a way that pays little attention to national interests.

The upshot is that the relationship between the Union's institutions is, depending on the context, either competitive or collusive.[1]

[1] See F Vibert, *The Rise of the Unelected: Democracy and the New Separation of Powers*, Cambridge, Cambridge University Press 2007, 129–43.

For instance, while Parliament competes with the Member States in the Council and the European Council to control the Commission (just think of the jostling over who will become Commission President), it also sees the Commission as an ally against the Member States. Likewise, the Commission sees the Member States (as represented in the Council and the European Council) as a threat to its agenda-setting role, but also needs them in the legislative process to push its own regulatory ideas through. Parliament views itself as the voice of the people and understands its role in Union politics in the same way that opposition parties understand their role in national parliaments, but at the same time it is an integral part of the legislative process that needs to convince the Commission and the Council of its perspective. The Court, finally, seems above the fray in that it reviews the measures of both the Member States and the Union institutions, but it, too, plays a political role that aligns it, more often than not, with the Commission.

This logic of power-sharing comes at a political cost. One cost is its lack of transparency. The fact that the Union's institutions are pushed together by the compound nature of EU constitutionalism makes it hard to disentangle the different strands of this institutional medley (something that gets even harder because of inter-institutional agreements). The diffusion of powers entails the diffusion of responsibility and accountability. Little wonder that European citizens are confused and frustrated when they look to the Union (see the Introduction to this book); all they see is 'Brussels'.

Another cost comes from a lack of political leadership. Power-sharing means that no-one can claim a monopoly over executive or legislative powers, and no-one wins all the time. The lack of hierarchical relations is, of course, precisely the point of the Union's institutional architecture. But it also means that the Union has no strong or clear political leadership. Rather, leadership is a highly contested commodity. Again, little wonder that the American President is uncertain about whom to call when he or she wants to talk to someone in charge of the Union (see, again, the Introduction to this book).

II. COMMITMENTS: FROM MAKING LAW TO ENFORCING LAW

Analysing the Union's decision-making process is highly intriguing because it is so different from the state template of constitutionalism. Political scientists are endlessly fascinated by it. It is, however, only part of the EU constitutional system. Another central feature is the Union's strong court. The role the CJEU plays in Union constitutionalism can hardly be overstated. As we saw by recounting its history, the Court is the reason why many describe European integration as 'integration through law'.

The pivotal role of the European Court corresponds with the immensity of the task before it: How to make sure that 27 states, comfortably settled within their centuries-old history of sovereign state power and equipped with the ego and the tools that come with it, honour the agreements they have made with one another? How can we keep them from reneging on their commitments under international law, their strong national interests and democratic legitimacy notwithstanding? How, in other words, is it possible to push Member States towards compliance with Union law, and establish a culture of obedience that is akin to what we find in states?

The answer is by making EU law, and its enforcement, state-like. Union constitutionalism outsources enforcement to national legal systems without giving national legal systems the power to determine the substantive meaning of Union law. In legal terms, the solution is to grant EU law direct effect and primacy. This removes Member State parliaments from the equation since they lose political control over what the law of the land is and how it is applied. For instance, they can no longer interfere in the space of Union law and its application, either by failing to implement Union law or by passing national laws that contradict it. Direct effect and primacy also empower Member State citizens because they can enforce the rights granted to them in court without relying on a centralised enforcement mechanism. Finally, national courts are empowered because it is them to whom individual litigants directly appeal. They gain the power to overturn national laws if they conflict with Union law and reverse the judicial hierarchy within their state. After all, 'once a judicial decision has been weaponised with the doctrine of primacy, no other institution – not the government, not the parliament [and, one may add, not a higher court] – can overturn it'.[2] At the same time, it is the European Court which determines the substantive meaning of Union law through preliminary rulings.

This mechanism bifurcates Union constitutionalism in an interesting way. Decision-making is decidedly novel and does not fit the state template of constitutionalism, whereas enforcement of the results of that decision-making process is decidedly state-like. The former is about

[2] M Dawson and F de Witte, *EU Law and Governance*, Cambridge, Cambridge University Press 2022, 110.

sharing power, which is unfamiliar in states, whereas the latter is about coopting power, which is familiar because it entrenches the authority of Union law within the national constitutional settlement. The only novelty here is the fact that national courts play along, but that has been explained through the adjudicative and political power that is already bestowed upon them.

While direct effect and primacy have proven a spectacular success with regard to Member State compliance and the establishment of a genuine European rule of law,[3] they have also burdened EU constitutionalism with the problem of democratic deficiency. Removing stumbling blocks in Member States (such as domestic parliaments) also means removing key sources of democratic legitimacy. As for input legitimacy, the Union's decision-making process is incapable of supplying the same degree of accountability, deliberation, and representation as national decision-making processes. As for output legitimacy, institutional protection of national values decreases.

This problem is far more serious than it may sound, because it is exacerbated by four factors. First, direct effect and primacy have no legal grounding in the Treaties. It was the European Court which declared, in its 1963–64 judgments *Van Gend & Loos* and *Costa v ENEL*, that Union law had direct effect and enjoyed primacy. This gives rise to severe criticism up to and including the charge of a 'juridical coup d'état'.[4] While such an accusation may be excessive, it is fair to say that the emergence of direct effect and primacy through a 'judicial revolution', rather than through political consensus among the Member States, does little to furnish the Union with democratic legitimacy.

Secondly, primacy and direct effect open up EU constitutionalism to the critique of 'over-constitutionalisation.' The Treaties, this critique goes, contain hundreds of provisions that, in a state, would be ordinary law, not constitutional law. These provisions also exhibit a structural imbalance because they favour deregulation and force open markets. Since direct effect and primacy extend to all these provisions, they are (formally) very hard to undo and (substantively) create far more

[3] That is, as far as we can measure that success. For some doubts, see M Bobek, 'Of Feasibility and Silent Elephants: The Legitimacy of the Court of Justice through the Eyes of National Courts', in M Adams et al (eds), *Judging Europe's Judges: The Legitimacy of the Case Law of the European Court of Justice*, Oxford, Hart Publishing 2015, 197.

[4] A Stone Sweet, 'The Juridical Coup d'État and the Problem of Authority', (2007) 8 *German Law Journal* 915.

deregulation than Member States would have agreed to.[5] Again, this critique may be painting with a broad brush,[6] but it does signal a widespread democratic discontent with European integration.

Thirdly, Union law covers more and more policy fields, with or, worse, without express conferral of powers from the Member States to the Union. Competence creep is one of the most serious problems in European integration because it encroaches on policies and values of Member States even where they were intent on retaining regulatory autonomy over those issues for themselves. In the Union's state-like enforcement system, however, there is no reliable safety valve. The European Court has not established itself as a dependable guardian of Member State powers, and Member State courts would have to move against the CJEU, against its bedrock doctrines of direct effect and primacy, and against the European rule of law, if they were to disapply Union measures on the grounds that Union institutions have acted beyond their powers. While we saw instances of higher courts taking this stance, we also saw that doing so is an uphill battle.

Finally, the European Court does not simply enforce the bargains struck by the Union legislator, but sometimes strikes bargains with itself by giving itself the role of a regulator and legislator. In announcing the principle of mutual recognition in free movement law, for instance, the Court displaced the EU political process for harmonising Member State laws in the single market. The Court, in other words, crosses from enforcing law to making law, and brings the full weight of the Union's unitary and state-like enforcement system to bear on the tenuous and complex law-making system. This makes law appear not only self-extending because of competence creep, but also self-executing. The effect is significant depoliticisation. Often, Member States welcome such decisions because they are 'effective' and get integration 'done', especially when the channels of political decision-making are blocked (as they often are when the Council needs to decide unanimously). But usually they are blocked for a reason, and from the point of view of the dissenting veto player, at least, effectiveness is bought at the price of democratic accountability and legitimacy.

[5] See, for instance, D Grimm, 'The Democratic Cost of Constitutionalism: The European Case', (2015) 21 *European Law Journal* 460.

[6] For a rebuttal see, for instance, S Weatherill, 'The Beauty and the Beast: Is European Union Internal Market Law "Over-Constitutionalized"?', in T Ćapeta, I Goldner Lang and T Perišin (eds), *The Changing European Union: A Critical View on the Role of Law and the Courts*, Oxford, Hart Publishing 2022, 106.

III. POLITICS: FROM EXERCISING POWER TO CONSTRAINING POWER

Finally, EU constitutionalism alters the place, and the fabric, of politics as we experience it through domestic politics. The state template of constitutionalism, very broadly speaking, goes back to two basic assumptions of natural law theory: government ought to be legitimised by the consent of the governed, and should be limited by the innate rights of the individual. Today, these two assumptions translate into the relationship between democracy and fundamental rights. Democracy is how we legitimise exercising political power; fundamental rights is how we legitimise constraining political power. This well-known template locates politics at the point where political power is exercised, not where it is constrained. Politics uses consent and majority rule to translate societal preferences into a system of decision-making, often representative in nature and in the institutional form of a parliament. Constraints on power, in contrast, are imposed by law and guarded by courts. Here, law delimits the space of politics by setting boundaries that politics cannot cross. Those boundaries are the product not of majoritarianism, but of counter-majoritarianism. They establish a space of decision-making that is different from the one where political power is normally exercised. Decisions within that space are informed by values other than ideology or political power; they are based on law and knowledge. Neither of these values can be overridden by a majoritarian decision. It is, in other words, a space of expert knowledge that resists the simple logic of directly transposing current societal preferences into a decision.

EU constitutionalism reverses this relationship between exercising and constraining power by relocating the place of politics. The logic of knowledge moves to the point where power is usually exercised, while the logic of societal preferences moves to the point where power is usually constrained. The consequence is that exercising power is depoliticised, and constraining power is politicised.

As to the point where the Union exercises power, the logic of sharing power and balancing intergovernmentalism with supranationalism leads to institutions and processes that reduce direct input from societal preferences. Societal preferences are difficult to translate directly into the Union decision-making process because it is, of course, difficult to speak of a genuine European 'society'. The Union is not an institutional structure that a single political community has given itself, but the institutional form that several political communities are using to manage the relationship between themselves.[7] As a consequence, the Union's political authority is restricted by the limits of political community (see Chapter one). Rather than relying on political authority, which is in short supply, the Union relies mainly on processes that develop and channel knowledge-based judgements, not political judgements.

The argument here is not that states exercise power in a way that is disconnected from knowledge; they do not, of course. However, they apply political judgements to that knowledge, and that is what colours their decisions and defines their particular character. Nor is the argument here that knowledge-based decisions are unpolitical or unrepresentative; they are not, especially not those that are the product of legal knowledge. They have huge political consequences, if you think of our earlier discussion of market decisions in Chapter six. Yet, knowledge-based decisions, and their representational structure, are both very different from those of political decisions. Finally, the argument is not that all, or even most, of the Union's decisions are made in an unpolitical mode. Rather, the argument is that on a spectrum that stretches from judgements based on politics to judgements based on knowledge, the Union's decision-making process produces choices that are significantly closer to knowledge-based judgements than how decisions within the state template of constitutionalism are typically made.

The Union's institutional structure and daily operations supply plenty of illustrative material. The Commission is an independent body that is appointed, not elected; its working mode is managerial and technocratic. Yet it sets the legislative agenda because it enjoys the exclusive right to initiate legislation and uses that power to push Member States towards consent within the Council. The work of the Council itself is largely depoliticised; the overwhelming share of its decisions is made by COREPER and by countless working groups steeped in regulatory know-how and having little interest in politics. Independent agencies deal with the information base when making public policy. While they are set up in such a way as not to deal with policy itself, their influence on decision-making is far greater than their regulatory framework suggests. Networks of regulatory and competition bodies have sprung up and help to shape decisions. Even within major political bodies, legal services have become more powerful than ever. As Leino-Sandberg writes,

> The EU Legal Services are, in a way, the conscience of the Union and the practical guardians of the Treaties. In the fragile political community that

[7] S Weatherill, *Law and Values in the European Union*, Oxford, Oxford University Press 2016.

> is the Union, they play a key role in modulating the interplay between temptation and dynamism of political impulse, on the one hand, and the permanence and reliability of the Union's rules and processes, on the other.[8]

Indeed, an influential former Deputy Director of the Council Legal Service states that 'law is a natural instrument of the political debate'.[9] We have already seen how law takes the place of political regulatory decisions, and how the Court assumes a political decision-making role by crossing over from constraining the exercise of political authority to exercising political authority. The most pervasive critique the European Court faces is, after all, that it pursues its own political agenda. The exercise of much political power in the Union, in short, is in the hands of epistemic communities of service providers, central bankers, lawyers, risk assessors, and other experts who are far removed not only from the electorate, but also from politics itself. The reason behind this shift is, in itself, political. Member State governments bump issues up to Brussels in the hope of circumventing political opposition at home, which minimises political contestation within the Member States. They also have to make sure that the majority of Member States, the Commission and Parliament agree, which gets increasingly unlikely the more the issue is politicised. Knowledge-based choices, in other words, help in getting things 'done' because they reduce political contestation at both the Member State and Union levels.

Politics resurfaces, however, at the place where it was relocated, where the exercise of power is constrained. It is here where societal preferences play out. One example is legal doctrine, both in market constitutionalism and in fundamental rights law. The ground rule that prohibits or prescribes a certain state behaviour comes from the Union, which renders the Member State rule (and the values it protects) prima facie illegal. Member States only have the opportunity to justify their own rule. In other words, the act of Member State justification, which is part of the constraint on the exercise of Union power, is where national values and political contestation arise. Another example is the European Court's reversal in its jurisprudence on the extension of cross-border social rights in the context of Union citizenship. The European Court steamrolled Member States' sensibilities by disregarding secondary

[8] P Leino-Sandberg, *The Politics of Legal Expertise in EU Policy-Making*, Cambridge, Cambridge University Press 2021, 288.

[9] J-P Jacqué, 'The Role of Legal Services in the Elaboration of European Legislation', in A Vauchez and B de Witte (eds), *Lawyering Europe: European Law as a Transnational Social Field*, Oxford, Hart Publishing 2013, 43.

law and the constraints that Member States had set up there. Member State governments, fearing 'welfare migration' within the context of the financial and migration crises, threatened legislative override and non-compliance. Facing strong political pressure and bad press, the Court changed course.[10] Politics unfolded, not at the point where political authority was exercised, but where it was constrained. A final example is the political role of national constitutional courts. As the last line of defence with regard to competence creep, they act in a distinctly political manner when they decide to reject primacy and protect national values in the process. The language of law, in that respect, is indeed an instrument of political debate.

To be clear, the argument here is not that the limits on the exercise of power at the Union level are purely political, or that law, at the point where power is constrained, merely pretends to be law whereas, in reality, it is politics. However, the law carries a much heavier weight of political contestation on its shoulders than it does in the state template of constitutionalism. Needless to say, this changes not only the nature of political power in the Union, but also how it is deployed and plays out. Member States fight an uphill battle when trying to justify their own rules and values in the legislative process and in the Court, as well as when they try to stymie the effect of rules they do not agree with. Politics always looks like 'national egoism'.

Thus, the language and the meaning of what politics is finds a different home within the EU's architecture, at least to some degree. At the point where political authority is exercised, language points to politics but means expertise. At the point where political authority is constrained, language points to expertise but means politics. That reversal is a constitutional problem which damages both the legitimacy of the political process and the legitimacy of its limits.

IV. CHOICES

Finally, how will the Union's constitutional system fare in the face of present and future challenges? Three developments in the world are worth overviewing. First, the world is witnessing the return of geopolitics.

[10] Case C-333/13 *Dano v Jobcenter Leipzig*, EU:C:2014:2358. See M Blauberger et al, 'ECJ Judges Read the Morning Papers: Explaining the Turnaround of European Citizenship Jurisprudence', (2018) 25 *Journal of European Public Policy* 1422.

This poses the question of how the Union situates itself in the wider world. In order to compete with political powers like China or Russia, it will have to develop political strategies that require more long-term thinking, more centralisation, and an integrated vision that combines commercial and geopolitical thinking.[11] The impact on Union competences and decision-making will be significant. In the light of Donald Trump's return to the White House, competences would have to extend to the one area that Member States, to this day, have jealously guarded because they count it as the core of state sovereignty: foreign affairs. This will widen the Union's policy horizon and lead to much more intense contestation than already exists. It is an open question whether the Member States are ready to risk power-sharing in defence and foreign policy. Another open question is whether they will risk majority voting. Majority voting might be necessary to make decisions effective. The diverse Member State responses to Russia's aggression against Ukraine testify to the power a veto player would have. At the same time, removing veto-points would put enormous strain on the legitimacy of Union decision-making.

Second, the exhaustion of 'integration through law' and its expertise-based policy process has intensified demands to 'bring politics back in', but what does that mean? Policy fields like the single market depend on reliable enforcement to preclude the possibility of Member States cherry-picking the commitments they decide to honour. Would more 'politics' reverse integration? The 2024 elections have brought more populist parties to the European Parliament and made it more likely that radical groups will threaten core tenets of EU constitutionalism. Should they be sidelined in order to fence off the bitter conflicts that increasingly characterise domestic politics, or should the Union embrace them and accept the ensuing conflicts? Would that boost the Union's political legitimacy by making it more representative, more political, and, in the long run, more resilient, or would it destabilise it?

Third, the Union will have to find a way to deal not just with political contestation, but with constitutional contestation also. Member State constitutional courts have challenged primacy and the position of the European Court more generally. It appears there is a new willingness to police the boundaries of the Union's powers, in populist and non-populist Member States alike. The erosion of liberal constitutionalism in some Member States adds ample urgency to this problem.

[11] L van Middelaar, *Europe's Geopolitical Awakening, Groupe d'études géopolitiques*, Working Paper April 2021.

The Union's response so far has been to tighten legal control, mostly through infringement proceedings, with moderate success at best.

It is impossible to say how the Member States will react to these challenges, and what choices they will make in turn. One can easily imagine them either heeding the Court's exercise of authority when the Union finds itself on the precipice of a constitutional crisis or defying the Court even further. One possible source of resolution outside of the courts – Treaty changes – is unlikely. They require unanimity, which is becoming more difficult due to an increase in contestation between Member States because of domestic politics. It is therefore more likely that change will happen within the constitutional structure the Union already has, which places a lot of faith in the law.

That faith may be misplaced. Political and legal contestation arises from disagreements between people's deepest beliefs about what makes our community and what makes us citizens. The law can neither hold nor contain those beliefs. We may pretend it can, and treat winning a constitutional claim as the same as winning a political dispute. History, however, has taught us that winning the legal battle is not always the end of contestation; the law can reach its limits. The appropriate place for contestation, then, is the political arena. It is where constitutionalism is sustained and given meaning.

Index

www.ingramcontent.com/pod-product-compliance
Ingram Content Group UK Ltd.
Pitfield, Milton Keynes, MK11 3LW, UK
UKHW020032121026
15625UKWH00043B/331

9 781509 985104